Institution and Interpretation

Institution

and Interpretation

Samuel Weber

Afterword by Wlad Godzich

Theory and History of Literature, Volume 31

University of Minnesota Press, Minneapolis

This book is published with the financial assistance of the Graduate School and the College of Liberal Arts of the University of Minnesota.

Published by the University of Minnesota Press
2037 University Avenue Southeast, Minneapolis, MN 55414
Published simultaneously in Canada
by Fitzhenry & Whiteside Limited, Markham.
Printed in the United States of America.

Library of Congress Cataloging-in-Publication Data

Weber, Samuel, 1940–
    Institution and interpretation.

    (Theory and history of literature; v. 31)
    1. Criticism. I. Title. II. Series.
PN81.W344 1986   801'.95   86-3148
ISBN 0-8166-1297-8
ISBN 0-8166-1292-7 (pbk.)

The following chapters are copyrighted by Johns Hopkins University and are reprinted with its permission: Chapter 1, "Texts/Contexts: Closure and Exclusion," from *diacritics* 10.2 (June 1980):35–46; Chapter 4, "Capitalizing History," from *diacritics* 13.2 (summer 1983):14–28; and Chapter 9, "Ambivalence: The Humanities and the Study of Literature," from *diacritics* 15.2 (summer 1985):11–25.

Chapter 8, "The Debts of Deconstruction and Other, Related Assumptions," from *Taking Chances: Derrida, Psychoanalysis, and Literature*, edited by Joseph H. Smith and William Kerrigan (Baltimore and London: Johns Hopkins University Press, 1984), pp. 33–65, is copyrighted by the Forum on Psychiatry and Humanities of the Washington School of Psychiatry and is reprinted with its permission.

Publication history of remaining chapters: Chapter 2, "The Limits of Professionalism," *Oxford Literary Review* 5.1-2 (1982):59–74; Chapter 3, "The Debt of Criticism," *Critical Exchange* no. 15 (Winter 1984):17–26; Chapter 5, "The Critics' Choice," in *Reading, Writing, Revolution,* edited by Francis Barker et al. (Colchester: Publications of the University of Essex, 1982), pp. 147–58; Chapter 6, "The Blindness of the Seeing Eye: Psychoanalysis, Hermeneutics, *Entstellung*," revised and translated version of "Tertium datur," in *Die Austreibung des Geistes aus den Geisteswissenschaften*, edited by Friedrich Kittler (Bonn: Schöning Verlag, 1980), pp. 204–21; Chapter 7, "Reading and Writing—*chez* Derrida," *Tijdschrift Voor Filosofie* (Journal of Philosophy) 45.1 (1983):41–62.

The University of Minnesota
is an equal-opportunity
educator and employer.

Contents

Theory and History of Literature
Edited by Wlad Godzich and Jochen Schulte-Sasse

Introduction

A half-century ago, the French philosopher Gaston Bachelard published a short book investigating the ways in which traditional modes of thinking, both within the sciences and without, had been radically transformed by what he called "The New Scientific Spirit."[1] Although Bachelard was concerned above all with mathematics, physics, and chemistry, his interpretation of the changes taking place in those areas anticipates many of the tendencies that, in the past two decades, have begun to modify the manner in which the humanities, and in particular literary studies, are thought, taught, and practiced. A brief discussion of Bachelard's analyses can serve therefore both to introduce the alternative practices of reading and writing that comprise a major concern of this volume, and also to indicate that the forces at work in their emergence are not confined to the individual disciplines within which they are constrained, initially at least, to operate. What is at stake in the struggle between traditional modes of thought, whether in the experimental sciences or elsewhere, and the increasing number of intellectual practices that can no longer easily be assimilated to that tradition or comprehended by it, is nothing less than the *idea* and *ideal* of *knowledge* based on a notion of truth conceived in terms of the *adequatio intellectus et rei*. But whereas the "adequation" conception of truth presupposes both the *separation* of thought from its object and the *priority* of the latter over the former, it is the distinction itself that the operations of the "new scientific spirit" have rendered increasingly problematic.

The effects of such problematization, to be sure, extend far beyond the domain of "methodologies." The widespread "identity crisis" that is affecting a variety of different disciplines today is only the most obvious indication of a process of rethinking, the implications of which extend to the academic division of labor itself. As the binary, oppositional logic that has traditionally organized scientific inquiry ceases simply to be taken for granted, its institutional corollary, the procedures by which the disciplines and divisions of science and "scholarship" have demarcated their domains and consolidated their authority, is being subjected to renewed scrutiny. One of the most significant signs of this process in recent years has been the appearance of a variety of studies in different disciplines, often having no direct connection with—or even knowledge of—one another, which, independently of their specific methods, objects, and interests, problematize in varying ways the delimitations of the disciplines within whose sphere they are necessarily—if perhaps provisionally—situated.

What is increasingly being questioned today, perhaps more than at any time since the age of the Enlightenment, is the notion of intellectual and scientific *autonomy*. The autonomy of a scientific discipline, as traditionally understood—a tradition that still dominates vast areas of academic activity and of its institutions—presupposes a field that is self-contained, subject to its own laws, to principles or rules that are in essence independent of all that surrounds them, of all they are not.[2] In line with this ideal of *cognitive autonomy*, the initial and initiating concern of the established branches of learning has been to stake out territories and to secure borders. It is precisely this desire to establish impenetrable frontiers and unshakable foundations, Bachelard argues, that distinguishes the old from the "new scientific spirit." The practices of contemporary science entail a "diversification of axiomatics,"[3] and the recognition of an irreducible "multiplicity of basic hypotheses."[4] The concern with foundations that characterizes traditional thought is thereby supplanted by a more practical, strategic approach involving an effort to extend or otherwise put into play what could be described as *enabling limits*.[5]

Bachelard, to be sure, approaches the problem from the vantage point of *diversity* rather than that of *delimitation*: the objects and operations of modern science, he insists, are irreducible to any single or unified set of suppositions and hence to any one, self-identical reality. The complexity of the manifold reality of contemporary science renders the idea of autonomy inoperative. What has changed is the relation of identity to nonidentity, of inclusion to exclusion. The concepts and constructs of the new scientific spirit are relational rather than substantial, and as such, irreducibly *heterogeneous*, as Bachelard's interpretation of Pauli's principle indicates:

> Philosophically speaking, it is the systematical exclusion of the *same*, it is the appeal to the *other*. Within each system, or better, in order

for elements to constitute a system, mathematical diversity is essential to the components.[6]

The corollary of such "systematic exclusion" is the "mathematization" of scientific inquiry, or, more precisely, the supplanting of the traditional epistemic model, based on Euclidean geometry, by an algebraic one. Cognitive objects are henceforth to be identified not by reference to an intrinsic quality, their *form*, but rather in terms of their capacity to the *deformed* and *transformed*:

> The essence of a mathematic notion is measurable in terms of the possibilities of deformation that permit the application of this notion to be extended. . . . Mathematical thinking comes into its own (*prend son essor*) with the emergence of the ideas of transformation, correspondence, varied application.[7]

> One might say to the mathematical entity, "Tell me how you can be transformed and I will tell you who you are." . . . The keystone of all evidence is thus the algebraic form. In sum, algebra amasses all the relations and nothing but relations. It is only in terms of relations that different geometries are equivalent. It is only insofar as they are relational that they have a reality and not through the reference to an object, to an experience or to an intuitive image.[8]

This process of "algebraization"—of "deformation" and "transformation"—affects not merely the "object" of scientific inquiry, but also its subject, or rather, the relation of the two, as Bachelard's discussion of Heisenberg's celebrated "uncertainty principle" indicates. By demonstrating the impossibility of establishing simultaneously the position and velocity of an electron; by showing that the instrument of measure, the photon, alters the object in the very process of measurement, and similarly has its own frequency modified in the encounter, this "principle" strikes at the founding premise not only of traditional science, but also of the intuitive thinking that it sought to systematize (and to legitimize). This premise Bachelard designates as the "absolute of localization," a belief, he adds, that also lies "at the bottom of language" as it is generally used and construed.[9] Materialism and Realism, Baconian empiricism and Cartesian rationalism are both rooted in this "abstraction," for which "the localization"—or more precisely, the *localizability*—"of matter in a precise space" is taken for granted.[10] In short, the traditional conception that holds space and time to be measurable in terms of "the point and the instant" is irrevocably shaken by contemporary science.

To be sure, it is easier to indicate how the cognitive paradigm of Euclidean geometry is rendered problematic by modern science than to describe that by which it is replaced. One reason for this difficulty is the fact that the new "paradigm" can hardly be expected to have the same unity as the old. On the contrary, its complex disunity defies not only traditional science and knowledge, but also our intuitive experience and its familiar discourses. Thus, it is no empty rhetorical gesture (although hardly an unprecedented one) when Bachelard looks elsewhere for the language that will be needed to articulate complex and ambiguous realities of the new science: "What poet will give us the metaphors of this new language?"[11] Metaphorical this language will have to be, if it is to articulate "a mode of thought that draws support from its movement,"[12] rather than from the substantial being of a referent.

The prevalence of the *relational* over the *referential* dimension in contemporary science leads Bachelard, like Saussure some thirty years earlier, to be deeply mistrustful of the widespread conception and use of language that privileges its *denominational-representational* aspect over its *differential-signifying* function. He cites approvingly Heisenberg's caveat that "one should be particularly circumspect in using phrases such as 'in reality',," which satisfy the imagination but are cognitively "empty" and operationally inconsequential.[13] Only a radical rethinking and reworking of the metaphorical, figurative aspect of scientific language, Bachelard argues, can surmount "the difficulty of objective designation"[14] encountered by a science, the objects and concepts of which seem indelibly marked by a certain *duplicity*:

> All the basic notions can in a certain manner be doubled; they can be bordered by complementary notions. Henceforth, every intuition will proceed from a choice; there will thus be a kind of essential ambiguity at the basis of scientific description and the immediacy of the Cartesian notion of evidence will be perturbed.[15]

Thus, the world of contemporary science emerges as one of *Doppelgänger* and of ambiguous "choices," in which "time operates more by repetition than by duration,"[16] and where reality appears as a "spectrum of numbers" or even as "a double play of writing."[17] And yet, in this spectral world, choices must still be made and identities established, no matter how provisional, probabilistic, and aleatory these may be. It is the inevitability of such decision making, in a situation marked by irreducible ambiguity, that gives rise to a thinking nourished not only by ambivalence, but also by anxiety.

For upon what criteria will choices ultimately be based, when "it is the real and not knowledge that bears the mark of ambiguity"?[18] When the horizon traditionally delimited by being, reality, and truth no longer provides a reliable orientation for judgment? When, in short, the *res* addressed by the *intellectus* is simultaneously deformed and transformed in the process?

It will hardly be surprising, therefore, that the choices of such an intellect, which must both affirm ambiguity and alterity, and yet at the same time deny them, are marked by an "anxiety" to which Bachelard attaches considerable importance:

In place of that communion with a global reality to which the scientist would return with enthusiasm as to an original philosophy, should we not, in order to comprehend the evolution of the intellect, pay attention to the anxious thought, to thought in quest of an object, to thought that searches dialectical occasions to escape from itself, to break with its own frames: in sum, to thought on the way towards objectification?[19]

If the "anxious thought" of modern science is a thought in movement, we would doubtless do well to remember, with Freud, that anxiety is not just a flight *from* the self, but a flight *of* the self, and that therefore the "objects" to which it flees, far from constituting a pure and simple other, inevitably entail "more of the same." It is in this sense that Bachelard insists on the (apparently banal) fact that the objects of science are not individuals, but "classes":

Henceforth the real is accessible through its articulation in classes. It is at the level of the class that the properties of the real will have to be sought.[20]

For Bachelard no less than for Marx, there will always be a class in this text[21] and that class will be as much a theater of conflict as it is a classroom or laboratory, for reasons relating less to the persons involved than to the practices of science:

Scientific observation is always a polemical observation; it confirms or subverts a prior thesis, a given scheme, a plan of observation. . . . Naturally, once one passes from observation to experimentation, the polemical character of cognition becomes even clearer. For then the phenomenon must be sorted, filtered, purified, poured into the mould of instruments, produced on the level of instruments. These in- struments are in turn only materialized theories. The phenomena that emerge from them are marked by those theories through and through.[22]

The "polemical" character of scientific inquiry is thus not merely a result of the struggle to supplant previous theories—an important enough aspect, to be sure[23]—but also of the process of experimentation itself. And it is this that makes scientific reality not merely "ambiguous," in the sense of Heisenberg's Uncer- tainty Principle, but also *ambivalent*, *agonistic*, and *conflictual*. In such a situa- tion, where scientific activity inevitably entails the effort to determine the in- determinable, success can never be separated entirely from a play of conflicting forces, forces which, as recent studies have demonstrated, are in turn not ex- clusively scientific.[24]

The operations of science themselves—the "sorting, filtering, purifying" of "data," as well as their *inscription* and *circulation*[25]—thus entail a relation to alterity that can no longer be considered to be purely intrascientific. This is the point at which the perspective of the "institution," or, more precisely, of *institutionalization*, imposes itself: not, to be sure, as a magic term capable of resolving the problems of ambivalent cognition, but rather as an indication of the specific form such problems assume in the practice of modern science.

Although the perspective of institutionalization takes us beyond Bachelard, its necessity is clearly indicated by his remarks on the function of exclusion in scientific systematization. Exclusion, as described by Bachelard, is no less duplicit than scientific discourse in general. On the one hand, as we have seen, it inscribes an irreducibly heterogeneous "appeal to the other," into the constructs of contemporary science: in order for elements to be constituted into a system, the same must be excluded. However, this "objective" and quasi-dialectical role necessitates a *second exclusion*, which in a certain sense is directed against the first, since this time it is not the same that is excluded, but the different: that is, the very ambiguity that the system-building function of exclusion introduced:

> If, however, one should go the bottom of the chemist's certainty, one will discover that it too articulates itself in the form of progressive *exclusions* that put aside precisely those cases where there would be ambiguity. . . . The communion of minds realizes itself in negation. The perfect objective union is founded on a sort of non-object.[26]

To be sure, the exclusion being described here pertains to a "psychology of Determinism" that Bachelard associates with traditional rather than with contemporary science. And yet, even in the nondeterministic "epistemology of the probable" that he takes to be the most general philosophical implication of the New Scientific Spirit, ambiguity will still have to be limited, "excluded," if objects are to be determined — that is, cognized — in any way whatsoever. It is the tension arising from these two indispensable, inseparable, and yet mutually disruptive exclusions that results in the "strange ambivalence" that contemporary science imposes on the idea of reality.[27]

This ambivalent affirmation and denial of ambiguity and of indeterminacy is what characterizes the relation of "science" to an alterity it seeks to control but can never fully integrate or assimilate. No longer "grounded" in an order of being, however objectively or subjectively conceived, the only "intrinsic" support of science is its movement. But this movement *removes* science from itself, impelling it "to break with its own frames" in order to approach the enigmatic "objects" it addresses. Since these objects themselves can hardly check the centrifugal spin of science — for the very reasons that render it absurd to speak of "objects *themselves*" — the function of establishing identities, of imposing determinations and of enforcing lines of demarcation, can be conceived only as an effect of what we call "institutions" and of institutionalization.

On the condition, that is, that the process of institutionalization be construed differently from the way it has traditionally been treated in philosophy and, above all, in the social sciences. The dominant tendency, as René Lourau writes, has been to reduce the concept to only one of its elements: the maintenance of the status quo, and thereby to eliminate its dynamic, transformative aspect. The notion, Lourau observes,

> has been increasingly used to designate what I and others before me have called the *instituted* (*l'institué*), the established order, the already existing norms, the state of fact thereby being confounded with the state of right (*l'état de droit*). By contrast, the *instituting* aspect (*l'instituant*) . . . has been increasingly obscured. The political implication of the sociological theories appears clearly here. By emptying the concept of institution of one of its primordial components (that of instituting, in the sense of founding, creating, breaking with an old order and creating a new one), sociology has finally come to identify the institution with the status quo.[28]

By contrast, the notion of institution at work in the texts that follow is one in which *instituted* organization and *instituting* process are joined in the ambivalent relation of every determinate structure to that which it excludes, and yet which, qua excluded, allows that structure to *set itself apart*.[29]

II

An instance of such exclusion that has been of the greatest importance in the institution of modern literary studies is that which has come to define the literary object in terms of *work* and of *author*. The procedures by which texts have been rendered suitable for study, as meaningful objects to be read and taught in terms of their truth, have depended in large measure on a certain conception of the Author, held to be the constitutive source and defining principle of the Work. Roland Barthes put it quite succinctly in his celebrated essay, first published in 1968, on "The Death of the Author":

> To give a text an Author is to impose a limit on that text, to furnish it with a final signified, to close writing. Such a conception suits criticism very well, the latter then allotting itself the important task of discovering the Author (or its hypostases: society, history, psyche, liberty) beneath the work: when the Author has been found, the text is "explained"—victory to the critic. Hence there is no surprise in the fact that, historically, the reign of the Author has also been that of the Critic, nor again in the fact that criticism (be it new) is today undermined along with the Author.[30]

But if Barthes's obituary has proven premature, it is no doubt because the problem of authority is more complex than the passage quoted would suggest.

Is it possible to conceive of a "text" *without* limitation? Of writing without some sort of closure? And if not, the question then becomes not *whether* limits are imposed, but *how*? Barthes's response to this question, while anticipating the direction that a major segment of academic criticism was to take in the years following, also allows us to discern the difficulties inevitably encountered by any attempt to do away with one reign, that of the Author, by simply replacing it with another, be it that of the "scriptor" or that of the Reader:

> The reader is the space on which all the quotations that make up a writing are inscribed without any of them being lost; a text's unity lies not in its origin but in its destination. Yet this destination cannot any longer be personal: the reader is without history, biography, psychology; he is simply that *someone* who holds together in a single field all the traces by which the written text is constituted.[31]

The principle of delimitation is thus shifted from an archaeological instance, the author, to a teleological one, the "reader"—but the manner in which its operations are construed remains the same. The result is that "the birth of the reader" has proven to signify not "the death of the Author," as Barthes confidently predicted, but its resurrection.[32] This has not been without a certain logic. For as long as reading, writing, intertextuality, or any of the other categories that have been offered as alternatives to the classical dyad of author and work, are conceived of either in terms of *unity* and *totality*, or as their simple *negation*—as long, that is, as the attributes of the *work* continue to determine the hermeneutical horizon in which language is used and interpreted, the "reader" will ultimately be nothing more than a speechless stand-in for the (equally silent) author, while the critic claims to be porte-parole, heir and beneficiary of both.

The passage cited above provides ample confirmation of this: Barthes's attempt to replace the author by the reader inevitably leaves the last word to the logic of identity he ostensibly seeks to subvert: the "multiplicity" of the text is "focused" in and by a unified and unifying reader, who "is simply . . . *someone* who holds together in a single field all the traces. . . . " Such a function, to be sure, was precisely what Foucault, writing at about the same time as Barthes, attributed not to the reader, but to the author.[33] The fact that the desire for identity, unity, and totality should have proven so much more resilient than either Foucault or Barthes expected, testifies not merely to the power of Criticism, old and new, or to that of the institutions of learning and research through and in which it maintains itself, but, perhaps even more important, to the cultural investment placed in the notion of Reading itself. The character of this investment requires not, of course, that reading be taken very seriously, but on the contrary, that it be taken for granted.[34] It is precisely such self-evidence, however, that any *effective* problematization of "the author-function" (Foucault) cannot but disrupt. For how is reading to be distinguished from certain other practices—from hallucinating, dreaming, or fantasizing, for instance—without reference to a previously determined "object"—whether the latter be construed as a meaningful work or as a signifying text? Wittgenstein's discussion, in the *Philosophical Investigations*, of various occurrences of the verb "to read" (*lesen*), graphically reveals just how precarious the semantic unity of this all-too-familiar term is, with respect to the heterogeneity of its different uses.[35] And the same demonstration could undoubtedly be made concerning the notion of "writing," as Foucault's description of it suggests: "Writing unfolds like a game that inevitably moves beyond its own rules and finally leaves them behind."[36] But if the movement of writing takes it beyond the rules with which it starts, where, then, does it go? And is this process, however transgressive it may be, itself entirely without rules? If writing is *unruly*, is it lawless? If not, from where do those laws derive their force? How do they come to impose themselves?

To respond to such questions, what must be examined is not merely the authorial *function*, but the manner in which it is *assumed*.

III

Nowhere, perhaps, is the problematic necessity of this assumption more powerfully articulated than in *The Critique of Judgment*. Kant introduces his effort to work out the transcendental principle of judgment by making two moves that are of particular interest in the context of the previous discussion. First, he describes science and aesthetics as two forms of what he calls "reflective judgment"—that is, of judgments in which "only the particular is given," and "for which the universal has to be found."[37] Both scientific and aesthetic thinking, then, are said to be characterized by a certain *absence of cognition*; both entail a confrontation with the *particular* in which judgment is compelled to act on its own, as it were, in order to *find* the "universal (the rules, the principle, the law)" without which it would not be a judgment at all.[38] And yet, Kant reserves a particular place for "those judgments that we call aesthetical," since it is in them that "this perplexity (*Verlegenheit*: embarrassment) about a principle (whether it be subjective or objective) is mainly to be found."[39] For this reason, it is not Science, but the Beautiful and the Sublime that delimit the decisive area of the transcendental critique of judgment. This, then, is Kant's first move.

The second involves the manner in which reflective judgment is said to operate in its search for rules. Despite the lack of determining principles and laws, judgment, Kant insists, is not lawless; it has its own a priori principle, one that imposes itself as a rather remarkable and ineluctable *assumption*:

The principle can be no other than the following: As universal laws of nature have their ground in our understanding, which prescribes them to nature (although only according to the universal concept of it as nature), so particular empirical laws, in respect of what is in them left undetermined by these universal laws, must be considered in accordance with such a unity as they would have if an understanding (although not our understanding) had furnished them to our cognitive faculties so as to make possible a system of experience according to particular laws of nature. *Not as if, in this way, such an understanding really had to be assumed* (*Nicht, als wenn auf diese Art wirklich ein solcher Verstand angenommen werden müsste*) (for it is only our reflective judgment to which this idea serves as a principle – for reflecting, not for determining); but this faculty thus gives a law only to itself, and not to nature.[40]

The Bernard translation of this passage, which I have modified, is symptomatically suggestive. The German phrase enclosed in parentheses in the above citation is rendered as: "Not as if, in this way, such an understanding must be *assumed as actual*." By thereby transforming the adverb "really" (*wirklich*) into an adjective, and thereby substantializing it, Bernard tends to efface precisely what will prove to be the decisive issue, not just in the Introduction, but throughout *The Critique of Aesthetic Judgment*. What is at stake here is the *status* of the assumption of "purposiveness" (*Zweckmässigkeit*), *qua assumption*. Its own purpose, according to Kant, is to guide judgment in its effort to master the unknown. The problem, however, is: how can an assumption that judgment "gives . . . only to itself, and not to nature," and that therefore "ascribes nothing to the object (of nature) but only represents the peculiar way in which we must proceed in reflection upon [it],"[41] – how can such a purely "subjective principle"[42] constitute a transcendental – that is, a priori, universal – condition of the objective cognition of that "nature," in its infinite particularity, diversity, and heterogeneity? What does the making of such an assumption entail?

As is usually the case, it is easier to state what it does *not* entail. Most obviously, it does not imply an assertion about the nature of reality, nor about a particular state of affairs. In this sense, it involves what today might be called a "heuristic fiction": the assumption that another "understanding," like our own and yet sufficiently different from it, can accomplish precisely what ours cannot, that is, determine the particular object in question to be "purposiveful," *zweckmässig*, the product of a deliberate, conscious intentionality. This is the sense that Bernard gives to Kant's text: understood in this way, the assumption of purposiveness clearly does not imply a judgment about objective reality. This interpretation can hardly be contested, as far as it goes. The problem, however, is that it does not go far enough. The German, to be sure, is considerably less clear than Bernard's translation. By using the word "really" as an adverb, Kant questions the reality not merely of *what* is assumed, but also of the *assumption* itself. And indeed: what can the reality of an assumption be which seeks to comprehend the particular by first denying its alterity (assimilating it to a consciousness *like its own*), and then denying its denial by asserting that it is merely subjective? Can this double denial be contained within the space of a single, undivided consciousness – that of the judging subject? The subjunctive mode of Kant's phrase (*Nicht als wenn . . . angenommen werden müsste*) accentuates the uncertain status of an assumption that to be effective, must in a certain and complex sense seek to efface itself.[43]

The appeal to a constitutive, originating instance, as described by Kant, is as ambivalent as it is unavoidable, whenever and wherever available knowledge no longer suffices to comprehend the particular case at hand. If the exemplary instances of this situation are found on the one hand in science and on the other in aesthetic judgment, the absence of knowledge is more radical in the latter, which in turn would explain why the appeal to an "authorial function" would be more characteristic of it. Indeed, when one remembers the reasons for which Kant denies all cognitive content to what today we call "critical theory," one can begin to understand why the authorial assumption should have proven as resistant and as resilient as it has, some forty years after W. K. Wimsatt and Monroe Beardsley declared that "critical inquiries are not settled by consulting the oracle."[44] Paradoxically, by redirecting literary studies toward the "close reading" of individual texts, American New Criticism helped to reinstate the very authorial instance that Wimsatt and Beardsley sought to disqualify. The author has survived as the *principium individuationis* of literary studies.

But perhaps the question that needs to be explored is one that concerns not so much the survival of the "author-function" as such, but rather the manner in which it lives on; not whether or not such an assumption must be made, but rather *how* it is *performed* and with what consequences; the question, in short, of its *style*.[45] In this respect, a text such as *Tristram Shandy* and the responses it has evoked offer an excellent test case. Its "author," who as hero and narrator proves to be a function of the text rather than its foundation, is as impossible to pin down as to avoid. "The Critics' Choice" seeks to describe certain aspects of what is not just a dilemma but also a challenge to literary studies. Their future may well depend on the capacity to assume – rather than merely act out – the ambivalence that is their limiting condition, but also their greatest resource.

Institution and Interpretation

Chapter 1
Texts/Contexts:
Closure and Exclusion

Und gibt es nicht auch den Fall, wo wir spielen und—'make up the rules as we go along'? *Ja auch den, in welchem wir sie abändern—*as we go along.

*

Jemand sagt zu mir: "Zeige den Kindern ein Spiel!" Ich lehre sie, um Geld zu würfeln, und der Andere sagt mir "Ich habe nicht so ein Spiel gemeint". Musste ihm da, als er mir den Befehl gab, der Aussschluss des Würfelspiels vorschweben?

Ludwig Wittgenstein, *Philosophische Untersuchungen*

In an essay that was soon to become a classic of contemporary criticism, "Structure, Sign and Play," Jacques Derrida distinguished between two interpretations of interpretation:

> The one seeks to decipher, dreams of deciphering a truth or an origin that transcends play and the order of the sign, and for it the necessity of interpretation is lived as a kind of exile. The other, no longer oriented towards origin, affirms play and strives to pass beyond man and humanism, man being the name of that being which, throughout the history of metaphysics or of onto-theology . . . has dreamed of the plenitude of presence, of reassuring foundations, of origin and the end of play. (*L'écriture et la différence* [Paris: Seuil, 1967], 427; my translation)

These two interpretations of interpretation, Derrida wrote in 1966, "are absolutely irreconcilable, even if we live them simultaneously and reconcile them in an obscure economy"; moreover, "they divide—*se partage—*the field of what is called, problematically, the human sciences."

If I take the liberty of recalling a distinction that has doubtless become familiar, indeed all too familiar, it is precisely in order to question that familiarity. For what has become familiar is only part of the story, the alternative announced by Derrida, whereas the qualifications to which that part was submitted have drawn considerably less attention. Nor is this surprising, since the latter seem to take the edge off what would otherwise appear to be a clear-cut issue. Having stated the alternative, Derrida goes on to suggest that what is required is not so much a choice, embracing the one at the expense of the other, but rather reflection upon the "common ground" (*le sol commun*) of the two absolutely irreconcilable modes of interpretation, and upon "the deferring—*la différance*—of this irreducible difference."

What are we to make of this common ground? Without addressing this question further, Derrida's text nevertheless gives us at least two clues. First, what is described is not merely an irreducible difference, but a *struggle*. The two modes of interpretation "divide up the field of the human sciences *among themselves* (*se partagent le champ de(s) . . . sciences humaines*)"; this process of partitioning is no neutral operation; it entails the staking of claims, the effort to appropriate. The two interpretations do not simply have a common ground, they dispute it. This implies that the common ground is above all a battleground.

If the temptation to take sides, to make a choice, short-circuits the problem, it is because there are more "sides" to the battle than first meet the eye. For as a moment's reflection reveals, there are not simply two antagonists engaged here—nostalgic versus affirmative interpretation—but a third, the interpretive gesture of Derrida's text itself, setting the scene of a struggle it seems only to describe. This third interpretation is discrete, hardly visible as such, since everything in this essay, as in all others written by Derrida at the time, invites the reader to identify the authorial standpoint with the "affirmative" interpretation, and hence with the critique of the nostalgic yearning for origin. And indeed, ever since then readers have not hesitated to associate Derridean "deconstruction" with Nietzsche.

But if such identification is inevitable, it is not as simple as it might seem. For what is the "way" indicated by the name "Nietzsche"? ("Cette deuxième interprétation de l'interprétation, dont Nietzsche nous a indiqué la voie"). Here, in "Structure, Sign and Play," it is described almost as a symmetrical reversal of the "sad, negative, nostalgic, guilty, Rousseauistic face" in interpretation, as the "joyous affirmation of the play of the world and of the innocence of becoming." Yet this description—and this is the second clue—jars strangely with some of Nietzsche's most celebrated formulations of the interpretive process. In the *Genealogy of Morals*, for instance, we can read the following.

> Everything that exists, that has somehow come to be, is repeatedly reinterpreted in terms of new aims by a power superior to it, is repeatedly taken hold of (neu in Beschlag genommen), transformed and transposed to new ends; . . . *all* processes in the organic world entail overpowering and domination (ein Überwältigen und Herr-Werden), which in turn constitute new interpretation, manipulation (Zurechtmachen), in the course of which the previous "meaning" and "purpose" are necessarily obscured or entirely eradicated. (Werke II [Munich: Hanser, 1960], 818; my translation)

The process of interpretation articulated by Nietzsche here and elsewhere applies not so much to what Derrida describes as the "second" interpretation, the affirmation of play, of the "innocence of becoming," as to the interpretive practice of which that description is a part, but only a part. The allusion to Nietzsche suggests—but only implicitly, and hence only to a reader willing to interpret—that beyond the "irreducible difference" of nostalgic and affirmative interpretations, there is a third version, interpreting interpretation as a struggle to overwhelm and to dislodge an already existing, dominant interpretation and thus to establish its own authority. Could anything be less "innocent"?

No one was more aware—indeed, obsessed—with the simulacrum of such innocence than was Nietzsche. In a sense, this was precisely the brunt of his attacks against the Judeo-Christian and Platonic tradition. This tradition, in his view, had succeeded in playing the game of interpretation all the more effectively for denying that there was any game whatsoever. By concealing its genealogy as interpretation in the names of Truth, Being, Subject and so on, the tradition succeeded in establishing its own authority and driving all competitors from the field. The spectacle could not help fascinating Nietzsche, and even eliciting his grudging respect: the priests and philosophers were, after all, consummate performers. But their performance endangered the game itself. Thus, Nietzsche found himself in the difficult position of condemning those who had played the game to the hilt, on the grounds that their play jeopardized the ground rules. And yet the very passion of his condemnation suggests that not the players but the game itself may be ultimately responsible for the dilemma.[1]

An early essay, one of "Five Prefaces to Five Unwritten Books," discusses the manner in which the Greeks confronted a similar dilemma. In "Homer's Contests" (*Homers Wettkampf*), Nietzsche interprets the practice of ostracism as a means by which the Greeks sought to safeguard the "necessity of competition" against itself. The "original meaning of *ostrakismos*, as expressed by the Ephesians in banning Hermodor, was: 'No one should be allowed to be the best among us; if someone is, however, then let him be elsewhere and with others.' " No one should be permitted to excel, Nietzsche explains, "because then the competition would fade and the eternal vital foundations of the Hellenic state would be in jeopardy" (*Werke III*, 295; my translation). The gesture of *exclusion* thus emerges as a necessary move designed to save the agonistic process from its own tendencies toward entropy.

This is all well and good so long as we can distinguish between the contestants and . . . the arbiters. What, however, if and when the referees, umpires, judges, legislators, priests, philosophers, politicians are themselves competitors? Interpreters? Who is to exclude the winners then? Or is it the winners, on the contrary, who will exclude?

If these are some of the questions to be confronted along the way indicated by Nietzsche, a more immediate consequence of his conception of interpretation is that the latter must be regarded as something other than "joyous affirmation": if it is a play (*jeu*), it is a power play, a game that belies any simple opposition, such as "active" and "reactive." Interpretation, for Nietzsche, is—or begins as—reinterpretation, and its designs are never "innocent," if the word implies "disinterested." The 1966 text of Derrida did not say as much explicitly, but it practiced what it did not preach. In distinguishing nostalgic from affirmative modes of interpretation as two "absolutely irreconcilable" options, it did not forget to add that "we live them simultaneously and reconcile them in an obscure economy" (*ED*, 427). If that economy is obscure, it is doubtless because we are under its sway, as participants, contestants, even as we search for its rules.

The following remarks attempt to retrace the contours of that "obscure economy" of interpretation. Again, I shall begin with the familiar, with Saussure's theory of the sign. The "value" of a sign, Saussure argues, is determined not by what it represents but by its differential-diacritical relations to other signs. "The value of each term," he declares, "is determined by those which surround it," by its "milieu" (*Cours de linguistique générale* [Paris: Payot, 1960], 160: my translation). What, however, determines the *milieu*? What limits the differential-diacritical relations of signifiers and signifieds, or rather, how can we know that there is such a limit? If the value of a term is a function of its "pure difference" from "other terms of the system," what determines those other terms as a *system*, as *la langue*? In disengaging the process of signification from that of representation, Saussure sought to free language from its dependence on "extralinguistic" entities, and thus to construct an "integral and concrete object" upon which the self-contained and autonomous science of linguistics might be founded. But such a self-contained science presupposes an equally self-contained object, and the very gesture that sets up such an object simultaneously calls it into question: the determination of value as pure difference. For who is to say where the movement of difference starts and stops? What is to prevent it from fanning out on all sides, as it were, and thereby de-limiting what it is meant to determine?

The question of the status of the system, then, is absolutely decisive for the Saussurean enterprise. It is not a peripheral question, but one that strikes at the heart of the theory: no single signifier or signified can be determined apart from the play of difference, but that play itself must be limited in order for determination to take place.

The dilemma is visible in the section of Saussure's *Cours* entitled "The Sign Considered in Its Totality." There the underlying notion of "pure difference" as that which underlies the sign is revoked, or qualified. It is said to be an abstraction which holds only for signifier and signified "taken separately," in isolation; once the sign is considered "in its totality" we find ourselves confronted not merely by negative relations, but by something more "positive"; not by "pure difference" but by determinate "oppositions" (*Cours*, 166–67).

This shift in emphasis from difference to opposition is necessary if the systematic character of language is to be upheld. It turns on the manner in which signifier and signified *combine* to form individual signs. If Saussure's notion of difference, in its nonrepresentational aspect, had tended to undercut the very distinction between signifier and signified by having them appear as functions or moments of signification rather than as entities or dimensions, his emphasis on their combination seeks to reinvest the two orders with a more substantial character. The guarantee of this more stable relationship Saussure calls "linguistic institution": "Although signified and signifier are, considered separately, purely differential and negative, their combination is a positive fact; indeed it is the only sort of fact that the language-system (*la langue*) comprises, since the property of linguistic institution (*le propre de l'institution linguistique*) is precisely to maintain the parallelism between these two orders of differences" (166–67).

The question posed by Saussure's shift from the notion of difference to that of opposition thus acquires a new and important dimension; if the move is justified, it is because of something called "linguistic institution" (or perhaps: the institution of language), which has, as its proper function and property, precisely "to maintain the parallelism" between signifier and signified, and thus to guarantee the integrity and stability of the sign.

What is meant by linguistic institution? If it is that which allows us to consider language as a system, then it has two primary aspects: first, it is the "synchronic perspective" of the linguist, which studies language as "a system of pure values determined by nothing outside of the momentary state of its terms" (80). Second, if synchronic linguistics is not a mere figment of the linguist's imagination, it is because it has a *fundamentum in re*. This foundation is not simply empirical, since Saussure understood very well that the notion of a "momentary state" of language was a construction, a heuristic fiction. What is more surprising, however, is that this foundation is not purely linguistic.

> Synchronic linguistics will be concerned with the logical and psychological relations linking coexistent terms and forming a system, *such as they are perceived by an identical collective consciousness*. Diachronic linguistics, on the contrary, will study the relations linking successive terms not perceived by an identical collective consciousness and which replace each other without forming a system among themselves. (99–100, my italics)

The identification of "a system of pure values determined by nothing outside of the momentary state of its terms" is thus curiously dependent on something outside of the momentary state of its terms, the perception of "an identical collective consciousness." This establishes the crucial distinction between synchronic "system" and diachronic systemlessness, as well as the priority of the former over the latter: "It is evident that the synchronic aspect takes precedence over the other, since for the mass of speakers it is the true and only reality" (90).

Thus, the "reality" of language qua system is defined in relation to the *consciousness* of those who speak it: "In order to know to what extent a thing is a reality, it will be necessary and sufficient to discover to what extent it exists for the consciousness of subjects" (90). Of course, it is not the consciousness of the individual speaker that is meant here, but rather that of the sum of speakers comprising a linguistic community. Such an implicit communal consciousness is articulated in and by the synchronic linguist, who may thus be defined as the linguistic self-consciousness of that community.

The task of the synchronic linguist will consist, then, in gathering the "testimony" of "speaking subjects" in order to determine what is real for their collective consciousness, and what is not. To do this, the linguist must not merely observe certain phenomena, he must also force himself to disregard others: "For the speaking subject, their succession [that of the facts of language] in time is nonexistent: he is confronted with a state. That is why the linguist who wishes to understand this state *must disregard* everything that has produced it and *ignore* diachrony. He can enter the mind of speakers only *by completely suppressing* the past" (*Cours*, 81, my italics).

In order to regard, the linguist must *disregard*; in order to recognize he must *ignore*; in order to enter the minds of the speaker, he must *suppress*. He must, in short, repeat what Saussure assumes the speakers themselves do in speaking: forget time, history, and change, presumably in order to say what they mean and be understood. For Saussure never seems to doubt that the organizing principle of language is inseparable from the operations of understanding and communication, even while arguing that the process of signification, as differential articulation, is not reducible to the expression of meaning ("there are no preestablished ideas and nothing is distinguished before the apparition of language" [*Cours*, 155]).

In thus defining the "testimony" of speakers as objects of consciousness, what Saussure disregards, ignores, and suppresses is not simply an extraneous, empirical aspect of language; he disregards the forces that work to institute language, that endow it with a particular organization. In order to justify his reduction of difference to opposition, he constructs the opposition of synchronic and diachronic perspectives and defines it as absolute and irreconcilable (*Cours* 83). Diachronic factors act as a "blind force" upon synchronic systems (*Cours*, 127), but for the speaker and synchronic linguist the final effect of such action is precisely to create intelligibility and order. Diachronic action is the outer, enabling limit, transforming the chaotic play of difference into the transparent order of opposition—on the condition, that is, that the linguist not allow himself to confuse the two "perspectives."

Beginning from the insight that the identity of a term "is only truly determined by the aid of that which is outside of it (*Cours*, 160), Saussure seeks to determine that "outside" as diachronic "forces" which serve ultimately to contain and to delimit the internal coherence of the system.

This amounts to taking the "institution of language" — language as institution — for granted, as a given to be described rather than as a process to be understood. The question of how the play of difference ever comes to be systematically intelligible remains unaddressed.

Except, of course, in the famous example of the chess game, which in a curious and significant way disrupts the argument it is intended to illustrate. For, far from demonstrating that diachrony and synchrony are logically unrelated, it suggests that they cannot be simply opposed or separated. And it suggests this in a symptomatic manner: by offering an interpretation apparently unintended by Saussure, and thus not reducible to his consciousness, unlike the synchronic state it is designed to explicate. For the character of chess as a game makes diachrony and synchrony inseparable aspects of a process in which both subject and object, "state" and player are divided. In place of the fixed system we have the split "move"; instead of the unified consciousness we have the competing players.

What this "example" suggests, in conjunction with the unresolved problem of difference and opposition as aspects of signification, is that the differential articulation envisaged by Saussure may have to be construed along agonistic-conflictual lines. Or, as Jean-François Lyotard has recently put it in *La condition postmoderne*, "to speak is to struggle, in the sense of playing . . . speech acts are part of a general agonistics."[2]

If "to speak is to struggle, in the sense of playing (jouer)," what can be said of the rules of that game? Nietzsche's contention that every interpretation defines itself by seeking to dislodge and replace a previously prevailing interpretation can be related to the privilege Saussure assigns to synchronic as opposed to diachronic linguistics. The latter, of course, Saussure associated with the dominant school of historical linguistics against which he reacted and defined his own position. And yet, what I have tried to suggest is that the difference — in the sense of dispute — does not stop there, with what might be regarded as "external" polemics. Rather, difference is incorporated into the system itself, as its founding principle. What results is an inner tension that renders systematicity itself problematic: if the identity of a term depends on what surrounds it, the "institution of language" emerges as an open question. Saussure's injunctions to disregard, ignore, and completely suppress the past, history, the process of becoming, transformation, change, must, in this light, be seen not merely as a warning against the empiricist pseudoscience of historicist linguistics, but even more as a defense against the unsettling implications of his "own" principle of pure difference. For difference and diachrony are, if not identical, intimately related.

To identify language as a *state*, we must deliberately exclude its movement, for the individual speaker no less than for the linguist. The postulate of a "unified collective consciousness" is invoked as the objective correlate of this exclusion. The institution of language is thereby construed as the work of this consciousness. And yet the latter, as Saussure has argued, is itself a product of language.

If this is where our reading of Saussure leaves us, it is precisely where the American founder of semiotics, Charles Sanders Peirce, begins. In a series of essays published in 1868 Peirce develops his theory of signs precisely through a critique of the possibility of anything like a "synchronic perspective," which Peirce calls "intuitive cognition." This he defines as "knowledge of the present as present," as a cognition not itself "determined by a previous cognition,"[3] but which instead derives from, or relates directly to, its object. In an essay entitled "Questions Concerning Certain Faculties Claimed for Man," Peirce denies the possibility of establishing such a cognitive relation, whether in regard to external objects or internal ones. In both cases, he argues, we are necessarily dependent on the testimony of others, and "this remains so through life; testimony will convince a man that he himself is mad" (5.223).

The positive consequence that Peirce elicits from his critique of the possibility of "intuitive cognition" is that there can be no thought apart from signs. This assertion, however, only emerges indirectly, through a discussion of the question, "Can we think without signs?" The manner in which Peirce responds is no less significant than the content of his response: "This is a familiar question, but there is, to this day, no better argument in the affirmative than that thought must precede every sign. This assumes the impossibility of an infinite series. But Achilles, *as a fact, will overtake* the tortoise. *How* this happens is a question not necessary to be answered at present, as long as it certainly does happen" (5.250; first italics mine). Peirce addresses the question by analyzing the argument in the affirmative, not in order to demonstrate its fallaciousness, but rather its power. That power, he implies, has been one of sheer intimidation: by arguing that any negative response will necessarily entail an infinite regress, the proponents of the affirmative position have succeeded in imposing the priority of thought over sign. To deny this priority, they have argued, would be to fall prey to Zeno's famous paradox: for if all thought relates not directly to its object, but to signs, what criterion can there be for ever recognizing the object?

Against this argument of intimidation – a philosophical power play par excellence – Peirce responds with a symmetrically powerful assertion: "It happens all the time, even if we don't know how." Zeno's ingenuity notwithstanding, "Achilles will overtake the tortoise," "as a fact." I will return to the status of that "fact" shortly. For now, however, let us continue to follow Peirce's argument: "From the proposition that every thought is a sign, it follows that every thought must address itself to some other, must determine some other, since that is the essence of the sign" (5.253). The essence of the sign as described by Peirce recalls (i.e., anticipates) the conception of Saussure: the sign is not primarily a representation of an object, but something that "address(es) itself to some other . . . determine(s) some other." Peirce's formulation here deserves attention: it does not specify the addressee of the sign any further than to state that it is "some other." We should not fill in the blank too quickly, for instance with the word "thought," although that would not be entirely wrong. For the thrust of Peirce's entire argumentation here (against the derivation of thought from the object) as elsewhere (in his theory of pragmatism), indicates the importance of a certain indeterminacy. *Sign*, for Peirce, names the necessary determination of thought by something other than itself: another thought, an other-than-thought, but also an other-than-itself (i.e., other than an object present-to-itself). And perhaps above all, *other than the other itself*. The latter possibility is discussed at the conclusion of this essay, where Peirce addresses the question "whether a sign can have any meaning if by its definition it is the sign of something absolutely incognizable," i.e., sheer otherness, or the Kantian *Ding an sich*. In Saussurean terms, what is in question here is the possibility of a "pure difference." Peirce's response—recalling Hegel's critique of Kant—is that such a sign would entail a contradiction in terms, since there is no way of conceiving or conceptualizing alterity except as the other of cognition, which is nothing but a negative mode of knowledge. To generalize this other, to transcendentalize it, is to assert that we can know what we cannot know, and as such is unacceptable.

From this Peirce draws the conclusion that cognition must be conceived not as a static relation of knowledge to known, of sign to object, of same to other, but as a process: "The point here insisted on is not this or that logical solution of the difficulty, but merely that cognition arises by a *process* of beginning, as any other change comes to pass" (5.263).

The "fact" that "Achilles will overtake the tortoise" is thus also a process, one of "beginning" and of "change." That is the "difficulty" that Peirce does not claim to have solved, but with which he will grapple throughout his intellectual life. His semiotics, pragmatism, and phenomenology provide us with hints of a possible solution.

Semiotics. In the following essay of the 1868 series, "Some Consequences of the Four Incapacities," Peirce elaborates on the previously sketched conception of the sign: "A sign has, as such, three references; first, it is a sign *to* some thought that interprets it; second, it is a sign *for* some object to which in that thought it is equivalent; third, it is a sign *in* some respect or quality, which brings it into connection with its object" (5.283). The sequence here is significant: the "first" reference of the sign is to an interpreting thought, what Peirce will later call the "interpretant." What precisely such "interpretation" is, is explained in the second moment: the interpretant interprets by bringing the sign into a relation of equivalence with an object. Since such equivalence derives not from the object, as such, but from the interpretant, it is not absolute or exhaustive, but relative, "in some respect or quality." By thus construing signification and interpretation as inseparable, Peirce situates "diachrony" at the heart of the semiotic process. The latter is both temporal and historical. The process is not, however, diachronic in the sense of simple linearity. It is both pro- and retrospective. In addressing itself to an interpretant, the sign—or rather, since "sign" should be reserved for the process as a whole, the "representamen"—is prospective: a "thought suggests something to the thought which follows it, i.e., is the sign of something to this latter" (5.284). But the interpretant does not merely create, *ex nihilo*, its interpretation; "it only refers to the thing (i.e., the object) through denoting this previous thought" (5.285). The designation of cognition as a "process of beginning" and of "change" refers to the fact that in the sign-process there is no absolute beginning. The representamen and the interpretant are always already situated in a complex of previous signs and interpretations. As Peirce will put it in a later essay, "What Pragmatism Is": "There is but one state of mind from which you can 'set out,' namely, the very state of mind in which you actually find yourself at the time you do 'set out'—a state in which you are laden with an immense mass of cognition already formed, of which you cannot divest yourself if you would . . . " (5.416). The interpretive function of establishing an equivalence between representamen and object thus depends on, is relative to that "immense mass of cognition already formed." It is retrospective, implying a choice and combination of interpretive possibilities already existing; but it is also prospective, since the articulation of that choice or combination is itself a sign, a representamen requiring future interpretation. Ad infinitum? That is the problem. By introducing diachrony into the semiotic process, as interpretation, Peirce cannot avoid or evade the question of the *status* of the sign, and hence, of cognition itself. "But Achilles, as a fact, will overtake the tortoise." We will now have to look more closely at that *fact*.

Peirce's early attempt at a solution to the problem is notable, precisely inasmuch as it sidesteps, or perhaps dislocates, this question of facticity. It addresses itself, notwithstanding, to the problem of distinguishing "cognitions whose objects are *real*" from those "whose objects are *unreal*" (5.311). If cognition partakes of a process of interpretation whose limits are indefinite—each interpretation depending on prior interpretations and on future ones—how can we distinguish between true and false interpretations? Peirce therefore addresses the notion of "reality":

> The real, then, is that which, sooner or later, information and reasoning would finally result in, and which is therefore independent of the vagaries of me and you. Thus, the very origin of the conception of reality shows that this conception essentially involves the notion of a COMMUNITY, without definite limits, and capable of a definite increase

of knowledge. And so those two series of cognition—the real and the unreal—consist of those which, at a time sufficiently future, the community will always continue to reaffirm; and of those which, under the same conditions, will ever after be denied. (5.311)

Having eliminated the "object" as the origin or foundation of cognition, Peirce here replaces it by a transcendental, collective subject, the community of investigators. Although placed in an indefinite future, as though to stress the futurity of cognition, this community also transcends temporality, inasmuch as its "affirmations" and "denials" are construed as being constant and unchanging. Structurally, it performs the same function as Saussure's "unified collective consciousness," imposing a synchronic, systematic coherence on a process otherwise irremediably divided and divisive. Peirce's notion of the community of investigators is, in Kantian terms, regulative but not constitutive. Moreover, if it seems to define a certain direction or tendency implied in the notions of "reality" and "truth," it fails to account for the process by which "Achilles, as a fact, will overtake the tortoise." Peirce acknowledges this, in a letter to Lady Welby, and in so doing relocates, implicitly at least, the notion of truth: "I do not say that it is infallibly true that there is any belief to which a person would come if he were to carry his inquiries far enough. I only say that that alone is what I call Truth. I cannot infallibly know that there *is* any Truth" (*Semiotic and Significs, The Correspondence between C. S. Peirce and Victoria Lady Welby*, ed. Charles S. Hardwick [Bloomington: Indiana Univ. Press, 1977], 73). In other words, when we appeal to the notion of truth, we are referring to the kind of future consensus described as the community of investigators: what is "real" is that *reference*, not its *existence*.

Pragmaticism. Peirce's *"pragmaticism"*—so named to distinguish it from the theories of William James, considered by Peirce as psychologistic—embodies a second attempt to determine the nature of cognition, this time by addressing the question of the meaning of terms. In the light of Peirce's pragmatic "maxim"— "Consider what effects, that might conceivably have practical bearings, we conceive the object of our conception to have. Then, our conception of these effects is the whole of our conception of the object" (5.2)—a new dimension is added to his notion of the sign as that which "must address itself to some other . . . determine some other." For the "other" now is not entirely or simply another *thought*: it entails "practical bearings," "effects" that engage behavior, of a purposeful kind. Meaningful thought is construed as the attempt to establish belief in the place of doubt, to inculcate habits and thus to establish "self-control under every situation, and to every purpose" (5.427). Peirce conceives of meaningful thought as a kind of inner experimentation, in which hypothetical situations are constructed in order to devise appropriate responses. The following illustration indicates what the process is intended to achieve:

I remember that one day at my father's table, my mother spilled some burning spirits on her skirt. Instantly, before the rest of us had had time to think what to do, my brother, Herbert, who was a small boy, had snatched up the rug and smothered the fire. I asked him how he came to think of it so quickly. He said, "I had considered on a previous day what I would do in case such an accident should occur." (5.538. See also 5.487)

If this may be regarded as the *Urszene* of Peirce's pragmaticism, it suggests some of the problems that the latter cannot fail to encounter. First, the dangers or emergencies with which it struggles to cope are not purely external. The effort to establish self-control through the inculcation of "habits" is directed as much at coping with inner division as with outer challenges: "A person is not absolutely an individual. His thoughts are what he is 'saying to himself,' that is, is saying to that other self that is just coming into life in the flow of time. When one reasons, it is that critical self that one is trying to persuade; and all thought whatsoever is a sign" (5.421). To establish belief and habit means to establish an interpretation of one's words that will overcome the intrinsic divisions of those words as signs. "Doubt" is therefore not—as Peirce himself seeks constantly to convince himself—merely the "absence" of belief, its simple negation: it is a consequence of the divided structure of the sign. Within the individual subject, this takes the form of what Peirce calls "self-reproach" (5.418). The stronger the habit, the less this feeling of self-reproach will be. However, "the more closely this is approached"—that is, the "fixed character" imparted to action by habit—"the less room for self-control there will be; and where no self-control is possible there will be no self-reproach" (5.418).

Thus, both for "internal" and "external" reasons, the definition of meaningful thought as the establishment of fixed habits becomes self-defeating: internally, because it produces a kind of automatism that eliminates the self-control it is designed to achieve, and externally, because such fixed habits become, by virtue of their very fixity and hence inflexibility, incapable of dealing with changing and infinitely variable circumstances. The early Peircean notion of thought as the elimination of doubt and the establishment of habit would lead not to self-control and the ability to cope with danger, but rather to the blind automatism of something very like Freud's repetition compulsion.

This is surely at least one of the reasons why, as Peirce continued to work on his pragmaticism, the notion of habit as the goal of thought had to be transformed: precisely in the direction of transformation itself. And it is significant that this modification intervenes at a point in Peirce's thought where his theory of pragmaticism converges with his semiotics.[4] The question of the meaning of a term merges with that of "the interpretants, or proper significant effects, of signs" (5.475). Peirce distinguishes three kinds of interpretants: the "emotional interpretant," the "feeling" produced by the sign; the "energetic interpretant," the effort it engenders (which may be "a muscular one . . . but . . . is much more usually an exertion upon the Inner World, a mental effort"); and finally, "the logical interpretant." And here, once again, Peirce finds himself staring at . . . Achilles and the tortoise: "Shall we say that this effect may be a thought, that is to say a mental sign? No doubt, it may be so; only, if this sign be of an intellectual kind—as it would have to be—it must itself have a logical interpretant; so that it cannot be the *ultimate* logical interpretant of the concept" (5.476). The only logical interpretant that can escape this infinite regress—or progress—must therefore be not simply another sign, but "a *habit-change* . . . a modification of a person's tendencies towards action, resulting from previous experiences or from previous exertions of his will or acts, or from a complexus of both kinds of cause" (5.476).

This introduction of the notion of "habit-change," as opposed to mere "habit," alters the very conception of what an "ultimate" logical interpretant can be. It cannot be simply the propensity to act in certain ways under certain conditions; it cannot be simply a fixed result, the constant reiteration of the same. And, although it participates in the semiotic process, it is not simply a sign "in that way in which that sign of which it is the logical interpretant is the sign" (5.491). That sign, we recall, is determined as being in a certain, relative, and partial equivalence to its object. The final, logical interpretant, which is the site of that equivalence, is not itself equivalent, does not itself have an "object." We must keep this in mind when we read Peirce's final attempt at formulating this final interpretant: "The deliberately formed, self-analyzing habit—self-analyzing because formed by the aid of analysis of the exercises that nourished it—is the living definition, the veritable and final logical interpretant" [ibid.]. This final logical interpretant may be "self-analyzing," but the 'self' that it analyzes, "the exercises that nourished it," have no simple unity or identity. That "self" consists in all the factors contributing to habit-change, to "a modification of consciousness" (5.485) that entails a modification of behavior. If it necessarily involves repetition, it is in the sense assigned by Derrida to "iteration," which "alters."[5] As Peirce writes, "it naturally follows that repetitions of the actions that produce the changes increase the changes" (5.477).

This is why the "generality" of habit, and even more, of habit-change, is of a different sort from that of the sign, from "the verbal formulation (which) merely expresses it." If the habit is distinct from its verbal expression, it is because it is "the real and living logical conclusion." But its "reality" is not that of simple self-presence. Nor is it that of the anticipated community of investigators, asserting and denying the same in an indefinite future. Peirce's notion of "reality" takes us to his "categories."

And, more precisely, to his *phenomenology*, "the description of . . . all that is in any way or in any sense present to the mind" (1.284). Peirce allows for three distinct, interdependent but irreducible categories: firstness, secondness, and thirdness. Firstness he describes as "the mode of being which consists in its subject's being positively such as it is regardless of aught else" (1.25). Thirdness is the realm of reason and of law, and is epitomized in the irreducibly triadic structure of the sign. But here it is secondness that is of particular pertinence: it comprises the realm of fact and of actuality, "of causation and statical force" (1.325), of constraint, shock, and surprise. And of reality: "In the idea of reality, Secondness is predominant; for the real is that which insists upon forcing its way to recognition as something *other* than the mind's creation" [1.325]. The real is that which insists and resists, which disrupts and unsettles: "I call such forcible modification of our ways of thinking the influence of the world of fact or *experience*" (1.321). And again: "It is the compulsion, the absolute constraint upon us to think otherwise than we have been thinking that constitutes experience" [ibid.], and which calls forth resistance, "and resistance is effort opposing change." Habit, and habit-change, name one such effort: man "defends himself from the angles of hard fact by clothing himself with a garment of contentment and of habituation" [ibid.]. But this effort can never fully reach its goal; the garment must continually be changed. As with the dress of Mrs. Peirce, habits are incessantly under fire.

The second category, which includes "brute fact" and "brute force," experience and reality, is therefore "the element of struggle" (1.322). As "statical force," it entails the arresting of the movement of signs and of interpretation, and since it is also the "sheriff," without whom the law and judge (thirdness) would be impotent, such "arresting" can be taken quite literally.[6]

If "Achilles, as a fact, will overtake the tortoise," if indeed he will have (always, already) overtaken the tortoise, it is through the arresting facticity of a habit that is simultaneously a habit-change, pointed both toward the past and toward the future. Which is why the verbal formulation or "expression" of that habit-change will have to be in the "future conditional" (5.482). And which also explains why cognition, for Peirce, that process of "beginning" and of "change," necessarily entails violence: "This direct consciousness of hitting and of getting hit enters into all cognition and serves to make it mean something real" (8.41). For any such "fixation of belief," entailing the reaction to shock and surprise, as well as the effort to comprehend them, will inevitably have to exclude what it cannot contain. It will have to set its own limits by a reaction no less violent than the shock that calls it forth. Peirce's term for such enabling exclusions is "the acritically indubitable," which, he adds, "is invariably vague" (5.446).

As to the process by which such exclusions are effected, Peirce has little explicit to tell us; despite his anti-individualism, despite the historicity and sociality of his semiotics, the framework within which he poses the problems of the pragmatic aspects of thought remains that of the individual, struggling to cope and to gain "self-control." And yet, the very movement of his thought impels us beyond this framework. Criticizing Josiah Royce, he observes: "I find myself in a world of forces which act upon me, and it is they, and not the logical transformations of my thought which determine what I shall ultimately believe" (8.45). That such forces are intelligible neither within the scope of isolated individuals, nor within that of the community which is their idealized mirror image; that the established sets of interpretations from which we always take our point of departure require a more complex kind of analysis, is difficult to deny.

The formation and modification of what Peirce described as "habits" depend on collective traditions and the institutions through which they transmit and reproduce themselves. But if the institution of specific interpretations thus calls for the interpretation of specific institutions, Peirce will have sharpened our sensibility for the intrinsic and violent instability of both institution and interpretation and for the struggle they inevitably entail.

Chapter 2
The Limits of Professionalism

Some time ago a full-page ad appeared in the *New York Times Book Review* announcing that 1981 would be the year in which the freedom of "limits" was to be discovered. The ad was promoting a new book entitled *Limits—A Search for New Values*, and the title is a sign of the times. Events and processes with which we are all at least superficially familiar have, in the past few years, compelled Western industrial and capitalist societies to reconsider the status of their own limits, and to revise the previously prevailing view of them as borders to be extended, or as external boundaries serving merely to establish the integrity of the areas they demarcate. *The Limits of Growth* stands as just the most conspicuous symptom of this revision in our thinking about limits, in which we have come to conceive of them not as neutral and stable entities, but rather as active, volatile, and constraining factors that can no longer be taken for granted, factors that menace as much as they protect or contain.

This recent resurgence of the question of limits—entailing as it does a fundamental restructuring of power relations on a worldwide scale—has, I think, been most conspicuous in North America, and above all in the United States, where for as long as most people care to remember limits have been conceived as provisional markers in a process of continuous expansion, much like record performances in sports, which are there only to be surpassed at the next best occasion. If the motto of twentieth-century America has been "the sky's the limit," more and more Americans have come to discover that their sky is as close and as constraining as the ceilings of modern city apartments—and hardly cosy for being so close. The effects of this discovery have produced an alarming unraveling of the fabric of American society, a process that is radically transforming the world in which we live and work.

The breakdown of traditional frames of reference has directed attention increasingly to the problems of their (previous) stability—that is, to the questions of their institutionalization and of the possibilities, both positive and negative, that the crisis of such institutions brings with it. In a very limited area, this paper seeks to address some of these questions.

In a text written some ten years ago, dealing with frames and framing—"Le parergon"—Derrida argued, programmatically but in passing, that "deconstruction" would have to occupy itself increasingly with the institutional conditions of its own practice,

> with what is generally, and wrongly, considered as philosophy's external habitat, as the extrinsic conditions of its exercise—that is, the historical forms of its pedagogy, the social, economic or political structures of this pedagogical institution. It is by touching solid structures, "material" institutions, and not merely discourses or significant representations, that deconstruction distinguishes itself from analysis or "criticism." And to be pertinent, it works, in the most rigorous manner possible, in just the place where the so-called "internal" operation of philosophy articulates itself necessarily (that is, internally *and* externally) with the institutional conditions and forms of teaching and learning. And it drives this to the point where the concept of institution itself would be submitted to the same deconstructive treatment.[1]

This important statement is followed in Derrida's text by an allusion to future work ("But I am already getting into next year's seminar") which is in turn interrupted by one of those empty frames that are the joy and tribulation of the reader of "Le parergon" . . . Has that frame been filled in since? I think not, and if so, this is not without cause. The strategy of deconstruction in what I would call its orthodox form has focused on the particular ways in which systematic constructions simultaneously entail exclusions and incorporations, which render the system constitutively dependent on factors it cannot integrate or comprehend. But in thus elaborating the aporetic, nondialectical identity of the conditions of possibility and impossibility of systematic thought, such deconstruction has tended to downplay the forces and factors that always operate to institute and to maintain certain sets of paradigms, notwithstanding (or even because of) their intrinsically aporetic structure. In short, by focusing on the conditions of possibility and impossibility of systems, what has been neglected is what I would call the conditions of *imposability*, the conditions under which arguments, categories, and values impose and maintain a certain authority, even where traditional authority itself is meant to be subverted. To ignore such factors, of course, is to leave their force unchallenged and to suffer their effects without reserve.

This very problem is addressed in the work of Charles Sanders Peirce who, although certainly an early forerunner of deconstruction, was from the very start concerned with its other side: the fact that despite the tendency of semiotic processes to be open-ended and relatively indeterminate, determination takes place all the time, has always taken place, and will always take place, over and above the efforts of individual thinkers. In a previous article[2] I have attempted to indicate how Peirce's conception of semiosis leads him, first to a theory of "pragmaticism" and then toward the problem of *institutionalization*. I will try to carry this move a step further today. But before I begin, let me briefly summarize the steps that lead Peirce to the threshold of what, for want of a better term, I will provisionally call a "deconstructive pragmatics of institutions."

In Peirce's semiotics, the representational function of the sign, indispensable to all thought, is made to depend upon a third instance, which determines the ability of the sign to designate an object. This instance Peirce calls the "interpretant." The sign is only placed in relation to an object by another sign, which "interprets" it, i.e., which establishes a relation of equivalence between the sign as representamen and its designatum, the object.

This interpretant is itself split. It operates by referring to previously established interpretations, and hence is retrospective; but it also, as itself a sign, anticipates and depends upon subsequent interpretations. It is both retrospective and prospective. Considered abstractly, as an isolated process, this process of semiotic interpretation would be unlimited, and hence would, by itself, dissolve in total indetermination. But the process is never isolated, its point of departure is always fixed, locally determined. Peirce's critique of Descartes and of all subsequent *prima philosophia*, including the Husserlian *epochē*, asserts that absolute doubt is make-believe, a fiction of the ego designed to establish its self-identity. The effort of the individual mind to divest itself of all prejudice, of all prior knowledge and beliefs, is inherently impossible:

> There is but one state of mind from which you can "set out," namely,
> the very state of mind in which you actually find yourself at the time
> you do "set out"—a state in which you are laden with an immense
> mass of cognition already formed, of which you cannot divest youself
> if you would.[3]

This statement in itself is not strikingly original: what is, is the fact that such "states of mind" for Peirce are themselves products of interpretation, and more important, that such interpretation can never be regarded as inherently stable, given the semiotic process in which it is engaged. To establish or institute a state of mind, a particular interpretation can only involve an exercise of force, even violence, in order to arrest the inherent tendency of signs to refer to other signs, *ad infinitum*. This is why Peirce develops a notion of the "real," the "actual" or "experience" not as a given state of affairs, but as a violent shock, involving conflict, struggle, and resistance. Reality and resistance recover their etymological kinship in Peirce. The problem then becomes that of defining the conditions under which such a violent arrestation – in other words: institution – takes place.

Peirce himself is convinced that such a process cannot derive from the individual mind or subject; it must involve more general, communal factors. And although he himself never pursues this line of thought to the point where social and historical forces and institutions would necessarily enter the picture, he does indicate a possible direction such an inquiry could take. He does this in developing the notion of "habit" as that which limits and delimits the process of thought and interpretation. It is true that he construes habit primarily as a property of individuals – but it is no less true that his discussion of its function points us beyond the individual toward more general, social and historical factors. This, then, is what I want to develop here.

Among the many provocative peculiarities that confront the reader of Charles Sanders Peirce, not the least is the insistent emphasis placed on *habit* as the beginning and end of all thought, and as the decisive constituent of meaning. "The whole function of thought is to produce habits of action. . . . To develop its meaning, we have, therefore, simply to determine what habits it involves" (5.400). However complex this notion of habit may be in Peirce, however intricate his efforts to work out its import in relation to doubt, belief, and action, there remains throughout his writing the unwavering conviction that thought, in its essence, is *habit forming.* And this obtains not merely of untutored thinking, but of its most elevated form, *inquiry*: "Doubt . . . stimulates us to inquiry until it is destroyed" (5.373).

Peirce's "pragmaticism" conceives of thought as the effort to achieve control – above all, self-control – through the instilling of habits that will enable one to cope with emergencies, by anticipating them and devising adequate responses: "The decision upon the merely make-believe dilemma goes towards forming a *bona fide* habit that will be operative in a real emergency" (5.373).

What makes Peirce's use of the notion of habit so striking, at least to the contemporary reader, is the emphatically positive valorization assigned to the term. To be sure, it is true that as his thought evolves, Peirce introduces the notion of "habit-change" to describe the aim of intellectual activity, rather than simple habit formation (5.476ff). But he never seems to doubt that the basic function of thinking must be construed as an effort to anticipate danger and to devise quasi-instinctual and effective responses to it. The negative connotations of "habit," as a mode of behavior that can also entail a *decrease* in self-control, are almost entirely absent from Peirce's discussion.

This positive valorization of habit as the ultimate end of all thought appears all the more curious when one considers the exalted status Peirce sought to attribute to rationality as a mode of human behavior. This appreciation, he was well aware, did not fit easily into his conception of pragmatism. In 1900 he acknowledged as much in the context of a discussion of the role of higher education:

> Only recently we have seen an American man of science and of weight discuss the purpose of education, without once alluding to the only motive that animates the genuine scientific investigator. I am not guiltless in this matter myself, for in my youth I wrote some articles to uphold a doctrine called Pragmatism, namely, that the meaning and essence of every conception lies in the application that is to be made of it. That is all very well, when properly understood. I do not intend to recant it. But the question arises, *what is* the ultimate application; at that time I seem to have been inclined to subordinate the *conception* to the *act*, knowing to doing. Subsequent experience of life has taught me that the only thing that is really desirable without a reason for being so, is to render ideas and things reasonable. One cannot well demand a reason for reasonableness itself.[4]

And yet, despite the apodicticity of this last assertion, all of Peirce's reflections on the semiotic character of thought and on its pragmatic "purport" are precisely designed to provide "a reason for reasonableness itself": that of coping with possible dangers. Such a "reason," however, collides with Peirce's conception of scientific inquiry as an entirely disinterested activity, one diametrically opposed to the then-prevalent tendencies in American higher education, at least as Peirce saw them, "American education, for the most part, is directed to no other object than the welfare of individual scholars; and thereby incites *them* to pursue that object exclusively" (Wiener, 333). By contrast, Peirce's positive appreciation of the selfless and disinterested character of science was evidently intended as an alternative to the kind of self-serving motives then dominant in American academic life:

> No other occupation of man is so purely and immediately directed to the one end that is alone intrinsically rational as scientific investigation. It so strongly influences those who pursue it to subordinate all motives of ambition, fame, greed, self-seeking of every description that other people . . . fail, in many cases, to divine the scientific man's simple motives. (Wiener, 334)

In view of the decisive importance attributed by Peirce to the "community of investigators," as the ultimate instance in determining the value of individual insights and assertions, it is clear that such a community would itself have to be free from all particular and partisan interests if its authority was to be operative. Peirce, in statements such as those just quoted, sought to *defend* the essential disinterestedness of science and—for it amounts to the same—that of the community of inquirers, from the all-too-conspicuous *reality* of his time.

And yet, as I have indicated, such a defense collided not only with reality but also with Peirce's own thinking. For if thought, as a process of semiotic interpretation, constitutes itself through, and in, the formation and transformation of habits, and if habits are designed to enable one to cope with situations of danger and difficulty, then there is "a reason for reasonableness," and it is not necessarily one that is entirely rational. The reason for rationality would reside in the effort to ward off disaster, to maintain "control." This, in turn, would tend to suggest that the obvious discrepancy between Peirce's "ideal" community of investigators, free of all self-serving interests, seeking only the truth, and the real tendencies of self-interest he perceived in the American university system might be the inevitable consequence of what Peirce himself saw as the essence of thought: the effort to cope with reality and to maintain self-control.

But, it might be argued, there is a qualitative difference between "thought" *per se* and scientific inquiry. Ordinary, nonscientific thought might well be guided by individual interest and directed to the formation of habits. Scientific inquiry, on the other hand, could still be more disinterested, more concerned with the conditions under which habits are formed, rather than with the formation of particular habits themselves. And yet, even if scientific inquiry could thus be defined as that mode of thought which is animated by the habit of investigating habit formation as such, this in itself would hardly establish its intrinsically disinterested character. On the contrary: such a reflected mode of habit formation would seem merely the inevitable extension of less reflective forms of thought. For, as Peirce well knew, the aim of self-control is not served simply by the *formation* of a habit, once and for all; it requires modification of habits, in order to anticipate changing conditions and unprecedented emergencies. As Peirce observes: "Moreover—*here is the point*—every man exercises more or less control over himself by means of modifying his own habits" (5.487). Thought thus emerges, even in its least reflective forms, as a kind of inner, dialogical experimentation, aimed at anticipating the shocks and surprises that, for Peirce, constituted "reality" and "experience," in all of their "brute" force and facticity. Peirce's insistently proclaimed "realism" is not of a very consoling kind: the reality involved, if it is "independent" of what individuals may think about it, is not simply "outside" the mind; but it is not contained in it either: "For the real is that which insists upon forcing its way to recognition as something *other* than the mind's creation. . . . The real is active; we acknowledge it, in calling it the actual."[5] The essential characteristic of actuality, however, is struggle: the struggle to assimilate the shocks and intrusions of experience by—we return to our initial consideration—the construction of *habits*, also in the most literal (etymological) sense: Man, Peirce writes:

defends himself from the angles of hard fact by clothing himself with a garment of contentment and of habituation. Were it not for this garment, he would every now and then find his internal world rudely disturbed and his fiats set at naught by brutal inroads of ideas from without. I call such forcible modification of our ways of thinking the influence of the world of fact or *experience*. But he patches up his argument by guessing what those inroads are likely to be and carefully excluding from his internal world every idea which is likely to be so disturbed. (Buchler, 87–88)

The formation of habits, and their maintenance, thus involves a double gesture: *patching up* our garments, revising and reworking our habits, we not merely anticipate eventualities, but at the same time we deliberately (if unconsciously) exclude ideas and possibilities, in order to preserve and to strengthen the frontiers of our "internal world" against intrusions from without.

There is but one state of mind from which you can "set out" — namely, the very state of mind in which you actually find yourself at the time you do "set out." (5.416)

The "state of mind" from which Peirce sets out, or rather which allows him to construe thinking as an effort to anticipate and cope with the shocks of experience through the formation of habits — this state of mind shares certain salient features with more general tendencies characteristic of American society in the latter half of the nineteenth century, and which have been described by Robert Wiebe (in a book of the same name) as *The Search for Order*.[6] The tendency to see in the formation of habits an imperative and constructive necessity, a means of coping with danger rather than a danger itself, is reflected in Emerson's call for the development of a new culture: "It is a measure of culture, the number of things taken for granted," Emerson wrote, adding that culture is "all which gives the mind possession of its powers," and that "the whole state of man is a state of culture."[7] The sense of reality as a series of shocks, involving both potential risks and danger but also enormous opportunities; the need to devise a system of beliefs, habits, and practices capable of anticipating, ordering, and responding to those challenges; the emphasis on a certain development of "science" and "rationality," as key elements in the success of this project — all these were widely held convictions characterizing American self-consciousness in the latter half of the past century. Such sentiments were nourished by economic developments and their social repercussions: the rapid growth of the economy, as measured in per capita income, was accompanied by a no-less-striking concentration of wealth and inequality of its distribution. Socially, there was a decline of traditional local communities as the process of urbanization provided a geographic counterpart to the economic concentration taking place. Urbanization, industrialization, and what has been called "modernization" also meant an extension of commodity relations to virtually all sectors of social life, with its concomitant definition of individuals in terms of juridically equal commodity owners.

In this highly conflictural force field of expanding commodity production one form that the "search for order" took—and it is the one that interests me here—is the development of what Burton Bledstein has described as "The Culture of Professionalism." This "culture"—defined by Bledstein as "a set of learned values and habitual responses" (p. x)—was the collective effort of a significant part of the middle class to establish a measure of self-control, of status and standing, in face of rapid economic and social change. Although "more than an institutional event in American life" (Bledstein, x), the development of this "culture" entailed the transformation of a particular institution: the American university, which was fashioned into the privileged social instrument of professionalization. The thesis implicit in Bledstein's book, and which I want to discuss here, is that neither professionalism nor the university are fully intelligible in isolation from one another, nor in separation from the social processes to which they responded. For it is this that distinguishes his study of the phenomenon from almost all others written on it: professionalism is construed not merely as "a set of learned values," as an integral system, but, more to the point, as a set of habitual *responses*. This emphasis recalls the approach of Peirce, for whom every thought and action had to be construed as a response to, or inference from, another thought, action, or state of affairs.

But before we turn to just such a state of affairs, let us first attempt to describe some of the distinctive features of this "culture of professionalism." A professional was—and is—a specialist who lives from his work. He has undergone a lengthy period of training in a recognized institution (professional school), which certifies him as being competent in a specialized area; such competence derives from his mastery of a particular discipline, an esoteric body of useful knowledge involving systematic theory and resting on general principles. Finally, the professional is felt to "render a service" rather than provide an ordinary commodity, and it is a service that he alone, qua professional, can supply. The latter aspect of professionalism lends its practitioners their peculiar authority and their status: they are regarded as possessing a monopoly of competence in their particular "field." It is, then, the constitution of this "field" that provides important insight into the character and operation of professionalism. The latter has, understandably enough, often been identified with "specialization," that is, with the technical division of labor characteristic of modern forms of production and of knowledge. A recent instance of this attitude is furnished by John Higham, who argues that the attention devoted to professionalism is misguided:

> it is necessary therefore to ask: what distinctive characteristic of
> nineteenth-century knowledge impelled its creators and custodians to

turn their particular competences into professions? The obvious answer is specialisation. The multiplication and differentiation of bodies of esoteric knowledge made the new professions possible.[8]

Specialization may indeed be the "obvious answer," but it is not a convincing one. For although the specialized development of knowledge was surely one of the factors that "made the new professions possible," it does not suffice to explain the complex *ethos* — what Bledstein calls the "culture" — accompanying and indeed distinguishing the new phenomenon. For all studies of professionalism, even the most descriptive and functionalist, concur in identifying certain characteristics that differentiate the professions from specialized occupations in general. First and foremost, there is the tendency of the professional to present himself as relatively autonomous within his field. Such autonomy, however, does not derive simply from the specialized skills involved; the "services" rendered by a doctor, lawyer, or research scientist are not merely specialized (as are those of the auto mechanic), they are, in a crucial sense, *incommensurable*, and upon this incommensurability the distinctive autonomy and authority of the professional is founded. As Bledstein observes,

> Utilising his trained capacity, the professional person interpreted the special lines along which such complex phenomena as a physical disease, a point of law, a stage of human psychological growth, or the identity of an historical society developed in time and space. The professional did not vend a commodity, or exclusively pursue a self-interest. He did not sell a service by a contract which called for specific results in a specific time or restitution for errors. Rather, through a special understanding of a segment of the universe, the professional person released nature's potential and rearranged reality . . . Such was the august basis for the authority of the professional. (Bledstein, 89–90)

The incommensurability of the professional, of the "services" he *rendered*, and did not merely *sell*, sought to place his activities outside of the pale of ordinary commodity relationships. This was, and has remained, a decisive feature of the professional who, while offering his services for pay, nonetheless claims for them a *value* irreducible to that determined by the market. This claim of incommensurability has shaped both the techniques and the attitudes of professionalism. They are suggested in the passage just cited: the professional disposes over a body of systematic, esoteric knowledge, inaccessible to the layman and yet in itself coherent, self-contained, reposing on founding *principles*. These principles form the cognitive basis of laws, rules, and techniques, which constitute a *discipline*, and a praxis requiring a long period of training and initiation. Although a specialized branch of knowledge, such a discipline is regarded as comprising a coherent, integral, and self-contained domain, based on an equally self-contained "natural" state of things. "Nature" here designates above all the objective referent, the *fundamentum in re* which guarantees the legitimacy of particularized knowledge and the efficacy of its applications. The objectivity of such knowledge is invoked as the basis of a power, privilege, and authority that claims to transcend the limited partialities of social life: "Science as a source for professional authority transcended the favoritism of politics, the corruption of personality, and the exclusiveness of partisanship" (Bledstein, 90). But perhaps above all, professional competence is felt to transcend the self-interest of business and market relations.

The services rendered by the professional draw their "value" not from the usual exchange procedures of the market, but rather from the specific social *needs* they claim to fulfill. Although selling his skills as a private individual to other equally private individuals and therein no different from any other possessor of commodities, the professional professes to be concerned primarily with the public good, with the necessities of life and welfare. The professional, in short, seeks to define his services as exclusively determined by public need, and hence, as predominantly a *use-value*, not an exchange-value. It is precisely in the effort to distinguish himself from the businessman, on the one hand, and from the worker, on the other, that the professional finds it necessary to cultivate the professional ethos and "culture," the historical and social genealogy of which Bledstein has so remarkably described.

We see, then, that the emergence of professionalism may be understood as an effort not unlike that orienting the inquiry of Peirce: an effort to establish a measure of self-control, not, to be sure, on the part of isolated individuals, but on that of a group, seeking to define and to maintain a certain identity in the face of an extremely dynamic, unsettling, and powerful reorganization and transformation of society. What is of particular interest to us here, however, is the relation of such professionalization to the institutions and practices which marked the development of the humanistic disciplines in general, and those of literary studies in particular. The following remarks may be read as a first, tentative effort to elucidate this relation.

"Utilising his trained capacity, the professional person interpreted the special lines along which such complex phenomena . . . developed in time and space." The nature of that interpretation displays certain general characteristics, apparently common to professional disciplines as such, above and beyond their particular qualities. In order for the authority of the professional to be recognized as autonomous, the "field" of his "competence" had to be defined as essentially self-contained, in accordance with the "natural" self-identity of its "objects." In general, the professional sought to *isolate*, in order to control. Hence, the emphasis in the later nineteenth century on the elaboration of *principles*; once these were established, and with them the discipline, the emphasis could then shift to the identification of *rules*, where it has remained until today.[9] Bledstein describes a symptomatic instance of such "isolation": the treatment of the symptoms of hysteria:

> The scientific response of the trained physician was to seek a specific medical etiology in an individual case for a specific problem. Thereby he isolated a subject by minimising the significance of its social context and ignoring the root causes, which might require social and ideological reform. For instance, psychiatrists, neurologists, and gynecologists who treated such a "fashionable disease" of middle-class women as hysteria in the later nineteenth century were convinced that they were diagnosing a medical problem with a specific etiology, a predictable course of development, and an origin in an organic malfunction of the uterus. The disease stemmed not from society but from an individual's sexual organs (Bledstein, 109).

Hysteria, of course, was also the point of departure for Freud, who rejected such naturalistic, physiological explanations of the malady, tracing its etiology back to a structure of psychosexual conflict. The psychoanalytic method he thereby developed graphically redefined the relation of subject and object as well as the structure of each; the analyst could no longer be construed as a simple clinician or detached observer, nor did his training and knowledge enable him to isolate a self-contained object or sphere. Instead, he was progressively implicated in the conflictural history that, together with the analysand, he sought to repeat and transform. If the development of psychoanalytic therapy moved in the direction of ever-increasing activity on the part of its participants, analyst no less than analysand, this distinguished it from the characteristic relation of doctor and "patient," and more generally, of professional and lay client. For an indispensable feature of the professional's assertion of autonomy and authority was the corresponding passivity and dependence of the layperson, and in particular of the client. Here again, the traditional ethos of the marketplace — *caveat emptor* — was replaced by the injunction: *credat emptor*. As Bledstein remarks,

> Symbols of professional authority . . . reinforced the public's consciousness of its dependence. Indeed, the pattern of dependence was the most striking conservative consequence of the culture of professionalism. Practitioners succeeded by playing on the weaknesses of the client, his vulnerability, helplessness, and general anxiety. . . . The culture of professionalism tended to cultivate an atmosphere of constant crisis — emergency — in which practitioners both created work for themselves and reinforced their authority by intimidating clients. (Bledstein, 99–100).

In short, the culture of professionalism drew much of its force, its "social credit," credibility, from the cultivation and exploitation of anxiety. There is also reason to suspect that its general methods of interpretation reflected the psychic mechanisms of anxiety, as these have been described by Freud, in his essay, *Inhibitions, Symptoms and Anxiety*. In that text Freud portrayed anxiety as the reaction of the ego to a danger. Anxiety, he suggested, functioned as a danger signal, entailing the recognition (i.e., anticipation and recollection in one) of a situation threatening the integrity of the ego, i.e., its constitutive capacity to establish stable cathexes. The essence of danger for the ego Freud described as "separation" and "object-loss," phenomena that were associated with the helplessness of the ego to alleviate tension. Freud's analysis of this process—an interpretation of which I have attempted elsewhere[10]—suggests that the formation of stable cathexes by the ego depends on its ability to invest perceptions and representations with a relative power to endure, i.e., to remain identical to themselves. The operation of anxiety as a *signal* would thus converge with a process of identifying and retaining such perceptions and representations so as to maintain their self-identity against conflictual desires tending to disrupt such identity. The particular forms to which this general process might lead include the formation of phobias, of symptoms, as well as "defensive" processes such as that designated by Freud as "isolation." Let us begin with the latter (which, we remember, is also one of the features attributed by Bledstein to the method of professionalism):

> When something unpleasant has happened to the subject or when he himself has done something which has a significance for his neurosis, he interpolates an interval during which nothing further must happen—during which he must perceive nothing and do nothing. . . . The experience is not forgotten, but, instead, it is deprived of its affect, and its associative connections are suppressed or interrupted so that it remains as though isolated.[11]

Although Freud first relates this mechanism of isolation to obsessional neurosis, as is so often the case, he finds that this neurotic manifestation is merely an exaggeration of a far more common "normal" process of thought.

> The normal phenomenon of concentration provides a pretext for this kind of neurotic procedure; what seems to us important in the way of an impression or a piece of work must not be interfered with by the simultaneous claims of any other mental processes or activities. But even a normal person uses concentration to keep away not only what is irrelevant or unimportant, but, above all, what is unsuitable because it is contradictory. He is most disturbed by those elements which once belonged together but which have been torn apart in the course of his development. . . . Thus, in the normal course of things, the ego has a great deal of isolating work to do in its funciton of directing the current of thought. (Freud, 21)

For the emerging culture of professionalism, too, "genius was an act of concentration" (Bledstien, 267), entailing self-discipline as subjective condition for the mastery of a discipline, itself separated—isolated—from other disciplines. Limits and limitation were indispensable for the demarcation of the professional field, but once the latter had been established, the attention to borders (founding principles) became increasingly the exception rather than the rule. Attention was focused on the problems and questions emerging *within* the field, the coherence and even history of which was taken increasingly for granted:

> Within carefully established spaces, rituals and ceremonies began to dominate human relationships and to consolidate the emerging culture of professionalism. (Bledstein, 95)

If, then, "the culture of professionalism in America has been enormously satisfying to the human ego" as Bledstein (p. xi) asserts, not the least important factor in that satisfaction has been its ability to establish and to institutionalize a collective system of defense against anxieties deriving from American society. The general structure of that defensive system recalls two other aspects of Freud's discussion of anxiety. First, the formation of *phobias*. According to Freud, a phobia is formed as a means of defending against a conflictual or ambivalent desire. A "substitute-formation" is constructed, taking the place of the original desire, and displacing it onto a different object or representation, which can be more easily controlled:

> This substitutive formation has two obvious advantages. In the first place it avoids a conflict due to ambivalence . . . and in the second place it enables the ego to cease generating anxiety. For the anxiety belonging to a phobia is conditional; it only emerges when the object of it is perceived, and rightly so, since it is only then that the danger-situation is present. . . . All one has to do is to avoid the sight of it . . . that is, its presence . . . in order to be free from danger and anxiety. (Freud, 125)

The situation of a discipline, with fixed and unquestioned boundaries, facilitates a mode of thinking in terms of presence or absence, the either-or alternative so conducive to the phobic resolution of anxiety. Peirce's attempt to construe thinking and meaning in terms of "conditional possibility," and thus to extend controlled laboratory experimentation into a model of thinking in general, may be seen as an articulation of this phobic mode of behavior. What Whitehead described as the "professionalisation of knowledge" is yet another form:

> Its methodological procedure is exclusive and intolerant, and rightly so. It fixes attention on a definite group of abstractions, neglects everything else, and elicits every scrap of information and theory which is relevant to what it has retained. This method is triumphant, provided that the abstractions are judicious. But, however triumphant,

the triumph is within limits. The neglect of these limits leads to disastrous oversights.[12]

An understanding of the driving forces behind professionalization, construed not as a technical fact of the intellectual division of labor ("specialization") but as a *social relation* and as a defensive strategy, suggests that the "oversight" and "neglect of . . . limits" comprise an indispensable part of a phenomenon animated as much by anxiety as by a spontaneous desire to learn or to serve.

Second: the institutional structure of the culture of professionalism is identified by Bledstein with the career: the arrangement of the individual's professional life in terms of an ascending ladder of achievement. In place of the lateral ties of earlier local communities, as well as of emerging class structure, the progressive initiation, mastery, and exercise of a profession is presented in terms of upward mobility, the reward of rising achievement. Existing hierarchies of rank and privilege are associated with individual performance within an institutionally defined framework. Social and economic insecurity is thereby presented not as a function of conflict, not as the resultant of an agonistic field of forces, but as the linear order of ascending qualification, based on predictable, objective criteria. Here, again, the danger signal of anxiety finds its course plotted in advance, according to apparently transparent rules and regulations. Once the professional has succeeded in gaining admittance to the "field," he can hope to enjoy a measure of security unknown by other nonprofessional salaried persons: provided, of course, that he continues to accept and to practice the game according to its rules. The vicissitudes of a generalized and unpredictable *competition* are replaced by the calculability of *competence*. Having donned the habits of the profession, its practitioner can hope to be protected against the rigors of social struggle.

The process of isolating, as constitutive of the establishment of professions and of disciplines, requires itself an isolated, relatively self-contained social space in which to operate. Historically, this space was provided by the university,

> the matrix within which the culture of professionalism matured . . .
> the centre to which practitioners trace the theoretical basis of knowl-
> edge upon which they establish authority. (Bledstein, 289)

The university, as it developed in the latter half of the nineteenth century, became the institutional expression and articulation of the culture of professionalism. It was and remains the gateway to the professions, marking the transition from the local, geographically determined community of youth, centered around the family, to that "translocal" academic community, structured in terms of the professional disciplines themselves. The "insulation" or "isolation" of the American academic community from other segments of society is the negative prereq uisite of that demarcation that marks the professional perspective, above all that of the university professor. Positively considered, the establishment of the modern university was the institutional means by which the professional claim to a monopoly of competence could be established and maintained. The university, itself divided into more or less isolated, self-contained departments, was the embodiment of that kind of limited universality that characterized the cognitive model of professionalism. It instituted areas of training and research which, once established, could increasingly ignore the founding limits and limitations of the individual disciplines. Indeed, the very notion of academic "seriousness" came increasingly to exclude reflection upon the relation of one "field" to another, and concomitantly, reflection upon the historical process by which individual disciplines established their boundaries. Or the historical dimension was regarded as extrinsic to the actual practice of research and scholarship: history itself became one discipline among others. Functionalism and Operationalism were built into the organization of the university. The state of mind that resulted was incisively described, again by Whitehead:

> Effective knowledge is professionalised knowledge, supported by a restricted acquaintance with useful subjects subservient to it. This situation has its dangers. It produces minds in a groove. Each profession makes progress, but it is progress in its own groove. Now to be mentally in a groove is to live in contemplating a given set of abstractions. The groove prevents straying across country, and the abstraction abstracts from something to which no further attention is paid. But there is no groove of abstractions which is adequate for the comprehension of human life. (Whitehead, 282–83)

Whitehead's appeal to a holistic, organic reflection in order to supplement the limits of professionalism has been largely ineffective, because it—like all traditional philosophical attempts to transcend specialized knowledge—places itself over and above what it seeks to transcend. It is here that a deconstructive pragmatics might provide an alternative, in that it would work from the "inside" of the various disciplines, in order to demonstrate concretely, in each case, how the exclusion of limits from the field organizes the practice it makes possible, but in a way that diverges from the self-consciousness of the practitioners, as dictated by the ethos of professional competence. One way of exploring such limitations might be precisely to demonstrate how the apparently objective, denotative language of individual disciplines entails, necessarily but implicitly, a precise series of prescriptive "speech acts," involving injunctions and commands such as those that comprise the professional ethos in general. To make those prescriptive systems explicit, to reveal the strategic nature of apparently constative academic discourse, is a project that this paper has begun to explore.

Chapter 3
The Debt of Criticism:
Notes on Stanley Fish's
Is There a Text in This Class?

Whenever the codes and conditions that have assured the consensus necessary for communication begin to change radically or to break down, attention is inevitably drawn to the question of institutions. When the most important things can no longer be taken for granted, the process of *granting* imposes itself as a problem that becomes increasingly difficult to avoid. If such a development can be seen today as characteristic of much of modern thought, it is no accident that the field of literary studies seem about to become one of its privileged arenas. For the object that defines this field of study — "literature" — has traditionally been distinguished from other "objects" of study precisely by a certain *lack* of objectivity, whether as "mimetic," as "aesthetic," or as "fictional." And such a lack of objectivity has, from Plato onward, confronted the study of literature (or of art in general) with the problem of its *legitimation*, and hence, with its status as, and in regard to, *institution(s)*. To counter the Platonic charge that the poet is either a liar, a fool, a seducer, or all of these the traditional response has been to affirm, with Sir Philip Sidney, that "The Poet . . . He nothing affirmeth" (*Defense of Poesie*). But, as indicated, if the poet himself "nothing affirmeth," the critic, he, must affirm that very *nothing*. And, what is more, he must affirm it in the name of the poet, or of poetry. The extraordinarily problematic relation between what appears to be two radically different forms of discourse is thus posed: between a discourse that is alleged to be essentially nonaffirmative (nonreferential, nonobjective), and the alleging (affirmative, referential, objectifying) discourse, without which nothing essential could be attributed to "literature," not even its *name*. The discourse of criticism thus finds itself in a delicate—perhaps even aporetic—situation: it must seek to affirm the nonaffirmable, at the same time allowing the latter to speak for itself.

It is hardly surprising, therefore, that, until fairly recently, literary criticism much preferred to concentrate on the nature of its object, "literature," than upon the more thorny problem of its *relation to* that peculiar object. This was possible so long as certain founding conventions concerning the nature of that object were generally accepted as unproblematic. The most important of those conventions, because the most basic, was doubtless the conviction that literature did indeed constitute an *object*, which is to say, something *self-identical* and *self-contained*, whether as individual work or as collective canon. In recent years, however, a variety of factors have led to the questioning of this assumption, which has today relinquished much of its force as a founding convention. Such factors are too complex to discuss in a brief paper, being not merely intradisciplinary, but also inter- and even extra-disciplinary. Instead, I propose to examine a recent attempt to confront some of the effects that have emerged in literary studies as a result of the problematization of this founding convention. The work is Stanley Fish's book, *Is There a Text in this Class?*, and it is, I believe, quite symptomatic of the situation I have sought to describe. In it, Fish, in a most entertaining manner, recounts and reflects upon his critical development of the last ten years. Beginning with the question "Is the reader or the text the source of meaning?"[1] he arrives at the answer that it is neither; rather, it is the institutionalized set of assumptions and beliefs that define the community of interpretation and constitute the origin and end of literary meaning, and indeed that of literature itself. This is so because, strictly speaking, literature has no "self," no identity or meaning apart from that conferred upon it by the interpretive community. Apart from such a community of belief, Fish argues, neither texts nor readers can be said to exist. The traditional conception of the text as a self-contained and meaningful entity ignores the process by which language functions: namely, through the context in which it is read, rewritten, and interpreted. But such interpretation is equally context-bound: if individuals are the agents and actors in the game of interpretation they are not, qua individuals, its author or origin, for they too are situated within a tradition of interpretation, and this predetermines any moves they may make, whether affirmative or innovative. The true object of literary studies, therefore, is not this or that attribute of "literature," but rather the process of attribution itself: "knowledge of the rules is the real mark of professional initiation" (Fish, 343). Fish hastens to add that "this does not mean that these rules and the practices they authorize are either monolithic or stable. Within the literary community there are subcommunities . . . and within any community the boundaries of the acceptable are continually being redrawn" (Fish, 343). Such redrawing, however, is never simply arbitrary or the act of an isolated individual, since it always must take as its point of departure the existing institution. If Fish thereby claims to present his readers with "a principled account of change" (Fish, 367), its salient feature is that such change must inevitably take place *within* the institution that is thereby being changed. To speak of "rupture" or of "discontinuity" is therefore to miss the point—Fish's point—that all interpretation, including both its objects and its subjects, are always situated *within* a determinate, determinable set of assumptions and beliefs that are held in common: "changes are always produced and perceived within the rules of the game" (Fish, 358).

This, then, in brief, is how Stanley Fish "stopped worrying and learned to love interpretation," and it is also his message to all his colleagues in the profession of literary studies who have not yet learned this "simple" (Fish, vii) lesson, and hence, who are still more or less concerned with the state of their discipline and its prospects for the future. All they need do, he enjoins, is to follow his prescription, jettison the traditional constative (or, as he calls it, "demonstrative") model of literary criticism, which presupposes the essential self-identity of its object, "literature," and endorse a rhetorical (or "persuasion") model of their practice, which should be all the more inviting since it *costs* nothing, and allows critics to keep everything: "texts, standards, norms, criteria of judgment, critical histories, and so on" (Fish, 367). "We have everything that we always had . . . it is just that we do all those things within a set of institutional assumptions that can themselves become the objects of dispute" (Fish, 367). And when this latter eventuality materializes, it is no cause for concern, Fish contends, because this is precisely what enables us to arrive at "a principled account of change and . . . to explain to ourselves and to others why, if a Shakespeare sonnet is only 14 lines long, we haven't been able to get it right after four hundred years" (Fish, 367).

And yet, this powerful attempt to persuade "my opponents" that his position and prescription is not merely in Stanley Fish's own interest, but in theirs as well, this endeavor to "speak to (the) fears" of the profession concerning its own legitimacy, is more a symptom of the malady than its cure, or even palliative. And it is so precisely because there *are* opponents, and necessarily so, *within* the institution that Stanley Fish seeks to speak *to*, but above all, to speak *for*. The reason why professional literary critics are worried, today, and perhaps more so than for many years, is precisely *not* addressed by *Is There a Text in This Class?*, although it is in eloquent evidence throughout that book. If critics are worried today, it is because the "institution" or "community of interpretation" to which Fish so strongly appeals is no longer simply a *unified, undivided community*, "within" which the diversity of individual interpretations take (their) place. Rather, what bothers critics and what renders literary studies often an inhospitable place to live and work, is the fact there is no longer a generally held "set of institutional assumptions," since all such sets have themselves become "the objects of dispute." It is one thing to assert (justifiably, I believe) that every "fact" and "object" of interpretation depends on prior assumptions and "beliefs," that there can therefore be no "unsituated" or "acontextual" utterance, and yet quite something else to contend that critical controversies, challenges, and change always take place *within an institution*: that is, within a *delimitable, definable set* of commonly held assumptions. To argue, as Fish does, that "communication" or "understanding" imply just such a common situation is only to beg the question, for precisely the more interesting and profound controversies currently animating and disrupting the "institution" of literary studies cannot be reduced to such shared assumptions; such debates tend to put into question just what "communication" or "understanding" have traditionally been held to mean. Indeed, it is precisely because traditionally held "institutional assumptions" have "themselves become the objects of dispute" that Fish's invocation of "the" institution—that is, of a unified, well-defined set of "beliefs" or practices—is both topical, and yet also incapable of providing a "principle" for measuring "change", or accounting for controversy.

In short, what Stanley Fish would like to offer as an *answer* to the questions worrying literary critics today is precisely part of the *problem*: the *structure* of the institutional context "within" which every discipline must operate. And what his arguments indicate is that this problem cannot be adequately articulated so long as the unity of "the institution" is taken for granted. Rather, what has to be investigated and discussed is the process by which such unity is established, maintained, and disrupted. And here Fish's example is very instructive, for it demonstrates the incompatibility of the two notions of interpretation that he entertains, and the consequences of each. These two notions are first, interpretation as a process of *construction*, and second, interpretation as a more or less violent, agonistic *transformation*. The former is utilized in order to discredit the "essentialist" notion of literature as comprising a self-contained object upon which meaning is simply "conferred." Against such a conception Fish argues that the text only "is" whatever it is in and through the productive, constructive efforts of the community of interpretation, working through individual interpreters. However, the notion of production or construction is incapable of accounting for the *relation* of *individual* acts of interpretation to the more *general* interpretation of the "community" or the "institution." The individual interpreter finds him (her) self confronting a text that has already been interpreted in a variety of ways, and these interpretations constrain and determine the new interpretation. This new interpretation, however, in order to be viable, valuable, and interesting will have to modify the previous interpretations. As Fish puts it, "the space in which a critic works has been marked out for him by his predecessors, even though he is obliged by the conventions of the institutions to dislodge them . . . it is only because something has already been said that he can now say something different" (Fish, 350). A tension thus emerges between the given state of the institution, and its tendency to encourage or even demand innovation and transformation. As long as such changes do not call into question the basic premises that endow the institution with its particular identity, they can be rewarded and contained. But when, as today, those changes tend to affect the very founding assumptions of the institution, such containment can no longer be regarded as a given. This does not mean, of course, that such changes will themselves come from an extra-institutional space—which, as Fish insists, and I agree, would be a u-topia—but rather, that they will come from *another institutional region*, one not necessarily compatible with the dominant set of assumptions defining the discipline on which it intrudes. Fish, more than most critics, is keenly aware of and expert in the practices of "dislodging," and avoids the more explosive consequences of such agonistic tranformations by seeking to describe it as a succession of discrete temporal moments: there is never really ambiguity, ambivalence or contradiction, he asserts, but only an endless succession of intrinsical and self-contained univocal interpretive constructions: first one, then another, then yet another, a series of "successive contexts" (308). And since, according to this view, there *can* only be one interpretation *at a time*, there *will* only be one interpretation at a time, because there *is* only one institution at any one time, and this institution will decide which interpretations it can contain *within* itself, and which not. However, Fish's own account of how interpretation must not merely construct its object, but also *impose* it at the expense of other interpretations that it dislodges, demonstrates that the formal, definitional self-identity of discrete interpretations, and of institutions, is *intrinsically disruptive* by virtue of the agonistic process of interpretation itself. To the extent to which the existence of an interpretive institution depends on the "dislodging" of its predecessors and competitors, that existence will never be reducible to a single, undivided moment or a continuous stretch of time; nor will its interior space ever be simply the polar *opposite* of that which is *outside*. The self-identity of an interpretation will depend on what it attacks, excludes, and incorporates—in short, on its relation to and dependency on that which it is not, on other interpretations. The same, however, will hold of the beliefs and assumptions that inform such interpretation. Fish would counter that such a relationship of dependency is itself institutional; but if this is so, it demonstrates that the term "institution" cannot be understood as referring to a self-contained, unified, determinable system of beliefs or assumptions. Rather, it will mark the clash of such beliefs and assumptions, the conflict of systems. To argue that such conflict requires some common ground, albeit a battleground, resolves nothing, since it amounts only to asserting that in order for there to be conflict there must be contact, and that this in turn implies a structured, institutionalized space. This tells us nothing, however, about the forces and factors that delimit that space, which is precisely the problem that concerns critics today. For instance, in interpreting a literary text, an interpreter will not necessarily be limited to confronting those interpretations previously certified as inhabiting the discipline of literary studies, or even "the institution of academic America" (Fish, 320), as Fish puts it; he may also invoke interpretations emanating from other regions (philosophy, psychoanalysis, etc.), and these in turn may well challenge the unifying assumptions of the discipline of literary studies in America, at least as this is understood by a majority of its practitioners. In such a case—which is precisely what has been occurring in American literary studies—the debate and polemics that result will not necessarily be comprehensible in terms of any *given* institution or set of interpretive assumptions. Indeed, the results may not be *comprehensible* at all, which is not to say that they are necessarily worthless or gibberish, but rather that they may call for a new *practice* of interpretation, in which "understanding" or "comprehension" are no longer supreme categories or absolute values.

But one need not go quite as far to make the more obvious point that the process of "dislodging" that Fish himself construes as an indispensable and institutionalized element of interpretation is the condition not merely of the unity of the institution, but of its *intrinsic disunity* and instability—and, what is more important, perhaps, of its inherent ambivalence. For it is here that Fish's discussion is probably of greatest interest, and it is no accident that it is here that he develops a line of thought that can be traced back to Nietzsche. In the celebrated second book of *The Genealogy of Morals*, Nietzsche describes the emergence of the sentiment of *guilt* from the *debt* that each generation incurs with regard to its predecessors, a debt that increases with the power and performance of the indebted successors. In that same text, in what appears to be a parenthetical digression Nietzsche also formulates his theory of the agonistic nature of interpretation, which *imposes* its interests and aims on previously prevailing interpretive schemes. If we reflect on the relationship implicit in Nietzsche's account between this *interpretive imposition*, and the debt incurred by the present toward the past, we arrive at the very conclusion that Nietzsche himself seeks to deny, but that Fish (and others), indirectly at least, tend to suggest: that it is precisely the agonistic character of interpretation that necessarily transforms indebtedness into guilt, since the self-affirmation of any interpretation, as *criticism*—that is, as a discourse of *truth*—can only prevail and impose itself by denying its constitutive dependence on what it excludes, dethrones, and replaces. This in turn would account for two of the most prevalent traits of literary criticism, as discerned by Fish: first, the "aggressive humility" that marks the stance of the critic who sees himself as the true and devoted servant of the text itself (Fish, 353), and second, the fact that "at the heart of the institution [there] is the wish to deny that its activities have any consequences" (355), a wish, incidentally, that Fish himself utters at the conclusion of his book (370) (as though to assure or augment its persuasive force). For in denying that it *has* any consequences, criticism implicitly denies that it itself *is* only a consequence—and a most ambivalent one—of other interpretations. Its dependency on its other, source of its ambivalent identity, would be also at the source of the "aggressive humility," which defends against its intrinsic ambivalence (its structural disunity) by projecting it in the form of a Manichaean and external opposition, between the "good" text—self-contained and meaningful—and the bad critic, who, as parasite and usurper, becomes the alibi and straw man (or straw woman) for the *debt of criticism itself*, its "original sin," as it were. The construction of the good, meaningful text which the critic simply *serves*, together with the bad critic who *betrays* the text, would be the guilt-ridden attempt of criticism to avoid or evade a debt that is impossible to repay.

Perhaps this is what is really at stake in the debates to which *Is There a Text in this Class?* bears witness, and in which it partakes: the effort to come to terms with the debt of criticism. But if the notion of the "interpretive community" strives—unsuccessfully—to escape that debt by denying it, there are, we shall discover, other ways of attempting to assume it.

Chapter 4
Capitalizing History:
The Political Unconscious

In a book first published in 1955, *The Liberal Tradition in America*, Louis Hartz advanced a thesis which, if it has been largely bypassed by intellectual historians today,[1] could nonetheless be of considerable interest to English-speaking literary critics seeking to understand the situation of their discipline. Hartz argued that American liberalism, which he considered the dominant paradigm of political thought and action in the United States, could best be understood in terms of the European history from which, at a certain point, it detached itself. As a result of thus being separated from the conflictual dynamics of European history, American liberalism, Hartz affirmed, lost the sense of its own historical and social relativity and came to hypostasize itself as an absolute, a tendency that was reinforced both by the universalist and naturalist character of liberalist categories and values (which Hartz identified with the thought of Locke), and by the real absence of a strong, prebourgeois ("feudal") social tradition in the New World. Thus, the Lockean axiom of the natural liberty of individuals, "born free," which in its European context was endowed with a very nonnatural, polemical-strategic significance as an ideological attack on feudal values, appeared, in the new American setting, to be rather a statement of universal fact. To use the familiar terms of contemporary speech-act theory, the Lockean paradigm thus lost its performative connotations when it emigrated to America, where it imposed its authority all the more effectively by presenting itself as an essentially constative act. For Hartz, the result was a national history and culture blinded from its birth, as it were, to its own conditions of possibility and dominated by a liberalism that was as absolute and autocratic as its European model had been critical and dynamic.

The process of separation, which Hartz later designated as one of "fragmentation,"[2] thus entailed two, correlative, but not unambiguous gestures. The first was that of *universalization*. It was not that the Lockean tenet of naturally free individuals claimed universal validity, for that was true of the European paradigm no less than the American. Rather, the implicit but decisive context in which those claims operated was transformed drastically due to the absence of the historical antagonists against which Lockean thought developed its articulations. In short, without Robert Filmer, as the spokesman for a feudally oriented, aristocratic society, the status of Locke's thought was altered: it became *static* precisely for want of the other. Instead of advancing its claims to universal validity within a social and political sphere that was anything but homogeneous, it could present them as being coextensive with that sphere itself (which, in a certain sense, they were, since the emigrated American colonials did not reinstate the force of the European feudal past, but only that of its burgeoning bourgeois present). The Lockean paradigm thus was able to institutionalize itself as what Hartz calls an "absolutist" or "compulsive" liberalism that dominated—and still dominates—the American intellectual tradition.

The second gesture implied in this process, a correlative of the first, entails *the status of conflict*, ethically, epistemologically, politically. By thus universalizing itself, American liberalism no longer accepted the necessity of historical and social conflict as had been the case, inevitably, for its European version. As Hartz puts it, it lost "that sense of relativity, that spark of philosophy, which European liberalism acquired through an internal experience of social diversity and social conflict."[3] This does not, of course, mean that American liberalism denied conflict entirely—which would have been a rather remarkable feat—but rather, that it redefined the place and the nature of conflict, precisely by placing it *within* a "natural" context, which, qua natural, could not itself be considered as subject to conflict or to (legitimate) controversy. Thus, the most aggressive competition among private individuals and groups could be encouraged, whereas any challenge to the "natural" hierarchy subordinating public to private was not. Conflict was accepted only as a technical instrument in order to achieve ends that were held to be above (legitimate) conflict.

Whatever the merits of Hartz's arguments as an explanation of American political culture—and my feeling is that they deserve more serious discussion than they have received—they undoubtedly cast considerable light on the more recent transformation undergone by certain French thinkers as they have been imported into the United States (and, perhaps more generally, into the English-language universe of discourse). If authors such as Derrida, Foucault, and, to a lesser extent, Lacan, have been granted admission into the American Academy, the price they have had to pay has generally entailed the universalization and individualization of their work, which has thereby been purged of its conflictual and strategic elements and presented instead as a self-standing methodology.

Such a transformation is both ironic and revealing. It is ironic, because one of the most powerful impulses in the development of what in the English-speaking world has become known as "structuralism" and more recently "post structuralism" was precisely the profound suspicion of -isms, beginning with Lévi-Strauss's critique of the concept of "totemism," in which he saw the symptomatic effort of Eurocentric anthropology to project its own values and categories, in order to reduce and to appropriate alien, non-Western cultural phenomena. Although such a suspicion of universal values did, it is true, coexist for a while with the aspiration of establishing a new system of science with a claim to universal validity, such aspirations were rather rapidly abandoned. Thus, although the term "structuralism" is, of course, not a translator's invention, that of "poststructuralism," it seems, is, and in any case serves to obscure the antisystematic impulse at work in the thought of the writers thus designated. Indeed, labels such as "deconstruction" and "discourse analysis" serve to arrest the movement of the text to which they refer by implying that behind those writings there is a stable and static core that can be accepted or rejected as such.

What is revealing about this process of universalization is the institutional context in which it takes place. For the universalization of "poststructuralist" thinkers conforms to the intellectual ethos of the institution that monopolizes almost entirely their American importation: the University. The University universalizes, individualizes, and in the process excludes conflict as far as possible. Or rather, it delegitimizes conflict, in the name of pluralism. Pluralism allows for a multiplicity of coexisting, even competing interpretations, opinions, or approaches; what it does not allow is for the space in which these interpretations are held to take place to be itself considered conflictual. Its borders are given, and its structure, bipolar. Interpretations are right or wrong, better or worse, strong or weak, true or false, but the category of opposition, used to prescribe such alternatives, is itself held to be beyond dispute, and indeed is used to define conflict. The latter, in short, is held to be one theme among others, rather than an aspect of the process of thematization (or objectification) itself. "Scholarship" and "research" may investigate conflict, but they do not—or must not—as such partake of it. The function of "pluralism" is precisely to deny the necessity of conflict, in the name of peacefully coexisting diversity.

It may seem dubious to assert that the American university is actively engaged in the maintenance and reproduction of this "universalist" ethos, when it is more or less common knowledge that the temper of Anglo-American thought, as opposed to that of the European Continent, has been resolutely "nominalist" for many centuries. But, just as Hartz's use of Locke suggests, nominalism does not exclude universalism, although it certainly endows it with a different form from that determined by a more "realist" philosophy. As a recent example, I shall cite Stanley Fish's book, *Is There a Text in This Class?* At first glance, the position articulated there would seem to be resolutely anti-universalist. Since texts have no intrinsic meaning, but instead are constructed ever-anew by whatever particular interpretive assumptions "happen to be in force,"[4] the significance of texts can and does change all the time. There would seem to be, then, little place for universally valid statements. But if this holds for interpretive statements, it would seem not to be the case for the metacritical assertions that constitute Fish's own critical position. In a manner that is curiously reminiscent of Sartre, Fish reiterates that text and reader are *always in a situation*, *always* engaged *in* an institutionally determined activity, and so on. The theory thus implied by the "always-in" assertions must claim universal validity.

Fish's theory of institutional authority thus displays many of the same general tendencies Hartz discerns at work in American liberalism (although Fish himself might well demur at such a classification), namely: universalization, individualization, and the containment (or delegitimization) of conflict. This will doubtless seem a curious assertion to make concerning a critic who has obviously enjoyed and exploited the polemical aspects of the profession more than most, and moreover, one whose entire emphasis is placed on the nonindividual, communal, or communitarian aspects of the interpretive process. But the paradox is dissipated when one realizes that the concept of the collective, or the community of interpreters invoked by Fish, ultimately is nothing but a generalized, indeed a universalized form of the individualist monad: autonomous, self-contained and internally unified, not merely despite but because of the diversity it contains. And if there can be no doubt that Fish's own often highly polemical practice points up the importance of conflict, of the agonistic aspect of interpretation, his *theory* of the authority of interpretive communities functions not to explain such conflict, but to explain it away. And it explains it away simply by asserting that it is *contained* by—i.e., *within*—whatever monad (set of assumptions, interpretive institution, etc.) is said to occupy the critic. If conflict is a part of interpretation, and the latter is always situated *within* an institution, then institutions themselves cannot be subject to the conflict they contain. The institution thus emerges as the condition of possibility of controversy, and hence, as its arbiter.[5] Although the liberal mind has defined itself by the ethical exclusion or rather, by the containment of conflict as a historical process, such liberalism is being increasingly challenged today, even while it reacts with ever-more transparent intensity, and, often, intolerance. In short, the dissemination of contemporary French theory in the United States (and to the English-speaking world in general), far from merely reinforcing the liberal delegitimization of conflict, is also undermining it. And in so doing, this importation calls into question not merely the hitherto prevailing lines of demarcation, but also the manner in which those lines have traditionally been drawn. It is no accident that "margins," "borders," "framing," "exclusions," and möbius strips have come to designate, and to disrupt, the convenient opposition of "inside-versus-outside", which, as Hartz's entire analysis implies, dominates the liberal containment of conflict. It is also significant to recall that for the most part those French thinkers whose work has been most influential have themselves been situated on the margins of the French university system. For it has been the particular, although historically conditioned, genius of French society, deriving directly from its bourgeois revolutionary tradition, to have been able to reconcile institutionalization and change by establishing a series of elite institutions, thus allowing intellectual labor to develop in a climate that is relatively free from what Bourdieu and Passeron have rightly described as the "reproductive" constraints inherent in all *educational* systems. The Collège de France, Ecole Normale Supérieure, Ecole Pratique des Hautes Etudes, CNRS, Paris-VIII—these are the organisms that have enabled what Hartz aptly calls "philosophy" to survive in France. "Philosophy," in his sense, designates not simply a "discipline," but rather a mode of thought that remains imbued with "that sense of relativity . . . acquired through an *internal experience* of social diversity and social conflict."[6] I emphasize "internal experience" because it is precisely this which the positive disciplines, at least insofar as they are subject to the traditional strategy of legitimation prevalent within the educational establishment, must exclude. They must exclude or at least reduce the purport of their own inner disunity and internal conflictuality, and above all, of the inevitably conflictual process by which, through exclusion and subordination, disciplines define their borders and constitute their fields. And they must deny such exclusivity in the name of an ideal of knowledge, of science, and of truth that deems these to be intrinsically conflict-free, self-identical, and hence, reproducible as such and transmissible to students. Ultimately, such an ideal both reflects and supports the self-image of a society that imposes its authority precisely by denying the legitimacy of its structural conflicts, and hence of its relation to alterity. For the admission of the constitutive importance of such relations would amount to a disavowal of the categories of universality, individualism, and consensus that form the foundation of American liberalism, and of the institutions that perpetuate it.

This, then, explains the challenge of the recent import of certain French thinkers into an American academic scene alternately fascinated, and frightened, by the possible consequences of this incursion. For the tendency most visible today goes in the direction of a relegitimization of conflict with regard to intellectual activity, and this in turn cannot but affect, more or less profoundly, institutions that define such activity in terms such as "scholarship" and "research," words that already suggest the substantial self-identity of the "objects" they presuppose. Instead of the serene, detached character of such "scholarship," based in turn on a conception of cognition as an essentially constative process—whether construed as "discovery," "experimentation," or as "construction"—intellectual activity has come increasingly to define itself as a "performative" language game, although the notion of "performance" has often been equated with "productive," rather than understood as a form of play.[7] Nevertheless, the notion of "strategy" as it is applied to theoretical argumentation has begun to cease to be merely a synonym for "instrumental," as it still is in the writings of a John Searle, for instance,[8] and to recover its etymological connotation, with a reference to conflicting forces.

If the outcome, or even direction of these transformations are difficult to predict, it nevertheless seems highly probable that the reevaluaiton of the necessity and the legitimacy of conflict that is currently under way will impose a renewed concern and confrontation with Marxism. For the latter is a theory not only of the necessity of conflict as an *object* of study, but also as the medium in which thought itself operates. To the extent, therefore, that the liberal paradigm of consensus and conciliation is increasingly challenged, Marxism is bound to emerge as one of the most significant alternative models. If the Hartzian analysis of the liberal image of historical development as a kind of entelechy—as the unfolding of possibilities already contained, as it were, in germ, in the individual (or collectively individual) subject—then it is clear that the Marxist version of Hegelian dialectics, with its emphasis on struggle and conflict as the motor of all becoming, provides in one sense an extreme counterimage. And yet, as is usually the case with contraries, the Marxian model is often legitimized in terms of the same liberal categories it is attacking: the universality of cognition or of "science," objective necessity, an individualist conception of subjectivity.

It is precisely this aspect of Marxism, in conjunction with the political and ideological position of the Communist party in postwar France—with its claim to be the sole legitimate heir of the revolutionary tradition—that explains the critical, often hostile relations of most structuralist and "poststructuralist" thinkers toward Marxism. What is not immediately evident to many Americans, having grown up with the "red scare," McCarthyism, and a virulent tradition of antisocialist and anticommunist persecution, is the extent to which communism and Marxism could, within the capitalist society of postwar France, nevertheless have exercised an influence, especially on the intelligentsia, that would have let it appear increasingly as a *part* of the social establishment rather than as a challenge to it. Yet, if Marxism was criticized by Lévi-Strauss, Foucault, and implicitly, at least, by Lacan and Derrida, it was not because it insisted on the inevitability and legitimacy of conflict (as did American liberalism), but rather because it claimed to resolve it, once and for all.

In the United States, by contrast, the way in which Marxism has been systematically, and often hysterically, excluded from the pale of respectability has allowed it to become identified with the process of exclusion itself, particularly inasmuch as the latter has generally been denied to have taken place at all. If liberalism can be described as that form of exclusion which, wherever possible, denies its own exclusivity; which denies that exclusions are an inseparable concomitant of every possible inclusion; or which accepts exclusion only in order to exclude it (the traditional definition of individual freedom, limited only by that of other individuals)–then Marxism is the name of what liberalism most seeks to exclude, the inevitability of exclusion itself. As a theory of class conflict, Marxism does not ask *whether* but rather *which* exclusions are necessary. To this, American liberalism has traditionally responded: Marxism itself.

If this response has been uniquely effective, it is, Hartz argues, for the same reasons that liberalism has been able to install itself as a static and total worldview: the absence of a feudal past. Without Filmer to define and to demarcate the polemical thrust of Locke, the message of Marx loses its meaning.[9] The liberal notion of the natural liberty of the individual, "born free," expands to cover the entire horizon, leaving little room for socialist (collective) alternatives.

It is in this traditionally small space, but with a momentum drawn in large part from the "poststructuralist" incursion into the liberal enclosure, that Fredric Jameson's *The Political Unconscious* seeks to drive a wedge. It is a powerful, almost heroic attempt alternately to entice and to intimidate, to cajole and to browbeat its readers, presumably most or all members in good standing of the English-speaking "interpretive community," whose principal home base is doubtless American university departments of literature. And the way in which it goes about defining its task indicates that *The Political Unconscious* strives to appeal to the widest number of these colleagues in the broadest possible way: its goal is "to restructure the problematics of ideology, of the unconscious, and of desire, of representation, of history, and of cultural production".[10] Nothing less, it seems, is required if "the traditional dialectical code" of Marxism is to be adequately "defended" in the particular arena where Marxist criticism must operate, that of "the intellectual marketplace today" (Jameson, 10). Marxism may want to replace commodity relations, but in the meanwhile it must know how to sell itself on the market it hopes, someday, to abolish. Nor is this marketplace to be conceived of too simplistically, as constituting merely the *external* context of Marxist criticism. "Interpretation," Jameson declares, "is not an isolated act, but takes place *within* a Homeric battlefield, on which a host of interpretive options are either openly or implicitly in conflict" (Jameson, 13; my italics). However, this acknowledgment of interpretation as an activity that is not merely *collective*, but also *agonistic*, remains itself "an isolated act" within *The Political Unconscious*, and the grounds for this are already foreshadowed by the word I have placed in italics: "within." Jameson's use of the word here is all the more striking, since one would normally have expected the word "on," battles being usually fought *on*, rather than *within*, battlefields. But this shift responds to an imperative that dominates the theoretical arguments developed by *The Political Unconscious*, one that strangely recalls the position of Fish. Briefly stated, what the two books have in common, despite their obvious differences, is the priority they assign, axiomatically as it were, to the "in." For Jameson no less than for Fish, the interpretive process and everything that it entails, takes place *within* a space that is already delimited, and that therefore allows us, in principle, to comprehend the events that it is held to contain.

To be sure, the consequences that the two critics draw from this common conception are different. For Fish, the fact that the interpreter is *always in* a "situation" points to the role of the institution, of the interpretive community as the ultimate and decisive authority that defines the situation one is always *in*. The questions that this conclusion leaves unanswered are obvious enough. Above all, as Jameson's statement and Fish's practice suggest, there is the question of conflictual, agonistic interpretations and their adjudication or evaluation: do such conflicts indicate *conflicting* "institutions" (or "sets of interpretive assumptions"), i.e., a certain *exteriority*, or do they occur "within" an essentially *unified* institution? Can the alternative even be posed without recognizing that the relation between interpretation and institution cannot be the one-way street that Fish's affirmations tend to imply: you interpret as you do because you *are already in* an institution, *already* indebted to *a set* (i.e., single, unified) of assumptions, and so on. In short, a theory of *interpretive conflict* is required, and precisely this, Fish's "principled account of change" (Fish, 367) does not, and probably—given its own axiomatics, its *parti pris* for the Inside and for the Insiders—cannot offer.

If Fish, then, seeks to avoid the problems of historical and social conflict by reducing them to a discrete succession of self-contained, monadic moments (first this, then that, etc.), Jameson's strategy is to try to sell Marxism as the most powerful Insider of them all (albeit one that has been largely ignored and neglected until now):

> The priority of a Marxian interpretive framework . . . is here conceived as that "untranscendable horizon" that subsumes such apparently antagonistic or incommensurable critical operations, assigning them an undoubted sectoral validity *within* itself, and thus at once canceling and preserving them. (Jameson, 10; my italics)

Again, the pitch here recalls Fish's peroration at the end of *Is There a Text in This Class?*—"We have everything that we always had—texts, standards, norms, criteria of judgment, critical histories, and so on . . . it is just that we do all those things within a set of institutional assumptions that can themselves become objects of dispute" (Fish, 367). The last phrase, of course, points to the essential problem that Fish's position denies, rather than addresses. And it is this problem that Jameson seeks to resolve, in a sense by presenting "Marxism" as the operator that both reverses the question of Fish's title, and also transforms it, substituting for its question mark a resounding exclamation point: "There *Is* a *Class* in This Text!", Jameson assures us, and "Marxism" alone can tell us what it is, since only Marxism contains it. We will still have everything we have always had, everything that we have been taught and that we teach others, everything that gives us our daily bread and our (dwindling) privileges; for everything is "at once cancelled and preserved," "apparently antagonistic or incommensurable critical operations" are put in their proper places; that is, *we* are put in *our* proper places, places that are "assigned" to us as our *property* in exchange — for there is always a price, to be sure — for our accepting the authority of Marxism.

The deal is tempting, no doubt. And all the more so, since it is cushioned in a most attractive, self-critical, gift wrap:

> The ideological critique [of marxism] does not depend on some dogmatic or "positive" conception of [itself] as a system. Rather, it is simply the place of an imperative to totalize,

an imperative, Jameson adds, that can also be directed at the various forms of Marxism itself, in order to reveal "their own local ideological limits or strategies of containment" (Jameson, 53). As ideological criticism, then, Marxism is "simply" the place of the imperative to totalize, nothing more, nothing less. But is that place so simple to find, especially if its name can often be distorted or disguised by forms of Marxism that themselves must be subjected to "the imperative to totalize"? If Marxism can transcend such deficiencies, if it can be criticized in *its own name*, it is only because its own "place" is coextensive with another space that bears *another* name, that of History. Writ large. And it is with this gesture, capitalizing History, that Jameson takes up the challenge of "post structuralist" thought, which, as is clear throughout *The Political Unconscious*, is both the most immediate adversary and the (more or less) silent partner.

The "poststructuralist" challenge to History, as I have already suggested, entails a persistent suspicion of the teleological perspective of totalization in which historical "development" has traditionally been conceived. This suspicion goes back at least to Nietzsche, who, in *The Genealogy of Morals*, for instance, argued that the "assigning" of "purposes" as the "meaning" of a phenomenon is nothing but a mode of interpretation that seeks to impose itself by masking its particular, partisan character in the guise of the thing itself. A process that is not merely "performative," but agonistically and violently so, dislodging the previously dominant interpretive scheme in order to take its place. Such process can present itself as the mere "constatation" of a teleological or entelechical movement of its object, of which it is the simple porte-parole. History, then, whether as ethnocentrism (Lévi-Strauss), phallogocentrism (Derrida), the genetic/developmental stages of object development (Lacan), or as a strategy of power operating by the exclusion of discontinuity (Foucault), has been subjected to a reexamination that has tended both to question the attributes of self-identity, universality, and objective necessity hitherto attributed to it, and to redefine such attribution itself as part of a strategy that seeks to impose itself precisely by denying its own strategic, partisan character.

It is evident that such a move bears certain resemblances to the conception of thought as ideology developed by Marxism. The difference, of course, is that whereas Marxism retains the oppositions of "science" and "ideology," of true and false consciousness, as well as the notion on which these oppositions depend, that of historical objectivity as their indispensable and constitutive dividing line, most of the thinkers mentioned either explicitly or implicitly include all of these categories in the agonistic process itself.

Jameson's response to this challenge is to perform precisely the gesture that he seeks to exclude, by attributing it to "ideology": that of attempting to "contain" the adversary. This "strategy of containment"—which the ideology-critique of Marxism, Jameson asserts, seeks to expose through its "imperative to totalize" (but is not such an imperative itself already the mirror image of what it seeks to contain?)—consists of two gestures: acknowledgment and incorporation.

Acknowledgment:

> *The Political Unconscious* accordingly turns on the dynamics of the act
> of interpretation and presupposes, as its organizational fiction, that we
> never really confront a text immediately, in all its freshness as a thing-
> in-itself. Rather, texts come before us as the always-already-read; we
> apprehend them through sedimented layers of previous interpretations,
> or—if the text is brand-new—through the sedimented reading habits
> and categories developed by those inherited interpretive traditions. . . .
> [Hence,] our object of study is less the text itself than the interpreta-
> tions *through* which we attempt to confront and to appropriate it.
> (Jameson, 9–10; my italics)

After this, one might have expected a study of the procedures, mechanisms and approaches of interpretation in terms of their strategic, agonistic operation on "the academic marketplace." But such a discussion, presumably, would not simply "cancel and preserve" all competing critical positions, it would not simply assign them their proper place—it would displace them in a space that could no longer be safely contained by the "discipline" of literary studies, as we know it today. The analysis of the literary text, not as a self-identical *object*, but as an element in a highly conflictual, ambivalent power struggle, would have consequences for the organization and practice of the discipline of literary studies, as it is institutionally established, of which not the least disruptive would be the redefinition of its "borders," its relation to other disciplines and above all, to other modes of thought, whether these have been disciplined already or not. What would ultimately be raised is the issue of the existing definition and delimitation of knowledge, as well as the conditions of its practice: in short, the *discipline* and the *university*.

But the acknowledgment of the dependency of texts upon their interpretation remains just that: an *isolated* act without any further consequences.[11] Perhaps this is because the informing intention is not to disrupt "the academic market-place today," but rather to stake out the claims of Marxism "within" it. In any case, the terms in which the relation of texts to interpretation, and hence, to the "Homeric battlefield" *within* which the latter is said to take place, already an-nounces what is to come: if texts are only given to us "through" sedimented layers of previous interpretations, "through" sedimented reading habits, then they still remain what they are, in and of themselves, even after passing through those layers of sedimentation. The text may be *mediated* by its interpretations, but its meaning is not structurally constituted by these readings; rather, it is *con-tained* in the text, just as the text itself is contained within the space of History.

Here, then, is the meaning of History for *The Political Unconscious*: it is the name of that space which contains and comprehends everything else, including first and foremost, the "text." Hence, Jameson's insistence on the fact that His-tory and text are inseparable, but also nonidentical:

> History is *not* a text, not a narrative, master or otherwise, but . . . an
> absent cause [which] is inaccessible to us except in textual form. . . .
> Our approach to it and to the Real necessarily passes through its prior
> textualization, its narrativization in the political unconscious. (Jameson,
> 35; author's italics)

The text, then, is something that we—necessarily—must pass *through*, on our way somewhere else, to something as "prior" to the text as the latter is prior to our "approach to it": History, as "absent cause."

Viewed from a formal perspective—which is not necessarily the same as a formalist one—Jameson's defense of Marxism is caught in a doublebind: it criti-cizes its competitors as being ideological in the sense of practicing "strategies of containment," that is, of drawing lines and practicing exclusions that ulti-mately reflect the particularities—the partiality and partisanship—of special in-terests seeking to present themselves as the whole. But at the same time, its own claim to offer an alternative to such ideological containment is itself based on a strategy of containment, only on one which seeks to identify itself with a whole more comprehensive than that of its rivals.

If there is a difference, then, between "Marxism" and "ideology," it cannot be determined purely at the level of *form*, since both seek to contain and to com-prehend their competitors in the name of a certain objectivity. The difference, rather, must reside in the kind of objectivity appealed to. Which is why, toward the end of the long, introductory theoretical chapter, Jameson finally, after tell-ing us what History is *not*—a text, a narrative—attempts to tell us what it *is*:

> History is therefore the experience of Necessity, and it is this alone
> which can forestall its thematization or reification as a mere object of
> representation or as one master code among many others. Necessity is
> not in that sense a type of content, but rather the inexorable *form* of

events; it is therefore a narrative category . . . a retextualization of History. (Jameson, 102; author's emphasis)

If the Marxist comprehension of History is distinct from ideological strategies of containment, it is not, strangely enough, because of the *contents* of that History, but because of its *form*. Marxism, it turns out, *is* form after all, or rather, a certain kind of form. Not that of narrative as such, but that of a particular type of narrative, that which tells us "why what happened . . . had to happen the way it did" (Jameson,101). Necessity, then, the experience of which defines History, is that form of narrative which is ultimately, and in principle, self-identical; the story it tells could not be told otherwise, could not be changed, altered, or modified, without being falsified and losing its necessity. If History is thus the "absent cause," Necessity is the equally "absent story," the Idea (in the Kantian sense) of a Story, of a Text, of a Narration that could not be told otherwise than it is—and hence, which "is" not, which is absent, functioning only as a kind of regulative idea. But this idea is no mere fiction since through its putative absence it can be *invoked* to produce or to justify very real effects and practices: for instance, the legitimacy of judging actual, mundane narratives in terms of a text that is identical-to-itself, but whose identity is never immediately present-as-such. As an "absent cause," such identity—whether it is called "History," "Literature," "Work," "Author," or whatever—always requires an intermediary, a *critical* interpretation in order to be *heard*. It cannot speak for itself, but must be spoken for. And yet, it must also provide the basis for distinguishing between true and false interpreters, for is this not the essence, and justification, of the critical project and its practices?

And yet, if this is so, then the most dramatic of Jameson's attempts to provide a positive definition of History—"History is what hurts . . . what refuses desire and sets inexorable limits to individual as well as collective praxis" (Jameson, 102)—raises the question: hurts *whom*? The readers of *The Political Unconscious*? Its author? The brokers in the academic marketplace? Its customers? But what if all of these were searching precisely for some instance that might set "inexorable limits" to their "praxis," which, for want of authorized limits, was in the process of losing its sense of self-legitimacy? What, in short, if critics *desired* to be "hurt" in this way, as a lesser evil, rather than to court the risks of being left beside themselves, "beside the point," by desires they no longer controlled? Would "History," Jameson's History, still simply "hurt," or simply "refuse desire"? The desire, for instance, to capitalize (on) History?

It seems likely, on the contrary, that a good many of those whose existence is tied to the academic marketplace would be neither hurt nor frustrated by a History which can be described as follows:

This is indeed the ultimate sense in which History as ground and un-transcendable horizon needs no particular theoretical justification: we

may be sure that its alienating necessities will not forget us, however
much we might prefer to ignore them. (Jameson, 102)

Not to be forgotten, even by "alienating necessities," may yet be preferable to
the current uncertainties traversing the profession in regard to its social status
and its institutional future. To hear that "History as ground and untranscendable
horizon needs no particular theoretical justification" is doubtless music to the
ears of many scholars and critics for whom recent theoretical discussion has rendered the ground upon which the discipline has been based less than solid, and
its horizons anything but clear or "untranscendable."

Like Fish's "institution" or "interpretive commuity," then, Jameson's History
recommends itself as the best means of Saving the Text (and those who live by
it):

> It is in detecting the traces of that uninterrupted narrative, in restoring
> to the surface of the text the repressed and buried reality of this fun-
> damental history, that the doctrine of a political unconscious finds its
> function and its necessity. (Jameson, 20)

And, we might add, it is here that it also "finds" much of its appeal; like Fish,
Jameson could assure his readers (if he so chose), that the Marxism of *The Political Unconscious* will not be an engine of expropriation, but of appropriation:
that it will help them in their efforts to appropriate the text, to enrich themselves
by enriching the texts, that we will "have everything that we always had," only
more, better, and safer than before. It is no accident that Jameson recommends
Marxism in terms of its superior "semantic richness," which in turn is directly
related to its conception of History. The methodology outlined in *The Political
Unconscious* capitalizes directly on this notion of History:

> Such semantic enrichment and enlargement of the inert givens and
> materials of a particular text must take place within three concentric
> frameworks, which mark a widening out of the sense of the social
> ground of a text. . . . (Jameson, 75)

These three "frameworks"—the "symbolic" or "political" (in the narrower sense
of events); the "social," and the "historical"—can be described as "concentric"
only because their center is identified with the "inert givens and materials of a
particular text"—a text, in short, whose particularity coincides with its *inertia*,
the fact that it is, once and for all, in its proper place *within* History, that is,
within a story waiting to be told, once and for all, in the one and only way. Like
the movement of Capital itself, this story is never finished, but its end is always
in sight. It is, Jameson suggests, a "single, great collective story" with "a single,
fundamental theme . . . the collective struggle to wrest a realm of Freedom
from a realm of Necessity." This great struggle produces "vital episodes in a sin-

gle, vast unfinished plot" (19–20). It is this plot, then, that *The Political Uncon-scious* suggests it is the critic's business to discover. It is a plot that promises to keep critics in business indefinitely – on the condition that its unity, singular-ity, and self-identity are not themselves seen as an effect of interpretation, of narration, of "textualization" but rather as their center and frame, their ground and horizon.

But this plot, with its lure of limitless enrichment, contrasts strangely with the story it tells, and *The Political Unconscious* constantly returns to it like a criminal to the scene of the crime. The reader is thus led to reflect on the tension that pervades *The Political Unconscious*, between the "struggle" that is said to constitute the ultimate subject matter of texts and of their interpretations, on the one hand, and on the other, an essentially "constative" or "contemplative" con-ception of the process of interpretation itself. For notwithstanding the early re-mark about its agonistic, conflictual character, interpretation is described as a more or less faithful reconstruction, reproduction, or resuscitation of the "buried reality" – or treasures – of the text. Conflict is thus confined to the thematic ele-ment of literature, leaving its hermeneutical discovery to pursue its mission of "semantic enrichment" without any of the trials and tribulations associated with primitive accumulation as described by Marx.

The reason for this, of course, is that the problems faced by *The Political Un-conscious* are determined not by the needs of primitive accumulation, but by the crisis of overaccumulation. Translated into the particular area of literary criti-cism, this is manifest in the fact that the problems of the discipline arise not from a scarcity of interpretive productivity, but from its excess. The problem is not so much how to interpret, but how to valorize interpretation, at a time when it is in danger of asphyxiation from its uncontrolled proliferation. And it is here, in its response to this problem, that *The Political Unconscious* is most revealing of its own strategies and of the "battlefield" *within* which they are designed to operate.

What is at stake is the relation between individual and collective. For "in-dividualism" is one of the book's most explicit targets. "One of the most urgent tasks for Marxist theory today," remarks Jameson toward the end of the book, "is (to construct) a whole new logic of collective dynamics, with categories that escape the taint of some mere application of terms drawn from individual ex-perience" (Jameson, 294). It is from this standpoint that Jameson interprets the structuralist and poststructuralist critique of subjectivity; however, he does not seem to realize that the rapprochement could work the other way as well: that the problem of "individualism" might well be reinterpreted in terms of the aporias of constitutive subjectivity, a move that has been attempted by Derrida, Lacan, Foucault, but also, before them (albeit in a more Hegelian vein), by Adorno and Horkheimer. In this perspective, what could be more individualist than the notion of History as a "single, vast unfinished plot" ready to appropriate everything – all otherness – as a part of itself? What could be more individualist than the notion of Historical Necessity as a story that cannot be told otherwise (and yet which, necessarily, always is)?

What Hartz describes as the profoundly illiberal core of American liberalism, with its pretension to be the Whole, finds an exemplary manifestation in *The Political Unconscious* when Jameson describes the figure of *unity* implied by the Marxian conception of History, and by the collective self-fulfillment that defines it teleologically:

> The unity of the body must once again prefigure the renewed organic identity of associative or collective life . . . Only the community, indeed, can dramatize that self-sufficient intelligible unity (or "structure") of which the individual body, like the individual "subject," is a decentered "effect," and to which the individual organism, caught in the ceaseless chain of the generations and the species, cannot . . . lay claim. (Jameson, 74)

Despite the massive explicit emphasis on History, time, struggle, and narration, there can never be any question but that the synchronic perspective has the first, and last, word. To determine History as totalization, as a single, selfsame narrative, as a process of unification and of integration – ultimately, in short, as a movement of *identity* and of *presentation* – is to assume a point of view from which the whole can be comprehended, a position, therefore, that must be essentially detached from and outside of what it seeks to contemplate. And such a position, in turn, is only conceivable if that which it identifies is already, intrinsically and spontaneously, self-identical: that is, if its defining limits are held to be the product of that which they contain, a product of the interior they protect but do not constitute (for otherwise, the process of delimitation itself would intrude and disrupt every possible determination of an object, thus excluding any possibility of a position being simply exterior to that which it posits . . .).

It is here, then, that the category – although not necessarily the object – of individuality becomes a strategic necessity. To construe the collective or community in terms of a "self-sufficient, intelligible unity" is merely to universalize the individual, held to be the source and the goal of its being. Every such gesture rewrites the Declaration of Independence, as the independence of the self from the other, of identity from alterity, of sameness from difference. And the ambivalence inherent in all such hypostases of individualism becomes particularly evident and illuminating when Jameson takes us to the place in Marx's writings where this notion of a utopian, collective unity is foreshadowed. It is in the figure of the Oriental despot, described by Marx in the *Grundrisse* as the incarnation of a social unity that totally subordinated the differences of its constitutive members. It is here, Jameson asserts, that "the problem of the symbolic enactment of collective unity" is inscribed in the Marxian corpus, "by Marx himself"

(Jameson, 296). What is of interest here is not merely the fact that the model of collective unity seems situated at such a distance from the liberal individualism that dominates our political and social thinking, but also, that despite this apparent distance — or perhaps because of it — it seems so close to us.

But just what is it that "Marx himself" writes? Given Jameson's notion of Necessity as the Story of What Could Not Have Happened Otherwise, the response is particularly remarkable. For textually, there are *at least three* different versions in play here. First, there is the text of Marx "himself," who, in German, remarks that the *"Gesamteinheit"* — the collective unity — "is realized in the (Oriental) despot as the Father of many communities" (*"der Gesamteinheit — die im Despoten realisiert ist als dem Vater der vielen Gemeinwesen"*).[12] Then, second, there is the English translation used by Jameson, in which the term "despot" is rendered as *"the form* of the despot" ("a unity realized in the form of the despot"). And finally, there is a third version, that which occurs in Jameson's commentary, placed in quotation marks although it does not correspond exactly to either of the other two texts. For Jameson *alters* the other versions once again, this time to read: "the 'body' of the despot" (Jameson, 295).

Where, now, one is tempted to ask, is the "absent cause" that can justify these alterations and establish their "necessity"? Where, except in a powerful *desire* to see History and Necessity as the *body* of the father, the body, that is, of a patriarch who is father of all but son of no one, and hence whose body, unlike that of "the individual organism," is precisely *not* "caught in the ceaseless chain of the generations and the species" (Jameson, 74), but is the Immortal Body of the Father.

Is it not this desire to escape that "ceaseless chain," which determines at once the rejection of a certain *enchaînement* characteristic of the "metonymic" impulse of "poststructuralism," and the effort to replace it by a body which would be single, sane, and whole?

Needless to say, this is not — despite the connotations of the book's title — the body that psychoanalysis teaches us to expect, unless we identify psychoanalysis with the ego-psychology of the autonomous subject so dear to American liberal culture. If Freud insists that the ego is emphatically "a bodily ego,"[13] this body has little to do with the patriarchal body of the Oriental despot. The latter only becomes meaningful, for Freud, in the perspective of the parricide of *Totem and Taboo*, as the unattainable and ambivalent fantasy that only ceases to be destructive, precisely, by becoming part of a symbolic chain. In this symbolization the body is that which it has always been, "a place from which both external and internal perceptions may spring. It is *seen* like any other object, but to the *touch* it yields two kinds of sensations, one of which may be equivalent to an internal perception."[14] If the body, in *The Political Unconscious*, but not only there, to be sure, is thus introduced as a *prefiguration* of communal identity and unity, it is to help us forget that the body we *feel*, and *touch* — as distinct from that which we *see*, expose, or present—is neither whole nor unified, but a surface or limit in which external and internal perceptions are confounded and never entirely differentiated. The body is thus, as undifferentiated surface, the *matrix* of an ego whose perceptual-projective identity never fully escapes its ambivalent origins, but rather develops in function of them.

The notion of such a "body-ego," although first articulated by someone working in the sphere of what is commonly known as "individual psychology," is therefore considerably less "individualistic" in its categories than are the "Durkheimian or Lukácsean vocabulary of collective consciousness" to which Jameson resorts, in the putative absence of that nonindividualist, "whole new logic of collective dynamics" he anticipates and demands. But quite apart from the fact that such a "logic" is unlikely ever to arrive if we content ourselves with simply waiting for it, while continuing to use terms derived from the very individualism we hope, one day, to supplant—the very notion that such a mode of thought would be "wholly new" belongs to the same individualist thinking that construes sameness and otherness in terms of simple, and mutually exclusive (albeit "dialectical") opposition.

Rather than waiting for the New, we would probably do better to reexamine the Old, under the suspicion that this theory—if we can even conceive of its possibility—is probably at work already, not as such or full-blown, but in bits and pieces. To recognize it, however, we may well have to adopt a perspective quite different from that expressed by *The Political Unconscious*—mindful, of course, of the fact that different is not the same as unrelated. The following formulation of Jameson's can serve as a point of departure:

> This perspective may be reformulated in terms of the traditional dialectical code as the study of *Darstellung*: that untranslatable designation in which the current problems of representation productively intersect with the quite different ones of presentation, or of the essentially narrative and rhetorical movement of language and writing through time. (Jameson, 13)

Indeed, the dialectical notion of *Darstellung*, combining both the movement of representation and that of presentation, adequately names the hermeneutical perspective of *The Political Unconscious*, for which time is in fact a medium "through" which language "moves," and which construes the act of interpretation as an act of reconstruction, or rather, of resuscitation:

> Only Marxism can give us an adequate account of the essential *mystery* of the cultural past, which, like Tiresias drinking the blood, is momentarily returned to life and warmth and allowed once more to speak, and to deliver its long-forgotten message in surroundings entirely alien to it. (Jameson, 19)

But if the interpeter here, in the light of Marxism, recovers some of the sacral power of the priestly function out of which interpretation originally developed, this is also entirely compatible with a more serene, more bureaucratic and technocratic depiction of the interpretive activity, for instance, as it is said to characterize that third and widest of Jameson's three concentric frameworks of interpretation, the Historical:

> Within this final horizon the individual text or cultural artifact . . . is here restructured as a field of force in which the dynamics of sign systems of several distinct modes of production can be registered and apprehended. (Jameson, 98)

The interpreter here "restructures" with the aim of *registering* and *apprehending* words whose connotations can hardly be overheard. The purpose of such restructuring is precisely to render the force fields, the struggle and conflicts of History, appropriable by a contemplative, detached spectator, the traditional subject of scientific observation. History is thus to be made safe for cognition. Conflict is objectified, but the process of objectification itself is held to be outside the melee.

How different a picture of interpretation emerges in *The Interpretation of Dreams*, where, it is true, the "dialectical code" in which the notion of *Darstellung* is at home, is replaced by something more difficult to name, if not with the word used by Freud himself: *Entstellung*, displacement, disfigurement, dislocation. The interpretive process that it determines, however, provides a striking contrast to the academic serenity described in *The Political Unconscious*. "It should not be forgotten," Freud writes,

> that the work of interpretation must struggle against the very psychic forces to which we owe the distortion of the dream (*welche die Entstellung des Traumes verschulden*). It thus becomes a question of the relation of forces whether one's intellectual interest, capacity to overcome one's self, (*Selbstüberwindung*), psychological knowledge and skill in dream-interpretation enable one to master internal resistances.[15]

Interpretation, for Freud, does not reconstruct and resuscitate so that we may register and apprehend — it partakes of, and in a process of conflict that no totalization can ever comprehend. Which is why its effect is not simply the primitive or teleological accumulation of wealth, not the "semantic enrichment" of the phenomena it interprets, but their impoverishment as well. Or rather, a transformation in which enrichment and impoverishment become very difficult, perhaps impossible, to distinguish.

This is why, when Freud chooses a word to articulate the relation of *Entstellung* to "the forces" from which it proceeds, it is derived from "debt," *Schuld* (*verschulden*). The hermeneutics of *Entstellung* thus inscribe themselves in a tradition which can be retraced to *The Genealogy of Morals*, in which both history *and* interpretation are conceived as forms of a debt that is impossible to repay. By contrast, Freud—here and elsewhere—adds the implication that the debt in question cannot be construed as a static and stable obligation, but rather as an ambivalent and unresolvable tension. If the psychic conflict that structures the subject of desire precludes any enduring resolution, any kind of totalization, the process of interpretation cannot simply renounce such aspirations, either. For every interpretation must necessarily seek to arrest and to dominate the conflictual process of symbolization it seeks to comprehend. In the text just cited, the ambivalence can be retraced to the exigency of *Selbstüberwindung*—a term that means practically the opposite of its translation in the Standard Edition, which reads: "self-discipline," since what is both required, and stated, is the overcoming-of-self, i.e., of the ego. Such overcoming, however, the "mastering of internal resistances," still inevitably entails mastery, control, discipline, and hence, as such, appeals to the very ego that it seeks to "overcome."

It is only in the recognition of such ambivalence and in the articulation of its social and institutional consequences that the notion of "history"—but also that of "text"—may be brought into play, in a game whose rules are neither those of the "academic marketplace today," nor of the liberal tradition in America. For, as opposed to that tradition, to its compulsion to universalize, to individualize, and to delegitimize conflict, the players of this game will not have to ignore the fact that the rules themselves are at stake. And perhaps that, for once, will allow us to care for something other than just winning.

Chapter 5
The Critics' Choice

It would be difficult to find a work of world literature about which the opinion of critics has been more divided than is the case with *Tristram Shandy*. As Richard Lanham, one of Sterne's most provocative (and provoked) readers, has remarked, "even Milton has not been subjected to such precipitous reevaluation, such divergent appreciation."[1] In the twentieth century the poles of this divergence can be identified on the one hand with F. R. Leavis's cavalier dismissal of the novel as "irresponsible (and nasty) trifling,"[2] and on the other with Viktor Sklovskij's encomium of Sterne's text as "the most typical novel of world literature."[3] But such controversy merely continues a debate that began with the publication of the novel; eighteenth-century evaluation was no less polarized. For Samuel Johnson there could be no doubt that "nothing odd will do long, Tristram Shandy did not last,"[4] whereas for David Hume the novel was nothing less than "the best book that has been writ by any Englishman these thirty years."[5] Such contrary evaluations could be accumulated into an impressive list. But although this would not be without interest, I want instead to focus on two appreciations, dating from the nineteenth century, in order to indicate some of the issues at stake in the controversy. The first of these is to be found in Nietzsche's *Human, All Too Human*, in a section entitled "The Freest Writer":

Sterne is the great master of double entendre (*Zweideutigkeit*: innuendo, ambiguity), a term that should be taken in a far wider sense than is commonly done when it is applied to sexual relations. We may give up for lost the reader who always insists on knowing exactly what

Sterne thinks in each particular case, whether his face is serious or smiling, for it can be both in a single wrinkle (*in einer Faltung seines Gesichts*); he not only can be, he wants to be both right and wrong, mixing profundity and farce so that they become inseparable. His digressions are at the same time continuations and developments of the story; his moral maxims ironize all moralizing, his repugnance for the serious goes together with a penchant against taking anything to be simply flat or superficial. He thus provokes a feeling of uncertainty in the genuine reader as to whether one is walking, standing or lying down, a feeling most closely akin to that of being suspended in air (*ein Gefühl, welches dem des Schwebens am verwandtesten ist.*)[6]

Nietzsche's description of Sterne—which, incidentally, could also be read as a self-portrait—is remarkable in that it brings together a number of different traits to form a highly suggestive configuration. Above all, the motif of sexuality is related to that of language, to the effects produced on the reader, and finally to the designs of the author. Sterne's *Zweideutigkeit* deprives his readers of a fixed or reliable point of reference, a firm place to stand on. Such equivocation, Nietzsche implies, quite literally splits all statements, leaving the "genuine reader"—*den rechten Leser*—with little to hold on to. The reader who all the same insists on knowing what is *really* going on, who scrutinizes the text in order to discover the intention that guides it; the reader who searches for the true expression of the author, in order to distinguish what is *serious* from what is not, will find only a "fold," a wrinkled visage that suggests *both* seriousness and whimsy, at one and the same time.

Emphasis on Sterne's ambivalent innuendos also marks the second appreciation from the nineteenth century that I wish to discuss, although this one is as negative as Nietzsche's is positive. In his essay "Sterne and Goldsmith," Thackeray vents his grievances against the author of *Tristram Shandy* as follows:

The humour of Swift and Rabelais, whom he (Sterne) pretended to succeed, poured from them as naturally as a song does from a bird; they lose no manly dignity with it, but laugh their hearty great laugh out of their broad chests as nature bade them. But this man—who can make you laugh, who can make you cry, too—never lets his reader alone, or will permit his audience repose: when you are quiet, he fancies he must rouse you, and turns over head and heels, or sidles up and whispers a nasty story. The man is a great jester, not a great humourist. He goes to work systematically and of cold blood; paints his face, puts on his ruff and motley clothes, and lays down his carpet and tumbles on it.[7]

As opposed to the true humorist, who is as "natural" as he is "manly," Sterne is full of artifice; instead of laughing heartily as they do, "out of their manly chests, as nature bade them," "this man" is not manly enough; he neither sings nor laughs, he wheedles, whispers, and cajoles. And, what is worst of all, he schemes with (or against) his readers, never letting them alone or allowing them repose. What really seems to bother Thackeray is the sense of being a captive, if not captivated, audience; not only does Sterne "paint his face," thus hiding its true expression from view (a fact that Nietzsche counted in his favor), but Sterne also turns the tables: "He is always looking in my face, watching his effect, uncertain whether I think him an impostor or not; posture-making, coaxing, and imploring me."[8] The uncertainty that Nietzsche attributed to the "genuine" reader, Thackeray ascribes to the author, who is said to manipulate the reader, thus seducing him into complicity.

What is common to the appreciations of both Thackeray and Nietzsche, above and beyond the divergence of their evaluation, is the sense that *Tristram Shandy* puts the reader on the spot, while at the same time denying all certitude about just what, or where, that spot *is*. Is it "serious" or is it a "joke"? Is *Tristram Shandy* a novel, or is it a satire on the novel? Does it continue the tradition or reduce it to absurdity? Is it a precociously modern text, or the revival of a premodern, rhetorical style of writing? Or all at once? Or none of the above?

The sense of being placed in a double-bind has been most emphatically articulated by Richard Lanham, whose study of *Tristram Shandy*, one of the most suggestive of recent readings, is entirely suspended, as it were, on the horns of Sterne's cock-and-bull story. This is how Lanham sums up the quandary:

> We are damned if we do and damned if we don't. This strategy denies us a single point of view in the novel, a philosophic control as it were, and then continually alerts us to the need for one. Thus we must constantly search for a key, a basis for interpretation, and feel silly for doing so.[9]

Modern narrative theory has been eloquent in describing how the history of the novel has brought with it the progressive disappearance of the omniscient narrator and the proliferation of points of view. Such eloquence falters, however, when the same development begins to affect (or infect) the perspective of the critic himself, and not merely that of his object.[10] Lanham's study is in this respect exemplary: for while it displays an almost Nietzschean awareness of the traps and pitfalls of any single point of view in reading *Tristram Shandy*, it is honest and consistent enough to acknowledge that such a vantage point cannot be easily dispensed with if criticism hopes to be taken seriously. Since the dilemma thus described characterizes virtually all attempts to criticize *Tristram Shandy*, it is worthwhile retracing in some detail the manner in which Lanham articulates the problem and attempts to resolve it.

On the one hand, no one has been more sensitive to the obstacles and challenges that *Tristram Shandy* presents to its readers. To sum them up, Lanham cites a well-known passage from a letter written by Sterne to one of these readers:

Your walking stick is in no sense more shandaic than in that of its having more handles than one—the parallel breaks only in this, that in using the stick, every one will take the handle which suits his convenience. In *Tristram Shandy*, the handle is taken which suits their (the readers') passions, their ignorance or sensibility.[11]

Lanham comments

The twentieth century prefers to think that, seeing the novel whole for the first time, we grasp all the handles at once. In some ways this is true, but without belittling the excellent commentary of the last twenty years, have we too not grasped a single handle, the one that suits our passions, our ignorance, or our sensibility? Do we not look increasingly like Walter Shandy?[12]

What then emerges in the course of Lanham's study is that the adequate response to this challenge—if there is one—resides not so much in *what* handle the reader grabs, but in *how* he grasps it. Let us therefore examine Lanham's manner of seizing the handle, as it emerges in his reading of a scene that he presents as being exemplary for the overall strategy of *Tristram Shandy*. The episode is contained in the fourth volume of the novel, and it recounts the visit of Walter, Toby, and Yorick to the house of Didius, in order to learn from the learned scholars gathered there "whether the name" given erroneously to Walter's newly born son "can be changed or not" (IV.23).[13] Walter, you remember, had intended to have his child christened "Trismegistus," not Tristram. For Father Shandy, who—unlike many literary critics—attaches enormous importance to the power of names, this is an unmitigated catastrophe, one that he hopes to remedy if at all possible.

Before the question at hand can be submitted to discussion, however, an unfortunate incident takes place. Following dinner, a basket of hot chestnuts is set upon the table around which the scholars and their visitors are gathered. As everyone is in the process of helping himself, one of the chestnuts falls from the table into the unbuttoned codpiece of one of the scholars, Phutatorius, whose celebrated treatise *de Concubinis retinendis* is about to appear in its second edition. After a period of growing uncertainty, mounting agitation, anxiety, and just plain pain, and presumably after a St. Vitus-type-dance executed by Phutatorius, the chestnut finally falls to the floor, where it is picked up and eaten by Parson Yorick, "for no other reason," we are told, "but that he thought the chestnut not a jot worse for the adventure." Phutatorius, and his colleagues, however, see in this gesture of Yorick's "a plain acknowledgement that the chestnut was originally his—and in course, that it must have been the owner of the chestnut, and no one else, who could have plaid him such a prank with it." (IV.27) In this incident Lanham sees the strategy of the entire novel concentrated: Yorick, he argues "performs . . . on the narrative level the role the wordplay performs on the literal—or imagistic—level. He takes a chance event . . . and capitalizes on its accidental humor to make wit."[14] In other words, the individual event is arbitrary and contingent, and to search out its meaning—as the critics have usually attempted to do with the novel as a whole—is to miss the point. For that point resides precisely in the ability to transform the contingency and arbitrariness of events into sources of pleasure, by making them into the material of wit. Yorick's act of picking up the chestnut and eating it is exemplary, because it demonstrates what the novel as a whole seeks to present—the manner in which, at least within the sphere of private life, reality can be transformed into a game of pleasure. In scenes such as this one, *Tristram Shandy* acts out its game in a manner that Lanham does not hesitate to qualify as "autoerotic":[15] that is, as a "performance" we are intended to watch and to admire, but in which the reader does not participate except as spectator. If it does not much matter what handle the reader grasps, it is because all are equally irrelevant: "*Tristram Shandy* is a closed system," which presents the reader with the spectacle of pleasure seeking; to grasp the handle that one desires is merely to continue the spectacle, to prolong the game, not to affect it. To read *Tristram Shandy*, then, is ultimately to behold it as a mirror of what we all do anyway, whether we know it or not.

But to behold the novel as a "closed system" still presupposes that there is a framework that encloses it. If such a framework is designed to keep the reader, and the novel, in their respective places, and above all to prevent the former from taking the latter too seriously, the material out of which the frame is constructed must in turn be taken very seriously. Lanham's authoritative sources, invoked in order to elaborate his conception of the "game" as a search for pleasure, include Freud. Toward the end of his book, he increasingly appeals to Freud's theory of jokes in order "to catch" what he calls "the paradoxical self" of *Tristram Shandy*. The novel, he argues, "seems to abolish the ego altogether . . . it eliminates character" by presenting us with "a collection of discrete, forever colliding selves, but no dependable sense of self"; it is "all acting and no action" (Lanham, 156–58). "The self persists," Lanham continues, only "if by it we mean Freud's tireless seeker after pleasure" (Lanham, 157). He then goes on to elaborate what he takes to be Freud's conception of the joke:

> The joke, for Freud, is the contribution of the unconscious to a general theory of comedy based on pleasure and—even more to the purpose for Sterne—on pure verbal play as the center and symbol of that pleasure. Through Freud's comic thesis we may, in fact, be able to catch the paradoxical self that *Tristram Shandy* both denies—in its conception of life as absurdist drama—and affirms. If we are indeed trapped in a self fundamentally dramatic, how do we know it is real? By its endless pursuit of pleasure . . . *Tristram Shandy* shows us defending ourselves against the pressures of culture and of instinct by

converting them to pleasure. It does not satirize this conversion. Sterne
stands it at the center of mortal life. (Lanham, 158)

If Nietzsche had argued that the "genuine reader" of Sterne must be prepared to
accept a situation in whch he does not know if he is coming or going, standing
or floating, Lanham's critical reading here seems to act out that very condition
of oscillation, by affirming and denying it. All sense of stable identity, of ego and
of self, is presented as role and as acting: "We lose our reference point. No norm
remains" (Lanham, 155); and yet, that loss itself is made into a new norm, a new
reference point, a center, a ground on which to stand, insofar as Lanham assigns
it an apparently unequivocal name: "pleasure." This is where Freud comes in. For
if *Tristram Shandy* can be seen as an enormous "cock-and-bull story," as one big
joke, Freud appears to provide the critic with a meaning or function of that joke:
the search for pleasure, based on "pure verbal play as (its) center and symbol."
In order to avoid the pitfall of taking Sterne too seriously, or rather of misconstru-
ing "the peculiar configuration of (his) seriousness" (Lanham, 15), Lanham thus
returns to a certain reading of Freud. The problem with this reading, however,
is that it addresses a text—Freud's study of *Jokes and Their Relation to the
Unconscious*—which is every bit as treacherous as is *Tristram Shandy*. To attempt to extract from it a handle that will enable one to get hold of *Tristram
Shandy* involves the same kind of pitfalls and traps that Lanham seeks to avoid
in the case of Sterne. Let me briefly indicate what some of these pitfalls might be.

Lanham's reading of Freud's Joke-Book is based on a thesis advanced early
in the text, according to which the joke is a "developed game" (*ein entwickeltes
Spiel*): this game serves the pleasure-principle, Freud contends, by permitting
the adult temporarily to indulge the infantile desire to elicit pleasure from the
playing of games; this game-playing desire of the child has long since been inhibited by the development of critical reasoning in the adult, who must subor-
dinate play to the demands of the intellect, of morality, and of the reality-principle. The joke, by paying lip service to such rational demands, enables its
participants to recover the "original" and "pure" pleasure of "play," under the
cover of a rational, semantic facade. The meanings involved in the joke are
therefore nothing more than an external envelope ("*Hulle*") for the center
("*Kern*") they conceal and protect, and that consists in this pure pleasure of play.

It is evident that this thesis of Freud's provides Lanham with a model for reading *Tristram Shandy*: the individual episodes and motifs are deemed unimportant, except as occasions to indulge in the pleasures of pure play. This conception allows Lanham to arrive at his interpretation of the incident with the
chestnut, and of Yorick's role in turning pure chance into equally pure wit. This
reading, I shall argue, is as reductive of Sterne as it is of Freud. For despite the
theoretical language in which it is couched, Freud's treatment of jokes is no less
equivocal than the novel itself.

Once he has established the thesis that the joke is a developed game — a thesis he never explicitly rejects — Freud proceeds to complicate it in a variety of ways. Since I have attempted to analyze this text elsewhere,[16] I will limit myself here to a discussion of two points that are particularly pertinent. The first has to do with the nature of the game the joke is supposed to develop. Freud uses terms such as "original" and "pure" in order to characterize the pleasure the child takes in play, and he uses such terms because they enable him to portray the structure of the joke as essentially binary: the joke consists of a cover of meaning, designed to neutralize the "inhibitions" of the critical intellect, and a nucleus of play, reflecting its essence and its origin, the untrammeled principle of pleasure. However, once Freud enters into a discussion of the nature of that pleasure, it becomes clear — particularly if we place such discussion in the overall context of his thought — that the pleasure that the child derives from playing is not at all "pure" or "original," in the sense of a direct manifestation of the pleasure principle, but rather a derivative pleasure: that of the narcissistic ego in the process of formation. If the child enjoys verbal play, free of the constraint of meaning, it is not because of any intrinsic "purity" of such play but because of the experience of repetition and of recognition it affords; recognition of the same, through variations of repetition and of difference, provides the pattern for the narcissistic recognition of the self in others on which ego formation is, in part at least, based. This point is important, since it suggests that the split in the subject, of which the joke, like all manifestations of the unconscious, is an articulation, is not of a binary character, between two, self-identical, preconstituted poles (Meaning and Pleasure, Reason and Instinct, Seriousness and Play); rather, each of the poles is already split from the very start, as it were. This has consequences for the notion that Lanham — and many other readers of Freud — construe as the basic and founding principle of psychoanalysis, that of the "pleasure principle." One consequence is that this principle is not pure or original, but is divided and divisive in its inception. If Freud begins, in *The Interpretation of Dreams*, by oscillating in his designation of the basic motif of human action, calling it both the "Pleasure" and "Unpleasure" Principle (*Lust- and Unlustprinzip*), such oscillation is not the sign of immaturity, but reflects a fact that was to emerge with increasing insistence as his thought progressed. The processes and phenomena that Freud attempts to isolate and to study can not be reduced to a single name or opposition because they reflect irreconcilable and structural *conflicts*: what he was attempting to describe was not a simple, undivided movement toward pleasure but *at the same time* a movement away from pain; not merely *desire* but also and simultaneously *defense*. In the passage I have quoted from Lanham there is a faint trace of this fact, when it is asserted that "*Tristram Shandy* shows us defending ourselves against the pressures of culture and of instinct." The difference, however, between Lanham and Freud — the Freud of my reading, at least — is that Lanham construes the self as defending itself against *external* forces, against culture and instinct, whereas Freud shows us the self fending (for) itself precisely by defending against itself, intrapsychically and intralinguistically, as it were.

The upshot of this is that the pleasure of play defended by the joke is neither "original" nor "pure": it is, from the very first, ambivalent and narcissistic. And this brings me to my second point. For if Freud is constrained to relativize and to undermine the useful but misleading simplicity of his original, binary conception of the joke, it is because the thesis of the joke as essentially the development of childhood play omits what Freud recognized as perhaps the most distinctive trait of the joke: the fact that it must produce laughter in order to function. As Freud insists again and again, a joke at which one does not laugh cannot be considered a joke. And the laughter he envisages is of a violent, explosive, uncontrollable kind. Such laughter, however, controverts the notion of the joke as developed play; such play could indeed be what Lanham takes it to be, self-enclosed and virtually "autoerotic." The joke, by contrast, is the most eminently and directly *social* of all the manifestations of the unconscious: it requires a social context, and three poles or participants: the teller (Freud designates him as the first person), the object (which Freud designates, aptly but for reasons I cannot go into here, as the second person), and the listener (the third person). Thus, Freud's conception of the joke moves from a binary to a triadic structure. This change amounts to much more than the addition of a single term to two preexisting ones. Freud's conception of the joke is triadic in the sense first fully elaborated by Charles Peirce, as a structure in which the interaction of three elements is requisite to the establishment of the identity of any one of them. In other words, first, second and third persons only *become* themselves, the joke only is a joke insofar as it interacts in such a way as to produce laughter. Freud's theory of jokes is thus "pragmatic" *avant la lettre*: the joke is produced post facto, as it were, by the aftereffect of laughter. And what is crucial about laughter is that it can only take place in (the) place of another, of a radical alterity, which Freud designates not merely as the audience or listener, but as the "third" person. This person is "third" in the sense of a grammatical third person, about which Benveniste has argued that it designates a nonperson;[17] in any case, Freud's discussion demonstrates that if the third person must not be construed as simply another first person, an alter ego, this derives from the nature of laughter itself. Laughter, Freud asserts, results from the momentary *"Aufhebung"* or lifting of inhibitions that normally stand in the way of desires: the semantic and syntactic aspects of the joke seduce and deflect the otherwise vigilant critical inhibitions, making them temporarily superfluous, and the energy otherwise absorbed in the maintenance of such inhibitions is channeled into laughter. The interaction of the pleasurable relief from inhibitions (*Aufhebungslust*) and the play of desire thus rendered accessible (*Spiellust*) constitutes the overall effect of the joke.

We begin to see that Freud's initial binary conception of two distinct and hier-

archically ordered pleasures — that of the semantic lifting of inhibitions and that
of the nonsemantic indulgence in play — cannot do justice to the complex dynamics of the joke process. Above all, the relationship between semantic content
and play is no longer presented as one of facade and nucleus, exteriority and interiority, accident and essence; the play that goes on in the joke is far more intimately connected to the inhibitions that normally prohibit it. An example may
serve to concretize this state of affairs. In his study Freud cites the following
joke:

> A man enters a cafe and orders a piece of cake; having received it, he
> changes his mind, brings it back and orders a glass of schnapps in-
> stead. He drinks it, gets up and is about to leave when the waiter runs
> after him with the check. "What's the matter," asks the customer. "You
> haven't paid for the schnapps," stammers the waiter. "But I gave you
> the cake in exchange." "You didn't pay for that either." "Of course not,
> I didn't eat it."[18]

Freud cites this as an example of a joke using pseudo-logic, providing "a suitable
facade for a piece of faulty reasoning . . . We might say that the customer
used the relation 'in exchange for' with a double meaning. But it would be more
correct to say that by means of a double meaning he constructed a connection
which was not in reality valid."[19] Freud refers to this kind of joke as one using
"nonsensical techniques," but it is clear that this particular use of "nonsense" has
its own sense; the *laws of commensurate exchange*, which constitute much of
the social "reality-principle," are turned against themselves in order to make way
for another kind of law, the *incommensurable exchange of desire*. The unequal
exchange of desire, however, is neither "pure" nor without rapport to the commensurate exchange it seeks to outwit; indeed, the example suggests what Freud
only indirectly touches upon: that all wit involves outwitting, that its search for
pleasure is necessarily tendentious, comporting an aggressive element, directed
toward representatives of the reality-principle, of logic, reason, and of commensurate exchange. In the story cited, this representative is the waiter, who himself
is both agent and victim of such exchange. In the joke as such, however, this
role is assumed by the third person, who is both the addressee of the joke and
its judge; for if the third person does not laugh, the joke falls through, and the
first person with it. For if the joke-teller is to succeed as "first person," he must
move his listener to laughter; he himself cannot laugh or get pleasure from the
joke, except indirectly, through the effects it produces. Indeed, the joke-teller
only becomes a first person, an ego, through the third person. The listener, on
the other hand, cannot consciously will or decide to laugh; his laughter must be
essentially involuntary, it must "break out" spontaneously, through the momentary lifting of unconscious (or preconscious) inhibitions. This is why this third
person is an other not merely with respect to the first person, but also in regard

to himself, to his self-consciousness. His laughter comes from elsewhere. And this is also why, as Freud repeatedly insists, we can never know precisely *what* we are laughing about; for to know would preclude our laughing. The effect of the joke, then, is to produce a certain state of nonknowledge, one that is not independent of what we know, but not identical with it, either. Rather, it entails what we do not *want* to know—what we *want not to know*—what we bar ourselves from knowing, the enabling limits of our consciousness. In the case of the joke, such limits are not simply individual: they are shared, involving a certain sociality. This is why each joke must find its proper audience, one that shares the same inhibitions the joke attempts to lift.

Far from representing the simple other of meaning, then, the joke puts meanings into play in order to reveal the repressed, excluded desires on which it depends. But those desires are never revealed as such, because they have no "as such," no undivided purity; they are narcissistic in nature, involving the effort of a divided ego to recognize itself in the other, the effort to reduce that other to itself. This is why in the course of his study Freud is forced to redefine what he calls "tendentious or aggressive" jokes: having first, according to his original binary logic, attempted to categorize such jokes as one of the two basic kinds of wit—tendentious *versus* harmless jokes—he then goes on to acknowledge that *all* jokes are, to some degree at least, tendentious, and that this aggressive, ambivalent tendency is inseparable from the relation of first to third person. The joke is always, to a degree, made at the expense of the listener.

We seem to have wandered a long way from *Tristram Shandy*—but have we? Perhaps this digression is just another of the many that constitutes its progressive-digressive history. The discomfiture of the critics, from Samuel Johnson to Richard Lanham, might well have to do with the traits that make *Tristram Shandy*, as Ian Watt has observed, very like a "shaggy dog story":

> If we find any discrepancy between our early expectations of what we would be given in *The Life and Opinions of Tristram Shandy, Gent.* and what he has actually been good enough to vouchsafe, that is just his joke; all he ever intended was, as we would say, a shaggy dog story.[20]

The assuredness of this evaluation is based on a premise that Lanham is acute enough to question: that we do, in fact, know what a joke *is* and what it is *not*, where it *starts* and where it *stops*. Where it starts is always the same: with its "author," with "Sterne," with his presumptive "intention": "all he ever *intended* was . . . a shaggy dog story." Secure in his conviction, Ian Watt is ready to conclude:

> As a novel, *Tristram Shandy* is, obviously, incomplete; but by Sterne's standards the question of completeness or incompleteness is irrelevant:

his narrative texture has harmony and consistency; and his basic premises always included the possibility of infinite digression and expansion. This structural freedom and open-endedness may occasionally have enticed Sterne into going too far, or too easily; there are intrinsic advantages in literary forms and traditions which impose their own discipline on the author, which force him to discover the implications of his subject more fully instead of freeing him to pick up another one at will; . . . Sterne reminds one at times of the youthful occupation of seeing how slowly one can ride a bicycle without falling off.[21]

For Ian Watt, the problem of falling off is Sterne's, not ours, as readers. But this assertion can only be sustained if the *critic* has indeed succeeded in distinguishing the *intention* that governs the welter of the text. No wrinkle or fold, no leering face need concern a critic capable of distinguishing the author as one who has failed to accept the "discipline" that "literary forms and traditions . . . impose." In failing to submit himself to this discipline, Watt contends, "Sterne" missed the chance to discover the implications of his subject more fully . . . ." But he never quite tells us just *what* that *subject* might be. Except, perhaps, a shaggy dog story. For Freud, the shaggy dog story was one of the borderline cases of the joke, in which the narrator tells the joke directly at the expense of the listener — who can only "revenge" himself by in turn becoming a first person, a re-teller of tales.

That *Tristram Shandy* is about such shaggy dog stories, that it contains them and stages them, is beyond doubt; what is less certain is the assumption that *therefore* its story has nothing to do with the "discipline" — or should we say, the "inhibitions" — of "literary forms and traditions." Indeed, the joke might just turn out to be at the expense of such traditions, and of those readers who accept their authority without question.

But instead of pursuing this line of questioning,[22] let me instead try to get back to our original subject, to the text of *Tristram Shandy*, and in particular to the incident of the chestnut. What the previous discussion of Freud suggests is that play can never be pure, original, or free from aggression. And if Lanham is correct in pointing to Yorick as the exemplary jester, it should not be forgotten that his jesting is, from the very beginning of the novel, inseparably bound up with *ambivalence*. Indeed, Yorick's very status in *Tristram Shandy* is marked by this trait — he is the one major figure whose death is inscribed in the text in the graphic form of the two black pages that stand both as its frontispiece and its gravestone. Much could and should be said about Yorick's curious position in this text: peripheral and yet central, he serves to demark and to delimit what is often referred to as the "world" of Shandy Hall. What I want to stress here, however, is the curious mixture of comic seriousness that overshadows this figure, whose sad story serves to point up the dangerous consequences of wit. For wherever Yorick appears to display his wit, aggression is never far away. And it is this aggressive undertone that sets the scene at Didius's house. For as it turns out, Yorick and Phutatorius have long been at loggerheads. Indeed, the Parson's very first gesture is received by the scholars as a challenge and a provocation: he tears up his sermon and hands the pieces around to be used as pipe lighters. Yorick justifies this act by observing that the sermon "came from my head instead of my heart . . . to preach, to shew the extent of our reading, or the subtleties of our wit—to parade it in the eyes of the vulgar with the beggarly accounts of a little learning . . . is dishonest. . . . For my own part, continued Yorick, I had rather direct five words point blank to the heart—" (IV.26). Although it is Uncle Toby who is about to reply to the phrase "point blank," there can be little doubt that the learned scholars also feel themselves to be targets of Yorick's jibes, fired off point blank.

This then sets the stage for the incident of the chestnut. The scene is highly charged from the outset, and what transpires only confirms the vulnerability of the protagonists—or should we say *antagonists*? Let us now reread the description of this "accident":

> You must be informed then, that Gastripheres, who had taken a turn into the kitchen a little before dinner . . . observing a wicker-basket of fine chestnuts standing upon the dresser, had ordered that a hundred or two of them might be roasted and sent in, as soon as dinner was over. . . . Didius, but Phutatorius especially, were particularly fond of 'em. About two minutes before the time that my uncle Toby interrupted Yorick's harangue—Gastriphere's chestnuts were brought in . . . laid directly before Phutatorius, wrapt up hot in a clean damask napkin. Now whether it was physically impossible, with half a dozen hands all thrust into the napkin at a time—but that some one chesnut, of more life and rotundity than the rest, must be set into motion—it so fell out, however, that one was actually sent rolling off the table; and as Phutatorius sat straddling under—it fell perpendicularly into that particular aperture of Phutatorius' breeches, for which, to the shame and indelicacy of our language be it spoke, there is no chaste word throughout all Johnson's dictionary. (IV.27)

When, after this account, the narrator labels the incident an "accident"—an evaluation that Lanham, as we have seen, unquestioningly adopts as the keystone of his interpretation—we would do well to pay attention to the qualification immediately attached to the term: "Accident, I call it, in compliance to a received mode of speaking." If in *Tristram Shandy* "compliance" with "received mode(s) of speaking" can hardly be taken for granted, here there are particular reasons for exercising caution. Lanham may well be correct in accepting the assurances of the narrator that Yorick is not the culprit; the fact remains that the event itself is scarcely described as being *unmotivated*. "With half a dozen hands all thrust into the napkin at a time," it is not accidental if something is set in motion. Indeed, it is the avidity of the scholars and guests that triggers the incident. In this light, the scholars' dinner recalls an account earlier in the novel, of another "party":

> There is nothing so foolish, when you are at the expense of making an entertainment of this kind [i.e., the novel itself] as to order things so badly, as to let your critics and gentry of refined taste run it down; nor is there any thing so likely to make them do it, as that of leaving them out of the party, or, what is full as offensive, of bestowing your attention upon the rest of your guests in so particular a way, as if there was no such thing as a critick (by occupation) at table—I guard against both; for . . . I have left half a dozen places purposely open for them; and . . . I pay them all court. . . . Gentlemen, I kiss your hands. . . . I beg only you will make no strangers of yourselves, but sit down without any ceremony and fall on heartily. (II.2)

Small wonder that the critics and scholars thus invited to the table of *Tristram Shandy* have felt ill at ease. For in grasping at the kernels of meaning—and is not this the traditional task of the reader, at least insofar as he is a *critic by occupation?*—one can hardly avoid the conclusion that one has been "had." Like Phutatorius, all that is left is for us to soothe our wounds with the texts we produce, "hot"—or rather "cool"—off the press. And also, to search out a culprit: Phutatorius, Didius, and the learned scholars are convinced they have found him in Yorick. Discomforted readers of *Tristram Shandy* have similarly found solace in something or someone they call: "Sterne": "that is just his joke," as Ian Watt writes, "all he ever intended was, as we would say, a shaggy dog story." If the critic has difficulty in identifying the meaning of the novel, he can at least seek refuge in *naming the identity of its author*. If the text seems to defy all efforts to determine its meaning, this at least appears to offer a handle we can hold on to. Even Lanham ultimately resorts to it:

> One perennial perplexity remains to plague us. When do we say Tristram and when do we say Sterne? . . . As a working distinction, we talk of Tristram when we mean the narrator of *Tristram Shandy* or confine our discussion to the novel. Speaking of the novel as written in a certain time and place, we may use Sterne.[23]

This sounds harmless enough and self-evident: most texts have been written by someone, in a definite time and place. But Lanham's very next sentence demonstrates that his use of the proper name *Sterne* implies much more than this:

> And so too of what Tristram does *not* see, his character as satirized.[24]

That is, the reference to the *Author* serves to legitimate the insights of the *critic*: what *he sees* that the *narrator* does not—and this is ultimately nothing less than the meaning of the novel as a whole—is presented as the reflection of an authority that is ultimately unquestionable because it is identified with that of the Author: "This is Sterne's point *and the novel's*."[25] It is also the critic's last—and decisive—resort in defending his own authority, his ability to differentiate between, as Nietzsche put it, the "genuine" and the duped reader.

What I want to suggest is that it is this kind of critical gesture that *Tristram Shandy* most powerfully invites, but also resists. If the supposition of an original, founding authorial intention is one of the most deeply ingrained, barely conscious gestures of critical interpretation, *Tristram Shandy* plays games with it as few texts have before or since. To elaborate the kinds of games it plays would entail nothing less than the practice of a different kind of reading, the nature of which the following passage from the novel can only begin to suggest:

> Of all the several ways of beginning a book which are now in practice throughout the known world, I am confident my own way of doing it is the best—I'm sure it is the most religious—for I begin with writing the first sentence—and trusting to Almighty God for the second. Twould cure an author for ever of the fuss and folly of opening his street-door and calling in his neighbours and friends, and kins-folk . . . only to observe how one sentence of mine follows another and how the plan follows the whole. (VIII.2)

"To observe how one sentence . . . follows another and how the plan follows the whole" is first and foremost to renounce the desire to resume the play of the text in a single statement or series of assertions which in turn are held to reflect the intention of an author. If "the plan follows the whole," it is the result of the play of language and not of a governing, anterior consciousness. Attention thus directed at transitions and juxtapositions, rather than at single propositions or unified groups of utterances, will produce different conclusions: "The mind should be accustomed to make wise reflections, and draw curious conclusions as it goes along," we read early in the novel (I.20). We would do well to take this phrase as literally as possible: such conclusions will be "curious" not simply because they are odd and unexpected, but because, in a certain sense, they do not conclude. They should not so much satisfy curiosity as suscitate it. And with this remark, I shall conclude, I hope, curiously.

Chapter 6
The Blindness of the Seeing Eye: Psychoanalysis, Hermeneutics, *Entstellung*

I

"I find myself for the moment in the interesting position of not knowing whether what I wish to impart should be regarded as something long familiar and obvious or as something entirely new and puzzling."[1] These words, with which Freud begins one of his last texts, "The Splitting of the Ego in the Process of Defense," seems an appropriate introduction to the remarks that follow, and not only because I too am uncertain about whether they will appear new and puzzling or merely all too familiar. Rather, a discussion of psychoanalysis and hermeneutics could hardly find a more apt place to begin than with this strange confession, which underscores just how pervasive the sense of uncertainty is in Freud's thinking. Indeed, were one to seek a single criterion in order to characterize what distinguishes Freud's writing so radically from that of almost all his students and followers, one could hardly do better than to examine the place it accords to the *unknown*. What is often described as Freud's remarkable attention to "style" derives not from the humanistic culture which, however vast and profound, was something he shared with many of his contemporaries (if not with his successors). Rather, the unusual rhetorical power of his work seems inseparable from its willingness to negotiate with the unknown and to acknowledge uncertainty not merely as an impediment or defect, but as an integral part of thinking and writing. If psychoanalysis has anything to contribute to hermeneutics – to the theory and practice of interpretation – it is probably bound up with this distinctive inscription of the unknown, which allows the writings of Freud to function as something other than merely an instrument of insight.

It is well known, of course, that psychoanalysis constitutes itself initially through Freud's encounter with the phenomenon of hysteria, "that strange state of mind in which one knows and does not know . . . at the same time."[2] What is less widely recognized, however, is the fact that this "strange state of mind" could only become an *object* of psychoanalytic interpretation to the extent that the latter was prepared and able to open itself to it, and indeed, in a certain sense, to participate in it. To observe this process at work, we need only examine the context in which the remark just cited occurs. Freud is recounting how one of his patients, "Miss Lucy R.," finally comes to accept his conjecture that she was in love with her employer. When asked why she hadn't mentioned this before, Lucy replies that she "didn't know—or rather . . . didn't want to know." This formulation incites Freud to write a long note, which deserves to be cited in its entirety:

> I have never managed to give a better description than this of the strange state of mind in which one knows and does not know a thing at the same time. It is clearly impossible to understand it unless one has been in such a state oneself. I myself have had a very remarkable experience of this sort, which is still clearly before me. If I try to recollect what went on in my mind at the time I can get hold of very little. What happened was that I saw something which did not fit in at all with my expectation; yet I did not allow what I saw to disturb my fixed plan in the least, though the perception should have put a stop to it. I was unconscious of any contradiction in this; nor was I aware of my feelings of repulsion, which must nevertheless undoubtedly have been responsible for the perception producing no psychical effect. I was afflicted by that blindness of the seeing eye which is so astonishing in the attitude of mothers to their daughters, husbands to their wives and rulers to their favorites. (*Hysteria*, 117n.)

Although Freud does not reveal to us just what it was that he "saw" and that "did not fit in at all with" his "expectations," the scenario is precisely the one he will use, some ten years later, to describe the way in which children deal with the perception of sexual difference.[3] It is therefore not entirely surprising that he should cite, as examples of "the strange state", cases involving relations of the sexes, in which *women* (mothers, daughters, wives) are particularly conspicuous.

Thus, the nonknowledge with which psychoanalysis, from its very inception, is not merely confronted but rather enveloped, is associated with a certain resistance to sexual difference. And this resistance, in turn, takes the form not so much of simple ignorance, but of a *desire not-to-know*. In order for such a desire to impose itself, however, there must already be a prescience of what it is one does not want to know. The unknown, then, with which psychoanalysis will be concerned, is far from the simple other or opposite of the known, but rather something that exists, as it were, *alongside* of it, as its condition of possibility and of impossibility at once. Although in a logic dominated by the law of identity, such a convergence would be untenable (except, perhaps, in a dialectical perspective of totalization), the laws that preside over the operations of the unconscious know no contradiction. The result of that nonknowing is that the conditions of (im-)possibility operate effectively as what I am tempted to call *conditions of imposability*.

Let us turn to one of the most striking instances of such an imposition—one that has considerable significance for the development of Freud's thought. It is related at the very beginning of the fourth case history in the *Studies on Hysteria*:

> In the summer vacation of the year 189- I made an excursion into the Hohe Tauern so that for a while I might forget medicine and more particularly the neuroses. I had almost succeeded in this when one day I turned aside from the main road to climb a mountain which lay somewhat apart (*abseits gelegen*) and which was renowned for its views and for its well-run refuge hut. I reached the top after a strenuous climb and, feeling refreshed and rested, was sitting deep in contemplation of the charm of the distant prospect. I was so lost in thought that at first I did not connect it with myself when these words reached my ears: "Are you a doctor, sir?" But the question was addressed to me, and by the rather surly-looking girl of perhaps eighteen who had served my meal and had been spoken to by the landlady as "Katharina." To judge by her dress and bearing, she could not be a servant, but must no doubt be a daughter or relative of the landlady's.
>
> Coming to myself (*zur Selbstbesinnung gelangt*) I replied: "Yes, I'm a doctor: but how did you know that?"
>
> You wrote your name in the Visitors' Book, sir." (*Hysteria*, 125; translation altered—S.W.)

This little scene can be read as nothing less than an allegorical staging of what might be described as "The Calling of Freudian Psychoanalysis." To be sure, we find ourselves confronted by a situation that Lacan was probably the first to thematize: the subject, here Freud himself, receives "his" message in inverted form from the mouth of another, indeed, of *the Other*, insofar as Katharina here can be seen to embody the sex that will never cease to exemplify the unknown for the "father" of psychoanalysis. This being said, however, it can hardly be denied that the interest of the scene resides more in its particular details than in any so general a pattern. Let us therefore dwell for a moment on some of those details.

The scene is set in the context of an outing; that is, of an attempt to escape, if only temporarily, the rigors of the everyday world, "and more particularly the neuroses." The "excursion" leads Freud first into the mountains, and then along a road that takes him off the beaten track, *abseits*, while holding out the promise of a spectacular view, to be enjoyed from the security of a "well-run refuge hut." The goal seems attained when, "after a strenuous climb," Freud finally sinks back in his chair and abandons himself to "the charm of the distant prospect."

Thus caught up in the panoramic view, oblivious to all around him, Freud is suddenly startled by a voice asking, "Are you a doctor, sir?" The question seems innocuous enough, and yet if we go back to the German text, we may begin to understand Freud's otherwise rather curious reaction: he is both startled and uncertain about whether or not he is in fact being addressed. The question that Katharina asks is, "*Ist der Herr ein Arzt?*" Literally: "Is the gentleman a physician?" The use of the traditionally polite form of the third person, now obsolete, leaves the question of its addressee far more open than the "you" would suggest.

Initially, then, Freud knows neither where the voice is coming from nor where it is going. He is also at a loss to explain where "the rather surly-looking girl of perhaps eighteen" with whom he finds himself confronted might have learned about him. Wrenched back to the world from which he had sought to escape, Freud finds that he had never really left it at all. Not merely because he is once again confronted by a problem of neurosis; but even more because he discovers himself again the prey of questions he had doubtless hoped to forget, if only for the time of a brief excursion: "Is the gentleman a physician?" And even more: "Are *you* that *gentleman*?" No place is sufficiently remote or off the beaten track to be beyond the reach of that voice and its equivocal questioning. *Freud is discovered for reasons that he will never cease to describe, perhaps most dramatically in one of his last works, Moses and Monotheism*, in which he observed that to disfigure a text and to commit a murder were in one respect similar: "The difficulty is not in perpetrating the dead, but in getting rid of the traces." (*S. E.* 23.43.) Freud has been found out because he too has, unawares, left a trace: he has signed his name and title in the guest book of the mountain inn. The attempt at flight, at abandoning one's cares to the magnificent view of the world far below, has foundered upon a signature. . . .

II

This little scene might well be considered to be an allegory of psychoanalytic interpretation itself. At first, and in the foreground, we encounter the effort to continue and to fulfill the project of traditional hermeneutics, that of uncovering meaning. One of the driving forces in Freud's development of psychoanalysis was his conviction that the established branches of medicine, above all, neuropsychology and psychiatry, had been hermeneutically deficient in failing to grasp and reveal the meaning present in all mental acts and especially in those arising without conscious deliberation or control: dreams, parapraxes, hysterical symptoms. The initial words of *The Interpretation of Dreams* are indicative of what might be described as the "rationalist" side of Freud's hermeneutical endeavor:

> In the pages that follow I shall bring forward proof that there is a psychological technique which makes it possible to interpret dreams, and that, if that procedure is employed, every dream reveals itself as a psychical structure which has a meaning and which can be inserted at an assignable point in the mental activities of waking life. (*S.E.* 4.1)

This rationalism consists in the double assertion first, that all psychic manifestations are meaningful, and second, that psychoanalysis alone can provide the key to that meaning.

In view of this and similar assertions, it is no wonder that *The Interpretation of Dreams* in particular and Freudian psychoanalysis generally should have been regarded and judged in the light of such claims. In the area of literary studies, for instance, the hermeneutical value of Freud's work was long held to be inferior to that of Jung, whose theory of archetypes appeared to address directly some of the more common symbolic motifs encountered in literature and art. Freud, by contrast, seemed strangely insensitive to such thematic recurrences. Few critics bothered to reflect on Freud's admonition of those who expected *The Interpretation of Dreams* to furnish a "key" or dictionary, with which all dreams could then be "decoded":

> My procedure is not so convenient as the popular decoding method which translates any given piece of a dream's content by a fixed key. I, on the contrary, am prepared to find that the same piece of content may conceal a different meaning when it occurs in various people or in various contexts. (*S.E.* 4.105)

And yet, although he insisted that there could be no general rule or code with which to assure the intelligibility of dreams, Freud also maintained, not only that they were all in principle interpretable—up to a point, al least—but, perhaps even more surprisingly, that they constituted themselves through, and as, interpretation.

It is in the tensions resulting from these two seemingly irreconcilable conceptions of the dream, the one stressing its idiomatic, even idiosyncratic *singularity*; the other, its structural dependence on interpretation—and hence, on a process which by definition entails repetition, alteration, and dislocation—that Freudian hermeneutics deploys its distinctive force.

The most characteristic articulation of these hermeneutics *at work* is probably to be found at the beginning of the seventh chapter of *The Interpretation of Dreams*, at precisely the point where Freud prepares to move from a descriptive analysis of the "dream-work" to a speculative theory capable of making good his initial promise to "insert" the dream "at an assignable point in the mental activities of waking life."

Before launching into the speculative part of his study, however, Freud sees himself constrained to confront a "difficulty," which, if left unresolved, is "capable of cutting the ground from under all our efforts at interpreting dreams":

> It has been objected on more than one occasion that we have in fact
> no knowledge of the dreams that we set out to interpret, or, speaking
> more correctly, that we have no guarantee that we know them as they
> actually occurred. (*S.E.* 5.512)

Indeed, Freud continues, "there is every reason to suspect that our memory of dreams is not only fragmentary but positively inaccurate and falsified."

What is at stake, then, in this anticipated objection is nothing less than the very "ground" upon which the entire *Interpretation of Dreams* is based: the dream itself, its status as an object of interpretation. All the more significant, therefore, is the strategy of Freud's response to this criticism: far from simply dismissing it or seeking to reject it out of hand, he *accepts* it, not as an objection, to be sure, but as an accurate *description* of what occurs, necessarily, in dreams and their interpretation. By thus accepting the pertinence of the remark not as it is intended, as a criticism, but as a description, Freud is able to reveal how and why the premise of this kind of objection is challenged by his approach to dreams:

> It is true that we distort dreams in attempting to reproduce them . . .
> but this distortion (*Entstellung*) is itself no more than a part of the
> elaboration which the dream-thoughts regularly undergo as a result of
> the dream-censorship. (*S.E.* 5.514)

To charge that the dream, as Freud has construed it, is accessible to us only through the distorting lens of a reproductive, interpretive, and even tendentious consciousness would be a telling critique of the previous discussion only if Freud had not insisted throughout precisely upon the fact that the dream itself must be considered to be a form of *distortion*, of *Entstellung*, a word which, as he will remark in *Moses and Monotheism*, signifies not only disfigurement, but also *dislocation*.[4]

The interpretation of a dream thus does indeed constitute a process of deformation; yet far from invalidating itself, this alone constitutes, paradoxically, its sole claim to legitimacy. For the dream "itself" is already an *Entstellung*: not merely by virtue of what Freud describes as "secondary elaboration (or revision)" (*sekundäre Bearbeitung*), but also because the specific mechanisms of articulation that constitute the distinctive language of the dream are all forms of *Entstellung*: a word that must read as an alternative to *Darstellung*, "presentation" or "exposition." The dream, as a conflictual wish-fulfillment, distinguishes itself from waking thought not by its content, but by its form, a point that Freud saw himself constrained to clarify in a long footnote appended in 1925 to the chapter immediately preceding that which we are discussing, and which deals with the "dream-work":

> I used at one time to find it extraordinarily difficult to accustom readers to the distinction between the manifest content of dreams and the latent dream-thoughts. . . . But now that analysts at least have become reconciled to replacing the manifest dream by the meaning revealed by interpretation, many of them have become guilty of falling into another confusion to which they cling with equal obstinacy. They seek to find the essence of dreams in their latent content and in so doing they overlook the distinction between the latent dream-thoughts and the dream-work. At bottom, dreams are nothing other than a particular *form* of thinking. . . . It is the dream-work that creates the form, and it alone is the essence of dreaming—the explanation of its peculiar nature. (*S.E.* 5.506–7)

The "form" of thinking peculiar to dreams, however, is that of a de-formation that dissimulates its deformative character by creating a representational facade. "*Darstellung*" thus becomes one of the means by which the dream achieves its goal of "*Entstellung*."

If Freud is thus able to respond to the objection that the dream is distorted by its interpretation, it is only by radically redefining the dream's ontological status; it can no longer be regarded as a self-contained, fully determinable *object*, susceptible of being rendered or represented faithfully—"*dargestellt*"—by an interpretation. Rather, the dream comes to be only through a process of revision and distortion that even the best of interpretations can only hope to continue.

What results from this conception of the dream is a situation of interpretation that is quite different from that presumed by a hermeneutics that defines its task in terms of *explication* or of *disclosure*:

> It must not be forgotten that in interpreting a dream we are opposed by the psychical forces which were responsible for its distortion. It is thus a question of relative strength whether our intellectual interest, our capacity for self-discipline (*Selbstüberwindung*), our psychological knowledge and our practice in interpreting dreams enable us to master our internal resistances. (*S.E.* 5.524–25)

The translation of *Selbstüberwindung* as "self-discipline" involves a shift in emphasis that is symptomatic of the redefinition of interpretation at work in this text. "Self-discipline" suggests a voluntary, deliberate activity of the conscious self, establishing a measure of control over its unruly impulses. While this is

by no means entirely foreign to the *Selbstüberwindung*, it is also far from ex-
hausting the word's connotations. Literally, what is involved is not merely a
genitivus subjectivus: an overcoming *by* the Self of obstacles external to it, but
at the same time and yet paradoxically, an overcoming *of* the Self, which, qua
conscious, deliberate volition, is inevitably an agent of dream-censorship. The
same paradox is indicated by the notion of "free association," designating the consciously initiated endeavor to circumvent the constraints enforced by consciousness in its efforts to control the tensions of unconscious desires and conflicts.

As a movement of *Entstellung*, then, interpretation must be conceived not as
the more or less faithful reproduction or re-presentation of an antecedent, self-
identical object, meaning, or "presence," but as a process of repetition and dislocation, the limits of which must always remain more or less problematic and un-
stable.

The question that thereby imposes itself defines the relation of Freudian
thought to traditional hermeneutics. It may be stated as follows: If interpretation
can no longer be regarded as *Darstellung*, and hence as constituted by a self-
contained structure or meaningful work, how are those delimiting forces to be
conceived, without which the very notion of *Entstellung* would dissolve into ut-
ter indeterminacy? Why, in short, is there something, rather than nothing at all?

III

This question is inscribed between the lines of Freud's writing from its earliest
articulation on. In his first effort at elaborating a systematic theory, the *Project
for a Scientific Psychology* of 1895, it has already acquired the form it will retain
throughout his work: how does the tendency toward displacement and discharge,
which seems characteristic of psychic behavior in general, come to be "bound"
or "inhibited" (*gehemmt*), so that "conscious, observant thought" and "memory"
may take place? Freud's response is really only a conjecture, a speculation that
he will then go on to "forget" for twenty years, before rediscovering it again,
as the long-sought-after "answer" to one of the enigmas of psychoanalysis. In
the "Draft," Freud speculates that what he calls "linguistic associations"
(*Sprachassoziationen*) are responsible for imposing a degree of stability on the
otherwise volatile dynamics of the "neurones."[5] In other words, the fact that the
psyche is inserted into an already existing, constituted language, with more or
less determinate "verbal images" (*Wortbilder*) is considered the basis for effectively "inhibiting" or arresting the tendency toward substitution and displacement
that Freud, in *The Interpretation of Dreams*, will identify as the "primary process" of psychic life.

The history of this "train of thought," which is introduced precisely to account
for the fact that our trains of thought are not incessantly derailed by desire, sheds

light on the question to which it sought to respond. In the first place, the inhibitory function attributed by Freud to such "verbal images" is predicated on his conviction that words, by definition, as it were, are "closed (few in number) and exclusive."[6]

When, however, a few years later, the same problem is taken up again in the last chapter of *The Interpretation of Dreams*, the indispensable emergency brake is no longer identified as "verbal associations." This idea will lie dormant— repressed?—for some fifteen years, until it bursts upon Freud as the explanation of the mechanism of repression. Since I have already discussed this return of the theoretical repressed elsewhere,[7] I will limit myself here to pointing out simply that this repression is quite revealing of Freud's theoretical evolution. For it seems likely that at least one of the reasons why Freud had to "forget" about his notion of "word-images" as an arresting and structuring force was his own discussion of verbal language in *The Interpretation of Dreams*. His analyses of the symbolic use of verbal language in dreams had shown that words were by no means always "closed" and "exclusive." Indeed, might not Freud also have been speaking to himself when he remarked:

> There is no need to be astonished at the part played by words in dream-formation. Words, since they are the nodal points of numerous ideas, may be regarded as predestined to ambiguity; and the neuroses . . . no less than dreams, make unashamed use of the advantages thus offered by words for purposes of condensation and disguise. (*S.E.* 5.340–41)

The study of dreams demonstrates that the problem of "inhibition" or closure cannot be resolved simply by pointing to the existence of words: their oneiric function is arresting, it is true, but only in the sense of interrupting and perturbing established semantic associations:

> It is easy to show that dream-distortion too profits from displacement of expression. If one ambiguous word is used instead of two unambiguous ones the result is misleading; and if our everyday, sober method of expression is replaced by a pictorial one, our understanding is brought to a halt, particularly since a dream never tells us whether its elements are to be interpreted literally or in a figurative sense or whether they are to be connected with the material of the dream-thoughts directly or through the intermediary of some interpolated phraseology. (*S.E.* 5.340–41)

What Freud has in mind, of course, is the way in which "the whole domain of verbal wit is put at the disposal of the dream-work" (*S.E.* 5.340–41). And indeed, it is only when he turns to the problem of the *Witz*, that the hermeneutical question of closure receives its decisive psychoanalytical articulation.

IV

Freud's study, *Jokes and Their Relation to the Unconscious*, marks the point where psychoanalytical theory is inextricably caught up in the very movement of *Entstellung* it has hitherto sought primarily to describe and to comprehend. Psychoanalysis itself is dislocated by the unsettling discovery — never complete nor fully conscious — that it can articulate the conflictual alterity of the unconscious only by going beyond the domain of the intrapsychic, and even beyond that of the intersubjective. It is no accident that the driving force of this dislocation imposes itself through the question of language, and more specifically through that of "verbal wit." If language in general, and its witty uses in particular, had emerged through the analysis of dreams as an indispensable element of the unconscious, this tended to indicate that the latter could not be understood exclusively in intrapsychic terms.

It is in this light that Freud's emphasis on the "sociability" of the joke assumes its full significance. Far from being merely a special case among the phenomena studied by psychoanalysis — an impresson that Freud encourages by contrasting the joke with the ostensible asociality of the dream — his investigation of the *Witz* demonstrates that the activity of the unconscious can be conceived only within a context that is linguistically predetermined, and hence, that entails a dimension of "sociality." On the other hand, if I place that word in inverted commas, it is to emphasize that its significance here can hardly be considered to be self-evident. Sociality is no more a key to Freud's thought than psychoanalysis is to society. Each must be rethought in the light of the alterations it imposes upon our previous understanding of the other.

Such rethinking is what constitutes the major hermeneutical interest of Freud's book *Jokes*. It occurs — as always in Freud's writing (and indeed, this is what gives it its force) — not so much in the individual pronouncements, which seek to appropriate the joke for psychoanalytic theory, as between the lines and against the grain of Freud's declared intentions. The latter seek primarily to comprehend and contain the joke within the theoretical framework previously established by *The Interpretation of Dreams*. Thus, the joke is portrayed as just another, although more social, form of conflictual pleasure-seeking, a "developed play." The problem with this approach[8] is that it fails utterly to account for what Freud himself recognized to be the specificity of the *Witz*: the laughter it elicits, which in turn reveals its social quality. Like the dream, the joke only "takes place" *after the fact*, as it were; but unlike the dream, the alterity of its "afterlife" can no longer be confined to the space of a single subject, however divided.

The joke thus emerges as a quintessentially "pragmatic" process: what it *is* only *comes to be* through the "effects" it produces. This is what makes Freud so uneasy about the status of the "examples" upon which he, like his many predecessors, must inevitably rely. Since by definition there can be no purely textual example of a joke, severed from the context in which it is received; and since that context can never be predicted or prescribed, no "example" that can be cited—inscribed—can ever be decisively authenticated. The joke is thus no more reliably "present" than was the dream.

The general conditions under which a joke operates, however, can be described, and it is here that the question of *Hemmung* returns. Laughter, as Freud conceives it, embodies, quite literally, the temporary release of energy otherwise used to sustain and to maintain *inhibition*: that is, to arrest what would otherwise be the unending slide of desire, as suggested by the (theoretical fiction of the) "primary process." The convulsive, spasmodic movements by which the body expels, as it were, its inner energies, suggest allegorically the kind of dislocation triggered by the joke, in which the self-contained subject becomes both the agent and the theater of an alterity whose transgression confirms and reproduces the *Hemmungen* it momentarily transcends.

The "sociability" of the joke, in this perspective, emerges as the form in which that conflictual alterity that marks the relation of the subject to language is *articulated*: that is, determined, transgressed, and maintained. The precondition for the joke is what Freud describes as "shared inhibitions," and the latter, he insists, must inevitably be both local and limited in their extension. At the same time, such limitation and localization are themselves inevitably dislocated, since they entail prohibition or proscription, and as such comprise a process of inscription that is addressed elsewhere.

This ineluctable alterity is (de-)figured by the ambivalent status of the addressee of the joke, its "third person." Such ambivalence entails not merely the mix of erotic and aggressive impulses that pervades the relation of joke-teller and listener. Rather, the "third person" is already in itself the site of a radical nonidentity by virtue of the fact that laughter and self-consciousness are, for Freud at least, mutually exclusive. Laughter breaks out *in place of* self-consciousness, in the place otherwise marked out by the shared inhibitions whose authority is sporadically and spasmodically disrupted by a body "beside itself." And when Freud suggests that one becomes a joke-teller—that is, a "first person," an ego—only after having *first been excluded* from the position of the *third* person, the "listener,"[9] he anticipates the famous phrase that Lacan translates as, "Where it was, I shall come to be."

I come to be in the place where *it* was, but could not remain: in place of a *listening* that culminates in *laughter*. Laughter, itself comprising recurrent movements, is unrepeatable as such, that is, in relation to the "same" story. It entails a repetition that precisely is not a return of the same, but a movement of violent effraction. Its singularity consists in this return of alterity, of the excluded, of the repressed. In the movements of voice and body, the bond between "what once belonged together but has been torn apart in the course of [the ego's] development"[10] is renewed.

What the joke reveals, however, is that "what once belonged together" is never simply "torn apart," but rather separated and differentiated into the form of an *opposition*, the paradigm of which, perhaps, is the proscription or interdiction. Within psychoanalytic theory itself, the exemplary instance of this process, which might be described as the "differentiation of difference as opposition," is undoubtedly the "castration complex." Here, the perception of sexual difference is interpreted in terms of the opposition of absence and presence, nonbeing and being, dispossession and possession, the invisible and the visible. Such "storytelling," or rather, such story-*listening*, emerges as the form in which the generalized play of metonymic displacement constitutes itself in and as the always-particular *game*, with its determinate *rules* and its particular strategies.

What psychoanalysis suggests — and this may be its most telling contribution, and challenge, to hermeneutics — is that the rules of this game are made not merely to be discovered and enforced, but also, and above all, to be broken and transformed.

Chapter 7
Reading and Writing – *chez* Derrida

I would like to preface my remarks with two citations.* Although I am writing in English, I shall take the liberty of quoting two passages, one German and the other French, in the original. The first is taken from an essay by Heidegger on Hölderlin's poem "Wie wenn am Feiertage. . . . " The text was first delivered as a lecture, in the years 1939 and 1940, before being published in 1941. In his opening words, Heidegger situates both Hölderlin's poem and the conditions in which he attempts to interpret it:

> Das Gedicht entstand im Jahre 1800. Erst Einhundertundzehn Jahre
> später wurde es den Deutschen bekannt. Norbert von Hellingrath hat
> erstmals dem Gedicht aus den handschriftlichen Entwürfen eine Gestalt
> gegeben und sie im Jahre 1910 veröffentlicht. Seitdem ist wiederum
> ein Menschenalter vergangen. Während dieser Jahrzehnte hat der
> offene Aufruhr der neuzeitlichen Weltgeschichte begonnen. Ihr Gang
> erzwingt die Entscheidung über das künftige Gepräge der unbedingt
> gewordenen Herrschaft des Menschen, der den Erdball im ganzen sich
> unterwirft. Hölderlins Gedicht aber harrt noch der Deutung.[1]

The poem was written in the year 1800. Not until 110 years later did the Germans learn of it. Norbert v. Hellingrath was the first, working from the manuscripts, to give the poem a definite shape, and to pub-

---

*The following is the text of a lecture held at the annual meeting of the Louvain Philosophical Society in 1982. The topic of the meeting was "Deconstruction." Given the importance of local considerations for the paper, no effort has been made to transform its oral character.

lish it in 1910. Since then yet another generation has passed. During these decades, the upheavals of modern world history have broken out into the open. Their march makes a decision inevitable concerning the future stamp of what has become the unconditional domination of man, subjugating the entire planet to himself. Hölderlin's poem, however, still awaits interpretation.

It is only after these initial remarks, however, that Heidegger proceeds to make the following declaration of method, which I propose as the first of my two epigraphs:

Der hier zugrunde gelegte Text beruht, nach den urschriftlichen Entwürfen erneut geprüft, auf dem folgenden Versuch einer Auslegung.[2]

The text here taken as authoritative is based, after renewed examination of the original manuscripts, on the following attempt at an explication.

My second epigraph is taken from Derrida's most recent book, *La Carte postale, de Socrate à Freud et au-delà,* and in particular from one of the missives that constitute the first section, the *"Envois."* One of the letters, or postcards, dated 10 June 1977, begins as follows:

ce qui resterait de nous a force de musique, pas un mot, pas une lettre. Encore en train—je t'écris entre Oxford et Londres, près de Reading. Je te tiens couchée sur mes genoux. En train de t'écrire (toi? à toi?) cette pensée pour Oscar Wilde. Qu'aurait-il pensé de cette carte? de l'inversion des noms et des places? Il la connaissait peut-être
il faut que tu comprennes, si j'écris *sur* la carte, comme aussi bien j'écrirais sur toi, et je l'aime, c'est pour détruire, que rien ne soit gardé qu'un support illisible, ou encore un cliché, rien qui ait mérité ou prétendu mériter d'être gardé. Et si nous ne détruisons pas toutes les traces, nous sommes sauvés, c'est-à-dire perdus.[3]

What would remain of us has the force of music, not a word, not a letter. Still on the train (underway)—I am writing you between Oxford and London, nearby Reading. I hold you asleep on my knees. While I write you (you? to you?) this thought for Oscar Wilde. What would he have thought of this card? of the inversion of names and of places? Perhaps he knew it
you must understand, if I write *on* the card, just as though I were to write on you, which I love to do, it's in order to destroy, so that nothing may be kept but an illegible support, or just a cliché, nothing that deserved, or could claim to deserve to be kept. And if we don't destroy all the traces, we are saved, that is, lost.

Were this text in French, I would probably have taken its title from this passage, and have called it: "Près de Reading." However, since I am writing in English, I shall have to forego this title—which, despite its apparent simplicity, poses formidable obstacles to translation—and instead adopt the one proposed by Professor Samuel IJsseling, namely: "Lire et écrire chez Derrida."

You will have remarked that I cite this title in French. This is related to a rather curious problem, which I would like to take a moment to explain, since it is intimately bound up with the topic I am about to address. The problem I am referring to is not the obvious and massive difficulty of defining a subject as enormous as it is elusive, since it can be legitimately equated with virtually every aspect of Derrida's work. This difficulty goes without saying, as does the fact that the title, "Lire et écrire chez Derrida" does not so much define a particular subject matter that would allow of anything like an exhaustive or even systematic treatment, but rather points in the direction of a series of questions, concerning what might be provisionally described as both the "theory" and the "practice" of reading and writing, "chez Derrida."

It is not, then, this problem that I wish to mention here, but rather something else, far more trivial perhaps, and a bit of an embarrassment. For having accepted, without any second thoughts, Professor IJsseling's suggestion that I hold my talk in English, I find myself, right at the outset, constrained to violate this agreement, if only briefly. My problem, in short, is that I cannot find a suitable translation for the title, "Lire et écrire chez Derrida." And, looking back, I now ask myself if it was not precisely this problem that caused Professor IJsseling, in his letter of invitation, written in an impeccable English and asking me to speak in English, to formulate this title of this paper . . . in French.

The difficulty, as you will doubtless have realized by now, is simply this: there is, in English, no adequate translation for the French preposition CHEZ. The apparent solution, "Reading and Writing *in the work* of Derrida," does not merely lack elegance, is not merely ponderous—it is also imprecise and downright misleading. It is imprecise inasmuch as the attribution or localization signified by the word *chez* is not to be equated with a relation of simple interiority or inherence. (*in* the work of . . .). And such a translation would be especially misleading in regard to a thinker, one of whose major motifs has always been the reassessment of the values of interiority, immanence, and inherence, as well as of the underlying opposition, "inside/outside," on which these values repose. To have translated the title simply as "Reading and Writing *in* the works (or: texts) of Derrida" would therefore have been to capitulate, in advance, to the challenge rather than to address it.

But how then should this challenge be *addressed*? Had I been asked to speak not in English but in German, the problem would have been resolved all by itself, at least insofar as the title was concerned. The latter would then have been

"Lesen und Schreiben *bei* Derrida," and I would probably have thought no more about it. Such was not to be the case, however. I had agreed to address you here in English, and I was stymied already, even before I had begun.

This dilemma, to which I could find no easy way out, left me no choice but to take the harder way *in* — that is, in the Latin sense of *in*: *toward* or *into*. Since what I discovered along this way is not without interest for *die Sache selbst*, let me take a moment to tell you about it.

My way led me first to a French-English dictionary (written in Paris, published in London, under the imprimatur of the Oxford University Press), which informed me that *chez* could be translated as "in," "within," or "among." None of these would do, to be sure, but they began to map out the contours of the problem. If "in" was too *inward*, "with" was too extraneous, whereas "among" implied a plurality of reference, no one, but many "Derridas." The latter possibility, to be sure, was by no means unsuited to texts such as *La Carte postale*, which take obvious pleasure in flaunting their "exappropriative structure."[4] The introduction to the book's first part, the *Envois*, ends with the following note:

> I regret that you (*tu*) don't have excessive confidence in my signature, under the pretext that we are many. It's true, but I don't say it in order to acquire any added authority. Or, even less, to be disturbing; I know the cost of that. You're right, there are doubtless many of us and I'm not as alone as I say sometimes when I can't keep from bemoaning it, or when I strive to seduce you.[5]

Nevertheless, despite such resonances, I could not bring myself, you will surely understand, to entitle this talk, "Reading and Writing *among* Derrida(s)." At the same time, I also began to realize that the difficulty raised by the resistance of *chez* to translation was not unrelated to the question of reading and writing itself, *chez* Derrida. The problem, in the title, and in that which the title was meant to indicate, entailed the difficulty of attributing predicates to a subject without claiming to establish thereby a relation either of simple identity or of simple difference. I therefore decided to take a further step along the way into the difficulty and to consult a work that is doubtless familiar to many of you, since its author, recently departed, is a Belgian. I am referring, of course, to *Le Bon Usage* of Maurice Grevisse, in which you can read that *chez* signifies *dans la demeure de* (that is, "in the abode or residence of"), and further, that it can be used in an extended sense, to mean "in the country of." The examples given by Grevisse to illustrate these two senses of *chez* are, first: *J'ai été chez mon père*, and second: *porter la guerre chez l'ennemi*. By contrast, Grevisse also notes the following abuse of the term and warns emphatically against it: "N.B. Do not use *chez*, as is sometimes done in Belgium, in the sense of 'near' or 'next to' (*près de, auprès de*), as in *Viens, mon petit, viens chez ta mère.*[6]

At this point I had to confess that the problem the Belgians seemed to have with *chez* was also my own, only even worse. For I was even more removed from the proper use of the word than they were: because the term or its equivalent was missing in my mother tongue, it seemed as if I was condemned to an improper, Belgian relation to this preposition, with which I could never hope to feel entirely at home. I could at best only approach or approximate the correct use and understanding of *chez*, but I would still be simply *près* or *auprès de lui*, and never *dans sa demeure*.

Having reached this stage in my bout with the recalcitrant preposition of my title, I began to wonder whether it could ever really be "my" title at all, whether I could ever have title to this title. My decision to accept the challenge nevertheless was motivated by three factors. First, I felt that I was probably not alone in feeling somewhat ill at ease with the term *chez* and in particular with the locution *chez Derrida*. I remembered the conclusion of one of the first books published under this name, *La voix et le phénomène*, which ended with the following affirmation:

> And contrary to what Phenomenology — which is always phenomenology of perception — has tried to make us believe, contrary to what our desire cannot fail to be tempted into believing, the thing itself always escapes.
> Contrary to the assurance that Husserl gives us . . . "the look" cannot "abide" (*"le regard" ne peut pas "demeurer"*).[7]

If, then, one of the motifs of the texts published under the imprint "Derrida" was precisely to indicate both the *desire* and the *impossibility* of ever being able *to abide*, that is of ever being fully able to use the term *chez* in the proper sense (*j'ai été chez mon père*), then the difficulties I was experiencing might be an integral part of the questions I was being asked to address. This, at any rate, was the first factor in my deciding to come. The second was that the problem I was having with *chez* was also shared by a good many Belgians, and hence, that despite the origins of the author of *Le Bon Usage*, I could probably count on a sympathetic hearing when I gave my talk, far from the capital of French culture. Finally — and this third factor is doubtless the most difficult to account for, and the most important — there was something in the invitation to speak on "Lire et écrire chez Derrida" that made it impossible for me to refuse; I felt compelled to accept, to assume a task that certainly surpasses my powers. Which is also why, when I came upon the bad, Belgian phrase, "Viens, mon petit, viens chez ta mère!" it was as if the words were directed at me in person, forming not an example to be avoided, but an appeal, indeed a command, to which I had long since acquiesced.

And so I decided — but was it really *I* who decided? — to come, or rather, to *go* — on with my explorations concerning the irresistible preposition that resisted all my efforts at translation. If *chez* would not come to me, I would go to it, and more precisely, to its antecedents. Here I made a rather important discovery. *Chez*, you will not be surprised to hear, comes from the Latin, *casa*, a word, however, that does not mean what one might expect, namely: house. For *casa* is by no means the same as *dómus*, and hence is not inscribed in the lexical chain that goes back to the Greek, *dómos*. *Casa*, which signifies a hut, cottage, or shepherd's cabin, thus stands somewhat askew from the main lexical-semantic line deriving from the root *dem-*, which, as Benveniste has shown, is the source of the words designating house, *construction*, and *domination*, and, above all, of the concomitant division of space into "outside and inside" (in Latin, *domi*: *foris*). With regard to this whole *economy*—and Benveniste reminds us that "dómos and [w]oîkos mean practically the same thing,"[8] *casa* stands apart, even if today, *chez soi* is often used, correctly, to designate precisely the intimate interior of home and hearth (*chez mon père*).

This discovery that the etymology of *chez* situated it on the periphery of what might be called the domestic economy of the House itself, with its Laws and its Masters, encouraged me to take one further step into the curious space that was thus opening up; I delved into the family circle of *chez*, where I encountered the following four cognates, listed in order of chronological appearance:

1. *Casenier*, going back to the thirteenth century, designated Italian merchants residing in France. Like its referent, the word itself is an émigré from Italy, derived from *casana*, bank, which in turn stems from it. *casa*, house, and the Arabic *khazina*, treasure. In the sixteenth century, the word undergoes a rather startling semantic transformation, accompanied by a minor shift in orthography: it exchanges its middle "e" for an "a" and acquires its modern meaning of a sedentary *pantouflard*, that is, a *homebody* (or *stay-at-home*). For the *casanier*, the wandering appears to be over; if you want to do business with him, you will have to meet him on his own grounds.

2. In the sixteenth century there appears the word *casemate*, another Italian émigré, this time from the word *casa-matta*, meaning literally, a madhouse, and figuratively, a false or phony house. The word was first used to designate the compartments constructed at the base of the outer walls of a fortress, from whose small openings the defenders could harass their enemies as these attempted to cross the moat and scale the ramparts. Sixteenth-century English lexicographers, such as Florio, the translator of Montaigne, speculated that the word came not from the Italian, but from the Spanish *matar*, to kill or slaughter. Still others traced its roots back far beyond *casa* to the Greek *khasma*, meaning "chasm," gaping hole, *béance*.

3. The third branch of the family goes back to the thirteenth century, when the word *case* appears, meaning first a little house, and then used to designate the cottages found in Senegal and the Antilles. What justifies its position as the third in my sequence, however, is that it only acquires its more modern meaning in the seventeenth century, when it comes to signify the spatial division, square

or box, on a game-board—a chessboard, for instance. Today, of course, *case* also signifies the subdivision of any space or volume, the cells of a beehive or those of the brain. But also the boxes in which things are put, permanently or provisionally, a *case postale*, for example. The verb, *caser*, has as its most general meaning that of putting things where they belong, in their proper place, where once put, they may be kept, safe and sound; *Caser une fille*, for instance, is to marry her off. But this most organized member of the family *chez* also bears the marks of the disorder it seeks to master: the *casier* is the inscribed record of infractions, whether judicial or fiscal; moreover, the word also signifies the net used to catch shellfish, as well as those pieces of furniture in which things— records, papers, bottles—can be placed and stored for future use.

4. Finally, the fourth and youngest member of the family, appearing only in the eighteenth century, is also the most frivolous: *casino*, the diminutive of *casa*, signified then as today a house where gambling, spectacles, and pleasures otherwise prohibited are permitted. The casino, then, is a house of organized, authorized transgression, and above all, of games of chance.

This then was the genealogy and legacy of the unprepossessing preposition that I was—and remain—unable to render in English. Reflecting on the results of this lexical-etymological survey, it struck me that every member of this verbal family seemed characterized by a certain ambivalence. *Chez* itself denoted both the proper place where one could abide and reside, and yet, at the same time, in an improper, abusive but widespread usage, a movement toward, an approach, implying in turn a certain disjunction, (auprès de), a certain remove from the economy and laws of a household. The fact that this ambivalent movement recurred in most of the cognates: in the shift from *casenier* to *casanier*; in the speculative uncertainty over the origins and meanings of *casemate*; in the ambiguous implications of the compartmental *case*, with its reference both to the rules of the game and also to their infraction; and finally, in the "little house" where infractions are authorized and chance organized—all this seemed both to reflect and to anticipate aspects of what might be meant by the title "Reading and Writing *chez* Derrida," while at the same time describing my own movements, as I was led by the very untranslatability of my title ever further from the apparent simplicity and unicity of a proper name, "Derrida," and ever more inextricably into an area where the property and propriety of such names could no longer be taken *for granted*. If "reading and writing" were ever to be adequately described, *chez* Derrida, it would have to be in terms that would at least begin to take the process of *granting* into account, and not merely its effects.

I therefore decided to proceed in the following manner. I would regard *chez* not so much as an arrow, pointing me toward a well-defined space in which "reading and writing" could be specified and specifically analyzed as the attributes of a selfsame subject. Rather, *chez* would be treated as a dash—a mark found frequently in the texts signed "Derrida"—a trait that serves to suspend the two parts of the title, dividing and joining them in a relation yet to be determined. I would therefore begin by discussing the left side of the title in a more general way, in order then to move to the right side and examine certain more particular instances of reading and writing, in one or two texts published under the imprint "Derrida."

Let me begin then, albeit belatedly, by noting that "reading and writing," although obviously inseparable and complementary, are assigned quite distinct places in what might be called the tragicomic drama of deconstruction. In the unraveling of the "phallogocentric" metaphysics of self-presentation, "writing" occupies a prominent position, plays the leading role, whereas "reading," although never absent, is more difficult to situate. Anticipating, I will suggest — retaining, for a while, the theatrical code — that its place is that of an "extra" (in French: *figurant*), an actor who has no lines to speak and whose main function is usually to get lost in the crowd. And yet, this crowd, which consists entirely of such "extras," turns out — as we shall see — to be that without which the main roles could never be played.

Nevertheless, in the perspectives first opened by deconstruction, it is a certain disproportion or dissymmetry in the relation of reading and writing that draws one's attention. The reason for this dissymmetry is perhaps this: that in regard to the role played by writing, reading appears to add nothing essentially new, to make no contribution of its own. If writing is the ambivalent locus of the most intense investment of Western thought in its effort to systematize itself, and hence, the predestined object of any strategy bent on revealing the limits of that system, the place and status of reading appears to be far more modest, less interested and less interesting. The disseminating description of writing as the repressed but irrepressible Other of Phonocentrism would seem to hold, *a fortiori*, as it were, for reading as well. Reading could thus be determined as the effort to reduce difference and repetition to a minimum, the effort of a representation to efface itself before that which it represents, in this case, the text, but without impinging upon or usurping the originality of its model. This interpretation of reading, however, would add nothing new to the general scenario of supplementarity or of *différance*: the effort of reading to reduce its repetitive-representative nonidentity with the text would be condemned from the start: if it succeeds, it fails, betraying the text by excess of fidelity, as it were, usurping the latter's prerogatives, taking its place or presenting itself as the double of writing; but if it fails, this too would condemn it to the very difference it seeks to efface; reading would fall short of its goal, its telos, the re-presentation of the text itself.

Considered in this light, then, reading adds nothing new to the drama of deconstruction; it merely repeats it: if writing is presented, within the closure of metaphysics, as the representation of a representation, as the signifier of a signifier, the repetition of a repetition, then reading appears only to reiterate all that once again, adding hardly a wrinkle.

Yet there is perhaps another aspect of reading—that is, of its position within the closure of metaphysics—that makes it a less likely candidate for a leading role in the dislocation of that closure. Given the predominant attempt to degrade and debase writing in regard to speech, to determine inscription as the fall into alienated exteriority, reading could be called upon to function dialectically, as the negation of a negation, the re-presentation of an irremediably extraneous representation—in short, as the vivifying actualization of a dead letter. This is, mutatis mutandis, the position adopted by certain contemporary "phenomenological" theorists of reading, such as Wolfgang Iser. But it is also a position masterfully analyzed, in the first publications of Derrida, as a writing that refuses to know its own name (precisely in order to establish a foundation for *knowing* itself). Here again, then, reading *as such* would seem to have no independent role to play, no strategic function in the unhinging of the metaphysical closure. Its place is merely that of the extra, the stand-in or understudy of the hero, which is to say that reading has no proper place of its own in the deconstruction of metaphysics. Since, however, that deconstruction is directed precisely *at the Proper*, it is not surprising that reading intrudes or impinges increasingly on the scene of writing, *chez Derrida*. And in so doing, it dramatically alters that scene—or rather, it alters the dramatic scene as such, and moves it instead in the *direction* of a narrative, a *récit*.

To illustrate this assertion I shall discuss the question of reading in regard to two texts, one published at the outset of deconstruction, *La Voix et le phénomène* (1967)—translated in English somewhat misleadingly as *Speech and Phenomena*—and *La Carte postale—de Socrate à Freud et au-delà* (1980). As we shall see, the latter text repeats, in a mode that might be called "parodic," many of the motifs of the earlier text, while displacing and altering them.

But first, let me begin by indicating what might still be called the hermeneutical position of *La Voix et le phénomène*, the stance it assumes in regard to the text it reads, by citing the following passage from the end of the book's introduction. The context is that of the "hold"—the *prise*—exercised over Husserlian phenomenology by the aporetic system of logocentrist metaphysics, which seeks to privilege the voice as the paradigm of a language construed as the reflexive self-presentation of consciousness:

> The nature of this "hold" is poorly conceived in the concepts habitually sanctioned in the philosophy of the history of philosophy. But our purpose here is not directly to meditate upon the form of this "hold" but only *to show it already at work (de la montrer à l'oeuvre déjà)*—and powerfully so—from the start, in the first of the *Logical Investigations*.[9] (my emphasis)

The project here asserted is essentially *deictic*: *to show, montrer*, something *already at work from the start*. To be sure, that something is anything but simple or self-identical: it is a *hold* in the process of *losing its grip*. But—and this is what interests me—that *hold* and that *grip* can still be *situated*, namely: *chez Husserl*. This is a citation, and again I will give you its context, which entails precisely the contextualization of a proper name, that of *Husserl* itself.

> Whether we consider expression, or indicative communication, the difference between reality and representation, between the true and the imaginary, between simple presence and repetition, has always already started *to efface itself*. Does not the [effort to] maintain this difference—*in the history of metaphysics and still chez Husserl*— answer to the obstinate desire to save presence and to reduce or derive the sign? And with it, all the powers of repetition?[10] (my emphasis)

The use of a proper name, "Husserl," serves to situate a process which can then be described and designated in self-reflexive terms: the constitutive, founding differences, in the history of metaphysics, "and still *chez* Husserl," "*efface themselves*." The reading undertaken in *La Voix et le phénomène* still *authorizes itself* in the name of an author, through the naming of an author to designate and delimit a process which, however conflictual it may be, still takes place, takes its place on the terrain indicated by a proper name: *chez Husserl*.

In a certain sense, then, *La Voix et le phénomène* is itself already inscribed in the repetition it describes: it *does* what it *describes*, and what in describing it attributes to an *other*: Husserl, Metaphysics. The question that emerges thereby has been stated with clarity in *La Carte postale*, in regard to Freud:

> What happens when acts or performances (discourse or writing, analysis or description, etc.) form part of the objects they designate? When they can give themselves as examples of that about which they speak or write? There is certainly no gain in self-reflexive transparency, on the contrary. An account is no longer possible, nor a simple report (*compte rendu*), and the borders of the whole (*ensemble*) are no longer either closed or open. *Their trait divides itself* and its interweavings can no loner be disentangled.[11] (my emphasis)

You will have remarked the repetition of the reflexive mode in the assertion that the "trait" of the borders, which are no longer open or closed, "divides itself." Nevertheless, this repetition functions very differently in the context of *La Carte postale* than in the earlier work. To indicate one aspect of this difference, it is sufficient to note that the title of the text from which the above citation is taken, is: "Spéculer—sur 'Freud'," and that the proper name is inscribed in quotation marks, that is, inscribed *as* a proper name; and indeed, the entire reading of *Beyond the Pleasure Principle* describes the effort of a name to establish and safeguard its property and propriety, an effort that neither succeeds entirely, nor simply fails, and that is as *impossible* as it is *ineluctable*.

The description of Husserl in *La Voix et le phénomène*, then, can also be read as a performance which forms part of the objects it describes. The primary such "object" can be designated as the will or desire to construe language as the medium through which consciousness can express itself in the pure interiority of the "living present." By demonstrating how the process through which such an *idealization* of language is construed, *chez* Husserl—namely, as an indefinite repetition of the same—also entails the irrevocable deferring of what it seeks to establish, the "living present," *La Voix et le phénomène* opens a perspective that has not ceased to direct the texts of Derrida: the perspective of a repetition that is not derivable from an origin but that, in its transformative, altering force, is irrepressible. *La Voix et le phénomène*, however, while retracing the disruptive power of this repetition, also assumes an argumentative stance that in turn repeats the repetition whose alteration and dislocation it describes. And it does this by appealing to the *proper name* of "Husserl" as an *author*, in order to situate and authorize its reading. In this respect, the deconstructive strategy of the text can be characterized by two assertions. The first is made in regard to the distinction between language as reality and as representation:

> *Husserl himself* gives us the means of thinking it [language] *against himself*.[12] (my emphasis)

The second concerns the consequences of those "means" that Husserl gives us:

> *In one and the same movement*, Husserl describes and effaces the emancipation of discourse as non-knowledge.[13]

The reading of *La Voix et le phénomène* thus *describes itself* as the simple repetition of a nonsimple, complex conflict, entailing the impossibility of repetition ever to be simply simple. But this self-description assumes the form—presumably in order to authorize itself—of the description of an *Other*, an *Author*, Husserl, defining a space in which one can be *chez soi*, even while there is self-conflict. The dynamics of difference, or of *différance*, is still—rhetorically and strategically, at least—contained and confined *within* the space of an *opposition*, Husserl *against* himself, "*contre lui-même*". The conflict is encompassed by a movement that, however riven and driven, can still be described as "one and the same."

When we shift from this movement to that addressed by the more recent text, *La Carte postale*, and in particular by its second part, "Spéculer—sur 'Freud' "—that is, the Psychoanalytical Movement, we can begin to take measure of the distance traversed. To be sure, that "distance" is already inscribed in the motif of repetition which is "already at work" in *La Voix et le phénomène*, if not before, long before. The project and prospect inscribed toward the end of the reading of Husserl was stated as follows:

> No doubt this work has already begun. What must be grasped is what goes on (ce qui se passe) in this interior [of the language of metaphysics—S. W.] once the closure of metaphysics has come to be named (*vient à être nommé*).[14]

What goes on within the closure of Metaphysics once it has been named, what has never ceased to go on, is that the being-named, the Being of the name, comes, comes and goes, be-comes without ever arriving at its proper destination, the telos of its Being. And this nonarrival, ever-coming, ongoing, in turn turns the "interior" of Metaphysics, or anything else for that matter, *inside-out*. For without the being of the proper name, without the being-proper to the name, no clear-cut distinction between within and without, before and after, in front and behind can be established, once and for all. Instead, the proper name is drawn, or rather *redrawn* into the iterative process—which is also a *procès*, a trial, an infinite proceeding—of language, as an effect, not as a cause, as a culprit rather than as an author. The motif of the signature underscores and gives relief to the analysis of the ego *chez Husserl* (in *La Voix et le phénomène*), namely, as the pro-noun indelibly stamped with the stigma of impropriety and alterity. Im-proper name, signature, title are all part of the iterative alteration of language, of the divided and divisive movement of the trace, which quite literally im-plicates, folds the frames and borders into the body of the text they were held to contain. Reading is no longer *Aus-legung*, ex-plication, but—if I may play on the German—*Ein-legung*, and it folds itself in with the rest.

All this cannot and does not leave repetition or its effects unaltered, simply the same. In *La Voix et le phénomène*, probably the chief of these effects, and certainly the most dramatic, was designated as the "testamentary" character of the inscription, its structural relation to the absence of its author, to the latter's death. This relation to death was described as that which is implied in all nominal and prenominal utterances, by nature of their very ideality; "I am dead" was described as the paradigm of "I am. . . ."[15] In "Spéculer—sur 'Freud' " this testamentary character of writing has acquired a new but perhaps decisive wrinkle: it is not merely the testament that is at stake in the operation of writing, but its *legacy*. And that "legs"—*le legs de Freud*—moves, even if it *goes nowhere* (like the *legs* of the horse in Little Hans, about which Freud never ceases to speculate, but which he can never definitively explain).

This movement has many aspects, but the one that interests me here is that which relates to reading—or rather, to the relation of reading and writing, *lire et écrire*. If writing is still described in this text as a movement of repetition, involving a certain alterity and nonpresence, the latter—alterity and nonpresence—are no longer formulated in dramatic categories of opposition, as

"Freud against himself," but rather as "a structure of alteration without opposition,"[16] a structure that above all is characterized by circulation and reversibility. Thus, the desire that we meet in "*Spéculer—sur 'Freud'* " is one that "obstinately" seeks not to "save presence," as though it were something already there, already possessed, but rather to write oneself, "*s'écrire*"[17]: to write one's Self and to write *to* oneself; to send oneself into circulation, dispatching oneself and above all, one's name, sending it off in the hopes of reaping a profitable return, as the name arrives at its proper destination. The dream of *La Voix et le phénomène*, the dream of "Husserl" and of "Metaphysics"—that of a purely interior soliloquy of the soul, qua *casanier*—is spent, and in its stead there is the *casenier* (with an *e*, the exiled merchant-speculator), who is also a bit of a gambler as well. Presence is no longer an original point of departure but at best, one of arrival; not something that can be kept but something that must be gained; not something that can be posed, but rather that must be *imposed*, upon others. Desire is no less obstinate, but it knows that property is theft, law based on violence, and that the key to Presence is power—and the Post. For whoever controls the postal system, controls the rest.

But it is precisely because of this rest that the postal system can never be fully controlled, and it is this story—more a narrative than a drama—that *Speculating—on 'Freud'* retells. it is the tale of how a *telos* is forever being replaced by a *tele*, although it is one that cannot be viewed, but at best, read:

> On the one hand, repetition, classically, repeats something that precedes it, it comes afterwards—as one says, for instance, that Plato comes after Socrates . . . or as one imagines that a tale (récit) reports something that would be anterior or foreign to it, or in any case independent of it. . . . But on the other hand, according to another, nonclassical logic of repetition, the latter is "originary" and, by unlimited self-propagation, it instigates a general deconstruction . . . But there is no "on the one hand . . . on the other." As in the epilogue or the "back room" (arrière-boutique) of *Plato's Pharmacy*, "one repetition repeats the other" and that is what makes the *différance*. . . . Two logics, therefore, in effect incalculable, two repetitions that do not oppose each other any more than they repeat each other identically and which, if they repeat each other, echo the duplicity that constitutes all repetition: it is only when one takes into "account" this incalculable double-bind of repetition—and even though it is not *presently* thematized by Freud—that one has a chance of *reading* the unreadable text which follows immediately, and to read it *as unreadable*.[18]

If "account" in the phrase just cited ("it is only when one takes into 'account' this incalculable double-bind of repetition") is inscribed within quotation marks, it is to indicate that the double bind cannot simply be taken into account. Which is also why the text which follows "immediately"—but also every text—is both structurally unreadable and yet destined to be read. It is structurally unreadable inasmuch as it can never be definitively delimited or situated (*casé*); it *is* only *as* the repetition of other readings, which in turn are the reinscription of other writings; and hence, the desire to repeat it once and for all, to read it properly, is inevitably frustrated. And yet, at the same time, this desire is also unavoidable: all writing, even the most self-consciously "deconstructive" (however oxymoronic that last phrase may be) cannot help seeking to repeat the "classical" form of repetition, repeating its object as more or less of the same. For this writing, too, must necessarily want to be read, to control, and to reappropriate the form of its repetition.

This is why, in *La Carte postale*, the soliloquy of the soul with itself has been replaced and supplanted by the writing of missives. This replacement does not merely entail the shift from the interiority of consciousness to the exteriority of the unconscious; rather, it implies a transformation of the space in which reading and writing take place. That space is no longer neutral, homogeneous exteriority, nor is it, as with Hegel, the dialectical precursor of time, itself the preface to the Concept. Rather, this space includes time, but in so doing alters both time and itself as well. For time is no longer defined by its most traditional attribute, that of irreversibility; it is eminently reversible, and space equally superimposable. In short, there is no unity of place as the synthesis of time and space, but rather only places that are split and superimposed, places that are constantly in movement, or rather, *on the move*, as in a game of chess or of chance, *sur le coup*—which is anything but a *coup sûr*, a sure thing. But this is also why in such a space writing, in order to take place, must forcefully, violently, endeavor to take the place of—from—Reading, from that which repeats it, but also alters it, and which is therefore not so much its *telos* as its *tele*, the gap between its inscription and its fulfillment, between *it* and its Self. In this reversible time and space of superimposition, one text reads another and is read by it in turn. But this turn never quite comes full circle:

> *Beyond* . . . [i.e., *Beyond the Pleasure Principle*] belongs in the tradition of the *Philebus*. The heritage is secured, Plato is behind Freud . . . It is also the *Philebus* that we read through the scene in *Beyond* . . . . . . But the *Philebus*, de-multiplying its scene, its authors and its actors, in turn reads *Beyond* . . . , *conducting the decipherment from afar, like a remote-controlled tape-head (tête-lectrice)* . . . *Beyond* . . . becomes in turn a supplementary chapter of the *Philebus*, a new scene recalling, in passing, other dialogues of Plato, the *Symposium* for example, etc. The two corpuses are each part of the other. They write each other (*ils s'écrivent l'un l'autre*).[19]

Plato is "behind" Freud, just as the "*Philebus*" is behind *Beyond the Pleasure Principle*: but behind *for whom*, in regard to what fixed point, that allows us to order space and time? Who follows whom, which text reads which? The question is unavoidable, but it is unanswerable. Or rather its answer *decides* nothing. For the doubling does not start or end with the two texts, the two Authors named. Their equivocal *correspondence* is repeated by—or repeats—yet *another correspondence*, one that *follows* them, and yet is also *behind* them: "It is also the *Philebus* that WE read through the scene in *Beyond*. . . . " But who or where is this *we*? Is it the presumptive—and legal—"author" of *La Carte postale*, published under the imprint of one "Jacques Derrida"? And if so, does this give us the point of reference we need in order to organize—*caser*—our reading? Is there any guarantee that the name "Jacques Derrida" functions any differently from the name "Freud," about which we can read:

> The proper name does not happen to efface itself . . . it comes only in its effacement, or, according to the other syntax, *it returns to efface itself* (*il revient à s'effacer*: it amounts to its self-effacement). *It only succeeds in effacing itself.* In its very inscription, fort: da. It keeps itself by, and from itself and that (*ça* = it, id) grants (*donne*) the "movement." It sends off (*Ça envoie*).[20]

The proper name sends off in effacing itself, its *emission* is its *omission* and this puts the addressee on the spot where he cannot abide or reside:

> In other words: already the "author" is no longer there, no longer responsible. He has absented himself in advance, leaving you the document in your hands. This is at least what he declares. He does not seek to convince you of a truth. He does not wish to reduce the power or the investments proper to each, nor influence one's associations or projections. Association is free, and this applies as well to the contract between the writing and reading of this text with its exchanges, engagements, gifts, including everything with which the performance tempts and attempts (*se tente*). This is at least what he says. [But] delivered to yourself you are more than ever tied to the cause . . . you can no longer get rid of the unquestionable heritage.[21]

The "we" of "it is also the *Philebus* that *we read* through *Beyond* . . . thus includes the reader of the text in which that "we" is inscribed no less than its "author." That is, it includes both and neither. More than both and less than either. The law of a certain repetition—which is the repetition of law—knows no bounds: the text that describes Freud, describing the game of fort-da and in turn being described by it; the text that describes Freud reading Plato, and in turn being read by Plato, also and simultaneously describes its own description of Freud describing. . . . But that description is not entirely its "own," any more than is that of Freud, for it too only "arrives" in "effacing itself," *in and as the reading that it prescribes and proscribes at once*: Près de Reading. Prescribes and proscribes since that reading—this one, for instance—is, structurally at least, in precisely the same position as the "text" it has been describing; and this "position," you will have long since realized, is one that in the strict sense it is impossible to occupy, at least for very long.

And so, perhaps, all there is left to do is to "speculate." That is, to begin and conclude by *borrowing*: from Nietzsche, for instance, as the following passage from *La Carte postale*, suggests:

> Borrowing is the law. Within each language, since one figure is always a borrowed language, but also from one discursive domain to another, or from one science to another. Without borrowing, nothing begins, there is no property (*fonds propre*). Everything begins with the transfer of funds, and *there is interest in borrowing*, it is even the first and foremost interest. Borrowing brings a good return, it produces surplus-value, it is the primary motor, the prime mover of all investment. One begins thus by speculating, by betting on a value (*une valeur*: a stock) to produce as though from nothing. And all these "metaphors" confirm, as metaphors, the necessity of what they say.[22]

You begin by borrowing, but with what do you end? The *casenier* leaves his house, his *casa*, to try his luck in the *casino*, where he places his bets in the *cases* of the game-table. He is really a homebody, a *casanier*, at heart, but his home is a madhouse, with a stench of slaughter about it, where nothing stays put, and all is askew. And so he foresakes the house of his father to heed the irresistible call, "*Viens, mon petit, viens. . . .*" And all that is certain is that he will never arrive *chez soi. . . .* This, then, is the story, my story, of reading and writing — *chez* Derrida. Feel free to do with it what you like. It's nobody's business but yours.

* * *

Postscript

I am by no means the first to have reacted to Heidegger's curious hermeneutical assertion cited at the beginning of this paper. In 1953 Detlev Lüders wrote a letter to Heidegger in which he confessed to a certain perplexity in regard to the passage concerned: "Ich verstehe nicht, wie ein Text auf seiner Auslegung beruhen kann; ein Text, denke ich, ist etwas im Wortlaut Feststehendes. Ihr Satz enthält das Paradox, daß der Text einerseits das 'Zugrundegelegte' ist, andererseits dennoch auf etwas beruht, das dadurch das noch ursprünglicher Zugrundeliegende wird; so daß der Text, von hier aus gesehen, nicht mehr das Zugrundegelegte heißen darf. Sie nennen ihn dennoch so." Heidegger's response is no less curious than the incriminated assertion itself. It consists of two parts. First, an explicit, verbal response to his correspondent. In his letter, Heidegger begins categorically enough: 'Sehr geehrter Herr Lüders! Sie haben Recht. Der angeführte Satz (Erl. S. 50) ist in der vorliegenden Fassung unmöglich. Ich werde ihn, falls es noch einmal zu einer Neuauflage kommt, streichen." Having thus apparently clarified the issue, Heidegger then continues: "Wenn Sie den Satz umdrehen, lautet er: "Der folg. Versuch einer Auslegung beruht auf dem nach den handschriftlichen Entwürfen erneut geprüften Text." In diese Form ist der Satz so richtig, daß er zu einer groben Trivialität und deshalb überflüssig wird." Herr Lüders "hat Recht," the statement is, as stated, "impossible," but the "possibility" that would resolve the "paradox" is perhaps even worse than "impossible"—namely, "eine grobe Trivialität." The reason for this is hinted at as Heidegger continues: "Die Frage, was 'ein Text' sei, wie man ihn lesen soll und *wann* er als Text vollständig angeeignet ist, bleibt freilich bestehen. Diese Fragen hängen . . . wesentlich mit der Frage nach dem Wesen der Sprache u. der Sprachüberlieferung zusammen." And Heidegger concludes this train of thought with the question: "Gibtes einen Text an sich?—" (Martin Heidegger, Gesamtausgabe, Bd. IV, 206–7).

"Die Frage, was 'ein Text' sei . . . bleibt bestehen," and it is perhaps the persistence of this question that motivates the second aspect of Heidegger's "response" to Detlev Lüders. This consists, simply, in doing nothing—in doing nothing to change, rewrite, or simply delete the incriminated passage. Herr Lüders "hat Recht," the lines are "impossible," but they were never changed, neither in 1963 nor in 1971, when the "Erläuterungen" were reprinted. The "paradox" of an impossible *Begründungszusammenhang*—inconsistent, but impossible to *avoid*—imposes itself, surely not by accident, in the relation of the "text" to its "interpretation," which also, as Heidegger indicates, entails the relation of *Sprache* to its *Überlieferung*. The latter term signifies, of course, "tradition," but even more broadly, it encompasses the pragmatic afterlife which appears to exclude any simple response to the question with which Heidegger "concludes": "Gibt es einen Text an sich?" It also indicates why the question of the text converges with that of a certain *timing*, the question of *when* a text may be completely appropriated: when, if ever. *La Carte postale* is doubtless an effort *to address* these questions, and again it can hardly be mere accident if the very first letter of the series begins with an echo of Heidegger's letter: "Oui, tu avais raison" (10). "You are right" is rewritten as "you were right"; it thus emerges not simply as a goal, but as a point of departure in an *Überlieferung* in which the question of the text is no longer addressed as such, but rather in which it addresses "us," as readers, as "addressees," inscribes "us," in quotation marks, on the margins of a correspondence, grasping after "right" and "reason" (recht *haben, avoir* raison), and yet never quite certain that we are not being "had."*

*I thank Professor IJsseling for having called this passage in the Gesamtausgabe to my attention, and also Jacques Derrida for pointing out its resonances in *La Carte postale*.

Chapter 8
The Debts of Deconstruction
and Other, Related Assumptions

To set us on our way, three epigraphs. The first, from an essay by Jacques Derrida, "My Chances/Mes Chances":

> Don't accuse me, therefore, of being, as you say in English, "self-centered." In truth I always dreamt of writing a *self-centered* text; I never arrived at that point—I always stumble upon others. This will end up by being known.[1]

The second, more to the point perhaps, is from Laurence Sterne's *Tristram Shandy*:

> The Mortgager and Mortgagée differ the one from the other, not more in length of purse, than the Jester and Jestée do, in that of memory. But in this the comparison between them runs, as the scholiasts call it, upon all-four; which, by the bye, is upon one or two legs more than some of the best of Homer's can pretend to;—namely, That the one raises a sum, and the other a laugh at your expense, and thinks no more about it. Interest, however, still runs on in both cases;—the periodical or accidental payments of it, just serving to keep the memory of the affair alive; till, at length, in some evil hour—pop comes the creditor upon each, and by demanding principal upon the spot, together with full interest to the very day, makes them both feel the full extent of their obligations. (I.12)[2]

And finally, the third, which is also the shortest, is taken from the preface to Nietzsche's autobiography, *Ecce Homo*:

Under these circumstances there is an obligation, against which rebel at bottom my habits, and even more the pride of my instincts, namely, to declare: *Hear me! For I am such and such. Above all, do not mistake me for another!*[3]

I

Readers of Jacques Derrida's *La Carte postale* will doubtless recall the following anecdote, recounted in a long footnote early in the *Envois*:

I feel obliged to note, here and now, that this very morning, August 22, 1979, around 10 A.M., as I was typing this page in view of the present publication, the telephone rings. The United States. The American operator asks me if I will accept a "collect call" . . . from Martin (she says Martine or martini) Heidegger. As is often the case in such situations, which I know only too well, since I must often call collect myself, I can hear vaguely familiar voices at the other end of the intercontinental line: someone is listening to me, awaiting my reaction. What is he going to do with the ghost or the Geist of Martin? I can hardly summarize the entire chemistry of the calculation that led me, very quickly, to refuse ("It's a joke, I do not accept"), after having the name of Martini Heidegger repeated several times, in the hope that the author of the farce would finally be named. Who, in short, pays: the addressee or the sender? Who ought to pay? The question is very difficult, but this morning I thought that I ought not to pay, apart from adding this note of thanks. (*La Carte postale*, 25–26)

It is to this "difficult" but decisive question—who pays, the sender or the addressee?—that these remarks will be addressed, in something less than systematic fashion. Let us begin, then, with this anecdote, in which, properly speaking, nothing really happens: unless, that is, the refusal to accept a collect call—one which is obviously a "farce," a "joke"—can be said to constitute an event of sorts. But even as a mere joke, the story is meager, without punch line or *pointe*, it would seem, unless the volatilization of the name "Martin," exchanging its gender or even its species, is to be considered a *pointe*.

And yet, if the fate of a joke depends, above all, on its timing, this one could not have come at a more propitious moment.

I know that I will be suspected of having invented the whole thing, because it's too good to be true. But what can I do? It's true, strictly and entirely true, the date, the hour, the contents, etc. The name of Heidegger had just been written, after "Freud," in the letter I am in the process of transcribing in the machine. (*La Carte postale*, 26)

In that letter, as in many others of the *Envois*, the writer—whom, for obvious reasons of convenience, but without seeking to prejudice an issue yet to be discussed, I shall henceforth refer to as "Derrida"—was ruminating upon that "old couple," Socrates and Plato, and in particular, upon their relative positions in the history of philosophy, but also as depicted on a postcard in an engraving by Matthew Paris. In this letter, Derrida remarks that the drawing calls into question the very "charta" upon which our entire "bildopedic culture" is based, one that prescribes that "Socrates comes *before* Plato," and hence, that "there is between them—and in general—an order of generation, an irreversible sequence of inheritance. Socrates is before, not in front of, but before Plato, hence behind him and the charta binds us to this order." Precisely this "order," however, is silently but all the more effectively *countermanded* by the remarkable postcard, in which "plato" is placed behind a Socrates who, for once, is shown writing.

Of this, Derrida reflects, even Nietzsche suspected nothing:

> He understood nothing of the initial catastrophe. . . . He believed, as did everyone else, that Socrates did not write, that he came before Plato, who wrote more or less under his dictate. . . . From this point of view, N. believed Plato and didn't overturn anything at all. The entire "overturning" has remained within the program of this credulity. (*La Carte postale*, 25)

The reference here is, of course, to Heidegger's reading of Nietzsche as the *Umkehrung*, the "overturning" of Platonism. And thus, we arrive at the fateful sentence, resuming all that has preceded, before it itself, perhaps, is resumed in the call that arrives just in time to punctuate its phrase:

> The entire "overturning" has remained within the program of this credulity. And this holds *a fortiori* . . . for Freud and Heidegger. (*La Carte postale*, 25)

Small wonder that the ghost or *Geist* of Martine (or martini) Heidegger should have picked this particular moment to intervene, for nothing less than his (her?) credibility and credit had just been called into question. The History of Metaphysics, programming and prescribing its proper overturning, including the very question—and the questioner—of the Meaning of Being: here is an assertion destined to drive the Sage of Todtnauberg straight to the nearest telephone booth in a vain attempt to assert his right of response.

But the call, not surprisingly, was refused, and we can only speculate as to what the response at the other end of the line might have been: amusement, shock, incredulity? "Not accepted; are you certain?" "*Nicht angenommen?*" Nor are we told if the callers ever called back. Or if the call was ever traced.

Indeed, all we do find out is that "my private relationship to Martin does not operate on the same exchange." To this "exchange"—this *standard*—we shall have occasion to return.

II

What *does* pass by the "same standard," it would seem, is Freud's relationship to Nietzsche, at least as it is described in "*Spéculer—sur 'Freud'* " (the second major section of *La Carte postale*). It is precisely Freud's refusal to assume his debt toward Nietzsche, and through the latter, toward philosophy in general, that constitutes Derrida's point of departure in posing the question of Freud's speculations. Or rather, it is not simply the refusal of a debt, but the astonishing *ease* with which it is performed, that fascinates Derrida:

> Freud . . . is so much at ease in such an embarrassing situation, he declines the debt with such rapid assurance, with such imperturbable facility that one cannot but wonder whether the debt in question is his at all, or whether it is not the debt of another? (*La Carte postale*, 280–81)

The passage referred to here is from Freud's *Autobiographical Study*, in which he distinguishes the character of his speculation from that of philosophy proper (*S.E.* 20.59). In this context he mentions the names of Fechner, Schopenhauer, and Nietzsche; if he has deliberately shunned the latter, Freud writes, it is because of the proximity of his insights to the results of psychoanalysis, a proximity that might have threatened Freud's "independence of mind" (*Unbefangenheit*).

What appears remarkable in this acknowledgment, as far as Derrida is concerned, is its matter-of-factness. To decline a debt with such facility is possibly the sign that it is not *one's* debt at all, but rather that of *another*. But, Derrida ruminates, perhaps this is not peculiar to Freud at all:

> What if the debt were always that of another? How one might both feel and not feel, in advance, acquitted and guilty of the debt of another if the latter, lodged in oneself by the effect of a singular topology, returns to itself [*revient à soi*: amounts to the same] in accordance with a filiation that has yet to be thought out . . . ? (*La Carte postale*, 281)[4]

The brunt of this question, concerning the subject of debt, its "rightful owner" as it were, is concentrated in the untranslatable ambiguity of the French phrase—one that recurs insistently in "*Spéculer—sur 'Freud'* "—*revenir à soi*; for if the subject of debt is another, and if that other is said to "return to the fold," the Self folded into that fold can be either the Other of the Other—that is, "oneself"—or that Other *itself*. Or perhaps both: oneself *as* itself. In which case, however, the Self (*soi*) would begin to lose much of its consoling familiarity, as that instance of synthesis and of identity in which differences are surmounted and alterities contained. Instead, this "self" would begin to acquire an uncanny aspect as a revenant (*à soi*) that never quite succeeds in returning.

Such a movement of revenants is described in regard to the celebrated *fort-da* game of *Beyond the Pleasure Principle*. The point of view of the narrator, spectator, theoretician, is that of the "PP": the pleasure principle, grandfather of Freudian metapsychology, but no more secure in its place than is the actual "PP" himself, Freud as grandfather of Ernst. Behind the seeming stability and unicity of an apparently proper name, Derrida unravels — or rather *weaves* — a network of threads (*fils*) within which each place is the overdetermined knot or scene of multiple scenarios: the spectator-speculator is interested in the spectacle he describes not merely as Grandfather (pp), but as father of Sophie, and as double of Ernst, with whom he identifies as the elder brother of a detested, younger rival. One result of such "demultiplication" would be to unleash a power of repetition that no stable structure could ever hope to comprehend, contain, or amortize in the name of truth. In short, the Freudian master-key, the Oedipus complex, would appear as only *one* figure among *others*. This is precisely the claim that emerges from Derrida's reading of the *fort-da*:

> But all the interweavings of fort-da (the scene of writing and of heritage that plays itself out there in ellipse, the abyss of its deferred report, the commutation of places, the leap of generations, the dissymmetry of contracts, in short, everything that *dispatches itself* in a graphics of repetition that dislocates the summary "triangle") can only be called oedipal if one names it by synecdoche, by means of only one of its effects, one of the most taut, I mean most tightly drawn and determined in its exemplarity. In its notorious and strict sense, the oedipal trait is only a rection for the leading thread of the spool. (*La Carte postale*, 362)

But if the "oedipal trait" or triangle "is only a rection" — and the connotations of the word are no less bizarre in French than in English — "only a rection" for the cast of the spool in the game of *fort-da*; if, in other words, it is "only" a reductive, regulative fiction, a part masquerading as the whole, it is nonetheless an ineluctable fiction, without which the trajectory of the spool would lack all determinate direction. The result is to remark the deceptive *necessity* of such reductive structurations:

> If one insists on subsuming the figure of *fort-da*, such as we have seen it functioning, under the name, Oedipus, this amounts to *remarking* a nebulous, vertiginous matrix (*en y remarquant une matrice nébuleuse et plus qu'abyssale*) in terms of only one of its effects, or if you prefer, of its offspring. It is as though one were to pull this nebulous matrix, with its chains of fusions or fissions, its permutations and commutations without end, its disseminations without return, by only one of its threads, only one of its sons (*par un seul de ses fils*). *It is true that this temptation (to form the trait out of only one of its threads/*

sons) is not a contingent limitation, for which one might not have to render an account. For it is as though one wished to have everything devolve upon, return to *(faire revenir à)* one of its sons (threads), in other words, to the mother as matrix, to a mother who would be nothing but that which she is. *(La Carte postale*, 362; emphasis added)[5]

The problem, which traverses *"Spéculer—sur 'Freud',"* becomes legible in the passage just cited: how can the noncontingency of the oedipal reduction be *taken into account*, if just some such reduction appears to be the condition of possibility of *accounting* in general? The dilemma is thematized, in *"Spéculer—sur 'Freud',"* as the problem of psychoanalytic speculation: if Freud, in describing the game of *fort-da*, is not merely representing an instance that can be explained in terms of the more general validity of the Oedipus complex (or of the pleasure principle), it is because what he is describing is also, and perhaps above all, his own process of writing, including the organization and articulation of his argument. This, in turn, displaces and reinscribes the significance of the scene that he is attempting to describe but that eludes all comprehension by mirroring, repeating, and dislocating the very theoretical scheme that seeks to comprehend it.

For the details of this dislocation, I must refer you to the text of *La Carte postale*, too vertiginously complex to suffer any résumé here. The hermeneutical facet, by contrast, can be summarized, as it is in the following passage, the ramifications of which are by no means limited to the putative "object" of Derrida's text—that is, to "Freud":

What happens when acts or performances (discourse or writing, analysis or description, etc.) form part of the objects they designate? When they can give themselves as example of that of which they speak or write? There is certainly no gain in self-reflexive transparency, on the contrary. An accounting is no longer possible, an account can no longer be rendered, nor a simple report or *compte rendu* given. And the borders of the whole are neither closed nor open. Their trait is divided. . . . *(La Carte postale*, 417)

Derrida describes Freud, in *Beyond the Pleasure Principle*, doing what he describes, performing the game of *fort-da* with the pleasure principle, just as Freud describes the boy playing with the spool. But in so doing, Freud's text does not merely repeat the scene it recounts: the oedipal triangle ceases to function as frame of reference once it is revealed to be only one version of a game that vastly transcends it. Hence, the repetition does not produce a "gain in self-reflexive transparency" but rather something very different. The measure of that difference, however, can only begin to be gauged when one remarks that the process just described—by which descriptions participate in what they describe—also applies, *a fortiori*, to the text that announces this as a general problem. "*Spéculer—sur 'Freud'* " can in no way be exempted from the "graphics of repetition" it "describes" at work in the descriptions of "Freud."

We begin to fathom the significance of the quotation marks that set off the proper name "Freud" in the text that speculates on it. If the temptation to form a trait out of only one of the threads (sons) of an irrepressible "matrix"—if this temptation is "not a contingent limitation," and if one cannot, therefore, be dispensed from giving an account of that noncontingency, then presumably the account will have to deal with the manner in which an irresistible process of repetition *assumes* the aspect and the allure of a *proper name*.

III

"*Spéculer—sur 'Freud'* " can be described as the "interminable story" (*La Carte postale*, 416) of making a name. As such, it also entails the recounting of an impossible accounting, the story of an ineluctable debt—and guilt (*Schuld*). No one was more aware of this problem than was Freud, as his remarks on the indebted, improper character of psychoanalytical discourse, toward the end of *Beyond the Pleasure Principle*, unequivocally demonstrate: without "the figurative language . . . [of] depth psychology," Freud remarks, "we could not otherwise describe the processes in question at all, and indeed we could not have become aware of them" (*S.E.* 18.60). Commenting on this passage, Derrida exposes the general law it implies:

> Borrowing is the law. . . . without borrowing, nothing begins, there is no proper reserve [*fonds propre*]. Everything begins with the transfer of funds, and there is interest in borrowing, it is even the primary interest. Borrowing gives you a return, it produces surplus-value, it is the primary motor of all investment. One begins thus by speculating, betting on one value to produce as though from nothing. And all these metaphors confirm, as metaphors, the necessity of what they say. (*La Carte postale*, 410)

If, however, "borrowing is the law" and the beginning of Freud's speculations, this explains why, in contrast to more traditional sciences or disciplines, psychoanalysis is inseparably bound up with the name of its founder. If its specificity is indissolubly linked to a fundamental indebtedness, something like a proper name is required in order to hold it together. But for this very reason, the "property" of that name will be even more fragile than is ordinarily the case in regard to the sciences. Freud's speculations, Derrida asserts, seek to take this fragility into account; they "will have consisted, perhaps, in claiming to pay in advance, however dearly, the charges of a return-to-the-sender" (*La Carte postale*, 353). But the "claim" is also a pretense (*prétendre*) that entails a "calculation without basis" (*sans fond*), a manner "to speculate upon the ruin of his name . . . which keeps what it loses" (*La Carte postale*, 353).

Perhaps the most ingenious, most radical stratagem in this project is that which consists in assuming the debt so totally as to render it inoperative. If "everything" can be said to "begin with the transfer of funds," then the very notion of debt itself tends to lose its force. The debt cannot be paid back,

> perhaps because economy itself has been transgressed; not economy in
> general but an economy in which the principle of equivalence would
> have been forced. All the movements in *trans-* would have violated
> this principle, and with it everything that could have assured a pay-
> ment, a reimbursement, an amortization. . . . This effraction—that is,
> the speculative transfer(ence)—would have rendered the debt either in-
> finite or insolvent, and hence null and void. It is the economic space
> of the debt that finds itself disorganized (*bouleversé*), immensely en-
> larged and at the same time neutralized. (*La Carte postale*, 415)

It is precisely this process that Derrida sees at work in the speculations of "Freud," endowing the latter with their paradoxical but characteristic "dual tonality": "Both grave, discouraged, gasping under the burden of the inexhaustible debt or task; and simultaneously flippant, cavalier, affirmative" (*La Carte postale*, 415). But is a debt thus generalized necessarily "neutralized"? Does the fact that everything begins with a "transfer" of funds—with a certain form of borrowing—necessarily "invalidate" the notion of debt? And what is the relation of such "forcing" of the principle of equivalence, to that noncontingent limitation at work in the Oedipus complex, and indeed, in all accounting and accountability?

These questions will compel us to return, in a moment, to the text in which the problem of *Schuld—debt* and *guilt—* is exposed in an unprecedented but decisive manner: to the second book of *The Genealogy of Morals*.

But before embarking on this inevitable detour, let us first consider the curious position in which we are placed, as readers of "*Spéculer—sur 'Freud,'* " in regard to Nietzsche. This text ("Speculer"), we are informed at its outset in a footnote, is in fact only the third part or "ring" in a chain of readings proceeding, in each of its parts, from a text of Nietzsche's. The first of these "three rings" revolves around the notion of life, the " 'modern' problematics of biology, of genetics, of the epistemology or of the history of the life sciences (readings of Jacob, Canghuilhem, and so forth). The second ring: return to Nietzsche, followed by an explication of the Heideggerian reading of Nietzsche. Finally, here, the third and last ring" (*La Carte postale*, 277n).

A certain reading of Nietzsche, then, is absolutely indispensable for the *mise-en-scène* of "*Spéculer—sur 'Freud'*." This reading, it is suggested, frames the analysis of Freudian speculation. That analysis offers us, here at its beginning, two distinct if interrelated aspects. The first still belongs to what I would describe as the classical "deconstructive" strategy: Freud, it is asserted, always related to Nietzsche in the form of a *denial* (*dénégation*). He mentions him, but only to dismiss him, to dispatch him. This motif is, to be sure, incontrovertible. It is supported not only by the passage from the *Autobiographical Study* cited by Derrida, but by others as well. A perhaps even more striking instance is provided by the minutes of the April 1, 1908 meeting of the Viennese Psychoanalytical Society, devoted to a discussion of the *third* section of *The Genealogy of Morals*:

> Prof. FREUD stresses above all his peculiar relation to philosophy, the abstractions of which were so uncongenial that he finally decided to give up the study of philosophy. Of Nietzsche, too, he is ignorant; an occasional attempt to read him foundered upon an excess of interest. Despite the much noted similarities he could still assure us, he said, that Nietzsche's thought had had absolutely no influence upon his own works. . . . Apart from [the motif of] infantilism, the mechanism of displacement is *not* recognized in Nietzsche.[6]

The logic of this response is already sufficiently familiar to readers of *The Interpretation of Dreams*: "No, I haven't read Nietzsche—he is too interesting. No, he hasn't influenced my work and I know nothing of his. Moreover, he has completely failed to recognize the mechanism of displacement." Derrida is thus amply justified in remarking a "denial" here, and then in going on to reveal its effects by pointing up a "return" of Nietzschean motifs in the speculations of Freud. The most striking, most "disruptive" such return relates to the thematics of power. Having analyzed the manner in which Freud pursues the problem of the pleasure principle in *Beyond* . . ., Derrida draws the following conclusion:

> It is indeed within the code of power—and not only metaphorically so—that [Freud's] problematic is situated. The question is always to discover who is "master" and who "dominates," who has "authority" and the point to which the PP can exercise power. (*La Carte postale*, 431)

Nietzsche, dismissed and avoided by Freud, thus imposes his "code" on the latter's speculations, taking his tribute in a debt admitted only to be denied.

However, this tells only part of the story: there is another "chapter," as it were, which comes not so much at the end but rather at what appears to be the beginning. And this other aspect, I submit, is no longer comprehensible within what I have called the classical strategy of deconstruction. For, as already mentioned, what fascinates Derrida throughout his reading of "Freud," and above all in the "scene" of the "denial" of Nietzsche (and of "philosophy"), is the very ease and the facility with which the putative debt is acknowledged and dispatched by Freud—*as though it were the debt of another*. Indeed, this aspect of Freud's *démarche* defines the very project of Derrida's "own" reading, which he describes as follows:

> I would like to render legible (*donner à lire*) the nonpositional structure of *Beyond* . . . , its athetical functioning, in the last instance, which, however, amounts to extracting it from the authority of a last instance, or indeed from that of any instance at all. (*La Carte postale*, 279)

This "nonpositional structure" of Freud's speculation, subtracting it from "the authority of a last instance, or . . . that of any instance at all," would, however, ultimately extract "Freud" from the project of a deconstruction. For the latter necessarily presupposes a governing intention, an effort to establish meaning, a *will-to-say-something*; what is at work in *Beyond the Pleasure Principle*, however, in the "athetical" reading that Derrida seeks to give it, is almost the opposite: instead of a *vouloir-dire*, we discover a vouloir-*rien*-dire. As we read in one of the letters of the *Envois* (18 May 1978), what captivates Derrida in *his* reading of *Beyond* . . . , is precisely the manner in which "it tells us NOTHING (*il ne nous dit* RIEN), doesn't take a step without then, with the next step, retracting it" (*La Carte postale*, 153).

What *can* be deconstructed here, by contrast, is not an intention to say nothing, to go nowhere, but rather all those readings of Freud's text that have tried to make it say something, be intelligent,

> all those readings as partial as [they are] canonical, even academic, [which mistake] the essential impossibility of arresting [Freud's text] at a thesis, at a conclusion posed in a scientific or philosophical mode. (*La Carte postale*, 279)

This is why even the most powerful "philosophical" theses—such as the Nietzschean theory of the will to power—cannot have the last word in regard to the speculations of "Freud." "The motif of power" may be "more originating and more general than the PP," it may be "independent of it and of its Beyond," but it still cannot impose itself fully upon Freud's most daring speculative notions: "The death-drive and the repetition-compulsion, however much they proceed from a drive for power . . . still exceed power" (*La Carte postale*, 432).

Nietzsche *almost* has the last word, then, but *not quite*. Not, at least, the Nietzsche of the will to power. For "there is only power if there is a principle or a principle of principles. The transcendental or meta-conceptual function pertains to the order of power" (*La Carte postale*, 432). What, by contrast, Derrida has remarked in the hesitation waltz of Freud's speculations is a movement that cannot be comprehended by a cognitive scheme of intention: a speculation that is not subordinated to the universal equivalent and supreme value, *truth*.

This, then, is the "Freud" of "*Spèculer — sur 'Freud'* " — the Freud who speculates on the impossible gambit of *writing-himself*; of constructing a network of circulation, of relay stations; and of paying the price in advance:

> [Freud's] speculation will have consisted, *perhaps*, in pretending (*prétendre*) to pay in advance, however dearly, the charges of a return-to-the-sender. (*La Carte postale*, 353; emphasis added)

But why, in this most programmatic, most "deconstructive" statement, that little most Nietzschean word, undermining the declarative tone with a barely perceptible hesitation — why the qualifying "perhaps"? Could it not be because of the peculiarly and openly contradictory manner in which Freud "assumes" and radicalizes his "debt," to the point where one can no longer be entirely certain just *whose* debt is at stake? An example of this "dangerous perhaps" (Nietzsche, *Beyond Good and Evil*, 10): When the "athetical reading" of "*Spéculer — sur 'Freud'* " declares itself to depend on an interpretation of *Beyond . . .* that is "selective, slanted [and] discriminating" (*sélective, criblante, discriminante; La Carte postale*, 279); and when, some pages later, *Freud's* rhetoric is also described as a "slanted strategy" whose "busy selectivity" is "no longer regulated by a reassuring model of science or of philosophy" (*La Carte postale*, 298) — then, *who* is repeating *whom*: Freud Derrida or Derrida Freud? And, if one responds that the distinction no longer makes sense, is one prepared to assume the consequences of its disappearance? Indeed, *are* those consequences assumable? The response depends, no doubt, on what one means by the word "assume" — a problem to which I shall return. But for the moment, let us note that the "athetical reading" advanced in "*Spéculer — sur 'Freud,'* " by undermining the possibility of establishing a decisive, final instance, "draws the textual performance into a singular slippage" (*dérive, La Carte postale*, 279) in which even "deconstruction" loses its footing. For the impossibility of establishing or identifying a governing intention also entails the impossibility of assuming that minimal "exteriority"[7] without which deconstruction is unthinkable. By contrast, "What happens when acts or performances . . . form part of the objects they designate" is that such exteriority is suspended and the deconstruction also emerges as "an example of that of which it speaks or writes." Which is doubtless why "deconstruction" in "*Spèculer — sur 'Freud,'* " is most conspicuously remarked in a scene where priorities and property rights are defended. I refer you to page 285 of *La Carte postale*, where the "brand name" of Deconstruction is defended against the "competition": French Heideggerians and Marxists, seeking to expropriate the term by rediscovering it in their respective texts of reference. It is precisely the necessity, and necessary absurdity, of such a defense that renders Deconstruction incapable of accounting for its debts, and for the question of debt in general. And it is this, too, which underscores the novelty of "*Spéculer — sur 'Freud.'* " At the very moment it is describing Freud's dis-

patching of Nietzsche, it also, in a certain sense, dispatches its readers by referring them to analyses that "Freud" refused to undertake, but that now have been
accomplished—but elsewhere, in a place that remains inaccessible to the reader:

> I will therefore be brief. To proceed in the quickest possible manner, I
> will recall for instance what was said concerning childhood, play and
> the lack-of-debt. What was said in regard to (à partir de) Nietzsche.
> How and with what the self-declared child indebts himself in a game
> that declares itself free of debt? Of the lack-of-debt upon which the
> game speculates in secret? And where to situate, according to what to-
> pology, the place of such a secret? (La Carte postale, 280)

Where, indeed, situate the secret if not precisely *here*, at this moment when the
text begins to speculate, on "Freud." A game that does not declare itself to be
"without debt," *sans dette*, to be sure, but that does immediately go on to declare
its other, "Freud," in hock up to his ears, and apparently—*perhaps*!—unwilling
to pay the bills. Unwilling, or unable? Yet, what if those bills were not *his* bills
at all? Or not simply, exclusively *his*?

Freud's will and wish not to know of, and not to owe anything to, Nietzsche
thus forms the paradoxical first act of Derrida's speculations on "Freud." Paradoxical first, because Freud, Derrida will go on to show, in fact continues to
play the game first "theorized" by Nietzsche—but in perhaps an even more radical manner, if one of the effects of that debt is to make theory, in a certain sense,
impossible. And second, the insistent reference to the "author"—in quotes—of
the *theory of debt* (not in quotes) is paradoxical, because it *does* what it purports
to *describe*: it refers to a theory of debt (first Nietzsche, then Heidegger), which
it then proceeds to withhold. Or rather, to promise: "As far as referring *Sein und
Zeit* to *The Genealogy of Morals*, insofar as *Schuldigsein* is concerned, I shall
attempt that elsewhere" (La Carte postale, 282).

Does this place us, as readers, in Derrida's debt—or him in ours? If a text, describing a certain refusal to assume a debt, ostensibly on the part of *Freud*, practices what it preaches, does what it describes, this does not, we now know, lead
necessarily to an increase in self-reflexive transparency. But just *where*, then,
does it lead? Perhaps the "author" of the theory of debt can give us a clue?

IV

It is curious that a promise, or something very much like it, should lead us back
to Nietzsche's discussion of debt in *The Genealogy of Morals*.[8] For that discussion, of course, proceeds precisely from Nietzsche's assertion that promising entails nothing less than the "essential problem of man" (*Genealogy*, 56). The opposition that Nietzsche establishes between "active forgetting," and its
disciplining through mnemotechnics—the establishment of memory, of anticipa-

tion, and hence, of the ability to promise—recalls in many ways Freud's distinction between primary and secondary processes, with its correlative categories of "perceptual identity" and "identity of thought." In each case, the articulation of the one process with the other, depicted as an apparently genetic development, but with distinctly structural implications, depends on what both Freud and Nietzsche designate with the word *Hemmung*: literally, "inhibition" or "blockage." Since the very notion of *Hemmung* strongly suggests the interruption or deviation of a continuous movement, it is not entirely surprising for Nietzsche to describe the decisive *Hemmung* as a consequence of the shift of life from water to land; it is this move out of the water and onto terra firma that is both ground and origin of what Nietzsche calls the "internalization of man": the development of a soul, of an interiority arises in direct proprotion to the blockage of any discharge into the external world: "The entire inner world . . . expanded and inflated itself . . . in the same measure as outward discharge was *inhibited*" (*Genealogy*, 84; Nietzsche's emphasis).

It is here that Nietzsche situates the origins of the *schlechtes Gewissen*, the "guilty conscience," and indeed, of guilt itself. But if Nietzsche introduces this section (sec. 16) by warning his readers that "my own Hypothesis on the origin of the 'guilty conscience' . . . will not gain a hearing easily and needs to be pondered, observed and slept over lengthily" (*Genealogy*, 84), it is not simply because of the phantasmagoric nature of the explanation, of its obvious lack of refutability. What makes this "hypothesis" so difficult *to hear*, as it were, is its disruptive implication for the fundamental opposition that seems to structure the entire three books of the *Genealogy*: That between nobility and *ressentiment*, between "active" and "reactive" values and behavior, between spontaneous self-affirmation and other-directed deviousness. The mythical "hypothesis" does not merely challenge such oppositions, it subverts the very force of *oppositionality* itself, in accordance with the suspicions uttered at the outset of *Beyond Good and Evil*:

> The fundamental belief of metaphysicians is *the belief* in the oppositions of values. It may be questioned whether there are indeed any oppositions at all . . . rather than simply foreground estimations, preliminary perspectives. . . . Indeed, it might even be possible that *what* comprises the value of those good and respected things is precisely that they are insidiously related, tied to, interlaced with those wicked, seemingly opposed things, and perhaps even of the same essence. Perhaps! But who is willing to worry about such dangerous perhapses. For that, we will have to await the arrival of a new kind of philosopher. (*Beyond Good and Evil*, 10; translation modified, Nietzsche's emphasis)

Nietzsche's hypothesis of the origin of the "guilty conscience" disrupts the governing opposition of his "story" precisely by virtue of its very *originality*: for what originates with this move from the aquatic to the land medium is *human being itself*, with *all* of the predicates that can be attributed to it, including not only the reactive qualities leading to resentment, but also the active self-affirmation constantly opposed to it. The move from water to land thus reveals the common origin of both nobility *and* resentment, active *and* reactive, internalization *and* externalization. Man only becomes "self-supporting" (*selbsttragend*) by becoming dependent: "From now on they were supposed to walk on their feet and 'carry themselves,' whereas hitherto they had been carried by water: a frightful heaviness lay upon them" (*Genealogy*, 84). This fateful move ashore is described, in German at least, more as the effect of a witty play on words, that is, more as a kind of *repetition* than as a clear-cut *alternative*. The choice was "entweder *Landtiere* zu werden [either to become land animals] oder *zugrunde* zu gehen [or to be destroyed, literally: to be *grounded*]." But this fateful joke is also one played at the expense of the "theory" that places resentment in opposition to its other: noble, aristocratic self-affirmation. This joke on the "dramatic" aspect of Nietzsche's story, however, also introduces an element that is perhaps even more *theatrical*: a *spectacle* necessitating the participation of *spectators*:

> Indeed, divine spectators were needed to appreciate the spectacle that thus began and the end of which is not yet in sight. . . . From now on, man is *included* among the most unexpected and most exciting lucky throws in the game played by Heraclitus' "great child," be he called Zeus or chance—man evokes interest in himself, a tension . . . as though he were not a goal but only a way, an episode, a bridge, a great promise. (*Genealogy*, 85)

It is only against the backdrop of this spectacle, with its interest, its tension, its promise—but above all, its spectators—that Nietzsche's discussion of *Schuld* can be appreciated.

The development of resentment out of a noble or aristocratic culture is marked by the emergence of the guilty conscience (*schlechtes Gewissen*), in turn characterized by a shift in the notion of *Schuld*. Nietzsche seems to tell us the story of two distinct, and indeed diametrically *opposed* conceptions of *Schuld*. The familiar, moral notion of *Schuld* as *guilt*, he argues, derives from an older, more pragmatic, more "material" notion, *Schuld* as *debt*. The opposition consists in the nature of the obligation thereby designated: whereas *guilt* is construed as a debt that is essentially *unredeemable* (by the debtor, at least), the earlier, more original, more tangible notion of *Schuld* was predicated precisely on the essential quality of its being *repayable*. Thus, if the essence of debt was originally to be "*abzahlbar*," if the derived notions of punishment and justice consisted in *Vergeltung*, retribution, it was, Nietzsche contends, because these concepts developed out of "the contractual relationship of creditor and debtor (*Gläubiger und Schuldner*)," which "in turn points back to the fundamental forms of buying and selling, barter, trade, and traffic" (*Genealogy*, 63). In this "prehistoric" period—a prehistory, Nietzsche remarks parenthetically (sec. 9), that "is present in all ages or may always reappear" (*Genealogy*, 71)—the notion of *Schuld* as debt is part of an overriding "logic of compensation" (*Logik des Ausgleichs*), one which prescribes that " 'everything has its price; *all* things can be paid for' " (*Genealogy*, 70). This "logic," which, Nietzsche insists, is *fremdartig genug* (strange enough) (*Genealogy*, 64), seems, at first sight at least, to consist precisely in the overcoming of "strangeness" (*Fremdheit*). For it is marked by what is apparently the unproblematic establishment of equivalences:

> In the oldest and most primitive personal relationship, that between buyer and seller, creditor and debtor . . . one person first confronted another person, one person first *measured itself* against another. Setting prices, measuring values, devising equivalents, exchanging—this preoccupies the earliest thinking of man to such an extent that in a certain sense it *is* thinking itself. (*Genealogy*, 70)

I shall return to the "strangeness" of this apparently unproblematic "logic of compensation." For the moment, however, let us retain the appearance of its straightforward simplicity, that of the establishment of a certain identity—"person to person"—by a process of evaluation and of *measurement* that coincides with "thinking itself." Let us retain this appearance, because without it, the contrast and opposition between the two kinds of *Schuld*, debt and guilt, are no longer as clear-cut as Nietzsche, in the more dramatic, more explicit aspect of his genealogy, would have us believe. For the shift from the notion of redeemable debt to that of unredeemable guilt is above all dependent on the loss of an unproblematic *standard of measurement*, the loss of binding equivalents. It is striking to note that this loss, the key component of the genealogy Nietzsche is developing, coincides with the emergence, precisely, of something like a genealogical consciousness. In a celebrated passage, in which Nietzsche anticipates, in certain respects, Freud's myth of the development of culture through guilt (*Totem and Taboo*), the emergence of the "guilty conscience" is portrayed as the result of an *interpretation* that is "exceedingly remarkable and perplexing" (the German word *bedenklich* suggests something both disconcerting *and* thought provoking; we shall have occasion to return to this word later, in another context):

> The civil-law relationship between the debtor and his creditor, discussed already at length, has been interpreted in an, historically speaking, exceedingly remarkable and dubious manner into a relationship in which, to us modern men, it is perhaps least intelligible: namely into the relation of the present generation to its ancestors. (*Genealogy*, 88)

And, Nietzsche continues, this *Hineininterpretieren* causes a logic to emerge which is very different from that analyzed earlier:

> The conviction reigns that it is only through the sacrifices and accom-
> plishments of the ancestors that the tribe *exists*—and that one has *to
> pay them back* with sacrifices and accomplishments: one thus recog-
> nizes a *debt* (*Schuld*) that constantly increases, since these forebears
> never cease, in their continued existence as powerful spirits, to accord
> the tribe new advantages and new strength. . . . The *fear* of the fore-
> father and of his power, the consciousness of being indebted to him,
> increases, in accordance with this logic, in direct proportion to the in-
> crease in the power of the tribe itself. . . . If one imagines this rude
> kind of logic carried to its end, then the ancestors of the *most power-
> ful* tribes are bound eventually to grow to monstrous dimensions
> through the imagination of growing fear and to recede into the dark-
> ness of the divinely uncanny and unimaginable: in the end the ancestor
> must necessarily be transfigured into a *god*. Perhaps this is even the
> origin of the gods, an origin therefore out of *fear*! (*Genealogy*, 88–89)

Here we would seem to have, quite clearly and unequivocally, the genealogy of resentment: the self-interpretation of the identity of the community situates the origin of that self *elsewhere*, in those forefathers held to be responsible for everything that the tribe has and is, for its very existence, its power, and its pos-sibilities. The result coincides with a well-known jingle of years gone by—"the more you have, the more you *want*"—that is, the more you have the more you owe. The "end" of this "logic" is, then, the establishment of this other as the "un-canny and unimaginable (*unvorstellbar*: unrepresentable)" God, to whom "the present generation (*die Gegenwärtigen*)" is tied by an unredeemable debt.

Nietzsche leaves the "origin" of this origin—of the fateful *Hineininterpre-tieren* of exchange relations into, or onto, the axis of generations—shrouded in darkness, no less uncanny than the effects it is said to produce. This is, on the one hand, in accordance with his conception of interpretation itself—dis-cussed several sections earlier (sec. 12)—as a *discontinuous* series of assaults, in which one scheme imposes itself on a previous one. And if Nietzsche stresses the discontinuity of these interpretive impositions, it is precisely because the ef-fectiveness of their power game depends in part on creating the illusion of a causal continuity, one which would thereby obscure the violence of the interpre-tive intervention as such, by presenting it as the intrinsic essence of the thing itself.

And yet, even in this general discussion of interpretation, it is clear that the "sequence of more or less . . . independently operating processes of subjuga-tion" cannot be entirely discontinuous, if only because it inevitably includes "the resistances encountered, the attempted transformations of form for the purpose of defense and reaction, and the results of successful counter-measures" (*Genealogy*, 78).

If every interpretive imposition is thus in part determined by the scheme it seeks to dethrone and to subjugate, the complicity of the particular interpretation which "projects" the exchange relationship onto the genealogical axis, with the notion of *Schuld* it is about to displace, is far more profound; indeed, it offers us what is perhaps the paradigm of that interlacing of opposites (*Verhäkelung der Gegensätze*) to which we have already referred.

The sign of this complicity—between *Schuld* und *Schuld*, guilt and debt—is nothing less than "the origin of the gods," as the uncanny, unrepresentable terminus *ab quo* and *ad quem* of the interminable *Schuld*. For this "origin" of the gods is by no means simply original or unprecedented: in the story Nietzsche is telling, it is itself a somewhat uncanny repetition of *another origin of the gods*, this time in the "prehistorical" world of simple exchange.

For, as we have already suggested, the "logic" of that exchange, of its *Ausgleichsform*, is in fact less simple than might first appear. Its *Fremdartigkeit*, its strangeness, lies in the peculiar kind of equivalences that are established. For what is striking, in Nietzsche's account of the "logic of compensation," is that it is ultimately no less "other-directed" than the culture of resentment to which it is opposed. We need only reflect on the following passage to discover such other-directedness at work in what appears to be the simple assertion of self:

> Let us be clear as to the logic of this form of compensation: it is
> strange enough. An equivalence is provided by the creditor's receiving,
> in place of a direct compensation for an injury (that is, in place of
> compensation in money, land, possessions of any kind) a kind of satis-
> faction (*Wohlgefühl*) in being granted a kind of pleasure as recompense
> and compensation—the satisfaction of being permitted to vent, without
> second thoughts (*unbedenklich*), his power upon someone who is
> powerless, the ecstasy "*de faire le mal pour le plaisir de le faire*," the
> enjoyment of violating the other. . . . The compensation consists,
> therefore, in a warrant and right to be cruel. (*Genealogy*, 64–65)

It is in the exercise of one's power to violate the other, the debtor, that the "universal equivalent" (Marx) is found, which in turn permits one sort of "injury"—a material debt, for instance—to be requited in a manner that, if no less "material," is yet of a quite different order: the production of *suffering* in the *other*.

The "strangeness" of this originary logic, by which the ideas of "debt and suffering" (*Schuld und Leid*) become "uncannily . . . intertwined" (*Genealogy*, 65), resides precisely in that moment which Freud, as we have seen, thought Nietzsche to have overlooked completely: that of an original, irreducible displacement or substitution. For the "equivalence" of debt and suffering is the effect precisely of a substitution, a shift or a displacement, through which the infliction of suffering becomes the equivalent of a property debt. The body of the debtor *replaces* the possessions he owes. The value of that body is determined by its position within the social hierarchy, in relation to that of the creditor. Society is thus the stage upon which the spectacle of cruelty—suffering as repayment—is acted out on the body of the other. And society is implicated because the demonstration of power cannot take place simply between two persons: it requires witnesses, spectators. It is this, perhaps, that most distinguishes the other-directed spectacle Nietzsche is describing from the Hegelian master-slave dialectic. For the efficacy of cruelty, as retribution, does not find its "truth" in the labor of the powerless other. Rather, the violation of the debtor by the creditor calls for spectators who are not directly involved in this process and yet without whom it could not operate *meaningfully*. For, despite the apparently "prehistoric" nature of such processes, what is at stake is the ability of "thinking" to set prices and to establish equivalences among objects and phenomena that remain, in a certain sense, incommensurable. "Meaning," therefore, entails precisely the recognition of that incommensurable equivalence that ties suffering to debt. But such recognition can only come from elsewhere, from others whose alterity has not been drawn into the power play of retribution. These others are the gods:

> What really arouses indignation against suffering is not suffering as
> such but the senselessness of suffering. . . . So in order to abolish
> hidden, undetected, unwitnessed suffering from the world and honestly
> to deny it, one was in the past virtually compelled to invent gods and
> genii of all heights and depths—in short, something that . . . will not
> easily let an interesting painful spectacle pass unnoticed. . . . The en-
> tire mankind of antiquity is full of tender regard for "the spectator."
> (*Genealogy*, chap. 7, p. 68)

"The gods conceived of as the friends of *cruel* spectacles" and the gods conceived of as the uncanny, unrepresentable ancestors to which the present descendants—*die Gegenwärtigen*—are irrevocably indebted: Are these two origins of the gods without a common thread? Or is it not rather the inextricably ambivalent relation to the Other that is here in play, in a play that reveals the ostensible opposition of noble and slave, aristocracy and resentment, to be two versions of a single but highly ambivalent story. For, if the relation of exchange could be "projectively interpreted," *hineininterpretiert*) into the genealogical relation of present and past, of descendants and ancestors, is it not because those uncanny "creditors" were already at work in the "contriving of equivalences" itself? The necessity of divine spectators, of the divine *as spectator* and as witness, confirms the irremediable indebtedness of even the most apparently spontaneous and direct retribution, its dependence on an alterity with which it can never dispense, since it is there *in* (*the*) *place of the other* that the "standard" of equivalence, the measure of value, must be established. But since that *place* is never accessible or determinable other than as that of an (excluded) addressee, the verdict or testimony that it emits can never be certain. For those spectators never speak for themselves, but only through others, through riddles or enigmas, which in turn must be interpreted. And since interpretation, as Nietzsche well knew, is simply another name for the power play of a certain indebtedness—one, however, that refuses to assume its *Schuld*—the words of those spectators can never do more or other than echo the spectacle they are held to behold.

Their "message," in the story we are rehearsing, is simply: *Schuld*. Debt, guilt: debt as guilt, guilt as debt. And if the two words are one, it is precisely because they seek to be two: *Schuld* as debt seeks to deny the structural dependency of the self on an other, by confronting that other as creditor to debtor. But despite the cruel self-affirmaiton of the creditor, his power and self remain indebted to another, whom he cannot control and with whom he can hardly even negotiate. For the creditor needs witnesses and spectators to testify to the (repayment of the) debt. But since that testimony is always mute, always equivocal, always as unreliable as it is indispensable, the repayment of the debt is never assured, never certain—never unequivocally certified or certifiable. And thus, sooner or later, the "friends of *cruel* spectacles" reveal themselves to be the uncanny, unimaginable, *unvorstellbare* gods, whom we must fear and hate as much as love.

V

If the theory of *Schuld* demonstrates, against its explicit assertions, that Schuld *is* Schuld—that is, that debt and guilt are inextricably interwoven in the irreducible reference to a certain alterity—then this is not without consequences for Derrida's reading of "Freud," or speculating with an unpayable debt. Above all, the generalization of this debt would not necessarily entail its neutralization or nullification (*La Carte postale*, 415). Nor would its accents be limited to that dual but opposed tonality that Derrida finds in Freud: "serious, discouraged," but also "flippant, cavalier, affirmative" (ibid.). Rather, Nietzsche's *Verhäkelung* (interweaving) of debt and guilt should sensitize us to possibilities of dealing with *Schuld* other than those of affirmation or resignation. Such possibilities, or tonalities, are often situated "within" the apparent unity of seemingly single words. I will limit myself here to what might constitute one such instance, in *Beyond the Pleasure Principle*. It occurs at the very beginning of the text, and it allows the reading of "*Spéculer—sur 'Freud'* " to set its scene and get underway.

The way is that strange "*pas au-delà*" that is both a step beyond, and no step at all. In other words, it is the effort of the PP to "write it/himself"—that is, to send himself a letter without ever moving from the spot, by paying in advance the costs of a return-to-the-sender.

The way, then, taken by "*Spéculer — sur 'Freud'* " is that of rewriting *Beyond the Pleasure Principle* in the discourse or code of that other PP: the Postal Principle. Such a rewriting, a letter in the *Envois* informs us, essentially takes care of itself:

> This whole vocabulary, this entire postal code . . . will go very well with all that imposes itself on me in the reading of *Beyond* . . . , that is with the typology of posting, postures, impostures, and above all, of the position (*Setzung, thesis*), the thesis, the athesis and the hypothesis. And it is the *postal*, the Postal Principle as differential-deferring relay that regularly prevents, delays, dispatches the deposition of the thesis, that prohibits all repose and incessantly deposes, deports and keeps the movement of speculation on the run. (*La Carte postale*, 61)

It is perhaps worth remarking here that in the list of words belonging to the postal code that impose themselves in the reading of *Beyond* . . . , one word is conspicuously omitted, although it is inscribed as the key operator of the series — the word "imposition." In what way does the word "imposition," which describes the intervention of the postal code itself, fall under the sway of that code, obey its rules, follow its laws? Or does its unremarked absence, here — and elsewhere — suggest that it is precisely the point at which the postal code ceases to be a code, that is, closed, systematic, self-contained?

The question imposes itself all the more after our brief detour to Nietzsche's *Genealogy*, since it is there that interpretation is described as a process of *imposition*, by which one discourse *prägt sich auf* — impresses itself upon — another. And if the problematic of *Schuld* involves just such an interpretive imposition — ultimately of a certain alterity or exteriority upon that which seeks to exclude it in the name of its self, of its power, and of its property — then we shall not be entirely surprised that just this notion of imposition should impose itself at the very outset of Derrida's reading of "Freud."

That outset, as we have already noted, begins on a double, and equivocal, tone: the one familiar, deconstructive, depicts Freud crassly denying his debt to Nietzsche, to philosophy — that is, to a certain philosophy. The second, or other accent, no longer deconstructive, is the wonderment over the ease with which "Freud" dispatches the debt. But in both cases, the Freud described is shown as a *sender* rather than as a receiver; indeed, he is characterized as one who refuses to receive (the debt or message of Nietzsche), in order more freely to "write himself": write of himself, write to himself, both while apparently only assessing the current state of psychoanalytical theory.

And yet, this is not the whole story either. Freud's ambivalent attitude toward philosophy, his effort to distinguish the nature of the "speculations" of psychoanalysis from those of philosophy, may also, Derrida surmises, comport the effort to redeem, or recognize, a debt that the philosophical notion of speculation has endeavored to exclude. And indeed, although "*Spéculer—sur 'Freud'* " does not make explicit mention of it, a certain aspect of Freud's suspicion of philosophy anticipates its own; for what animates this suspicion is the very *systematic* pretension of philosophy that has provided Derridean deconstruction with its privileged target. Thus, what Freud "rejects" here, at the beginning of *Beyond the Pleasure Principle*, is not simply a debt to philosophy as such—"en coupant court avec tel ascendant 'philosophique' " (in cutting off contact with a particular philosophical predecessor, (*La Carte postale*, 294)—but rather a debt to a philosophy that masks its own constitutive indebtedness with narcissistic claims to construct systematic explanations or arguments.

That this aspect of Freud's relation to "philosophy" would not be explicitly acknowledged in "*Spéculer—sur 'Freud'* " is all the more remarkable in view of the programmatic declaration, by Derrida, just a few pages earlier, that the purpose of his reading of Freud is

> to open [the issue of] what *holds together (tient ensemble)* the new position of the question of death in psychoanalysis, the apparently auto-biographical point-of-view of Freud, and the history of the analytical movement. What *holds together* does not maintain the form of a system. No concept of system (whether logical, scientific or philosophical) is perhaps capable (*habilité*) of . . . achieving such a bringing-together (*rassemblement*). Of the latter it itself is only an effect. (*La Carte postale*, 290)

Thus, *Freud's* "avoidance" of philosophy, as described in "*Spéculer—sur 'Freud,'* " appears also, and perhaps above all, as a certain avoidance of "Freud." The question, "what happens when [descriptions] . . . can give themselves as examples of that about which they . . . write?" folds back upon the text that inscribes it. As does the question posed at the outset of "*Spéculer—sur 'Freud'* ": "Comment spéculer avec cette speculation?" (How to speculate with this speculation?) (*La Carte postale*, 296)

The beginnings of a response, or of a strategy, in "*Spéculer*," is, then, as I have indicated, to translate Freud's speculations into the terms of the code that has "imposed itself" upon Derrida's reading of *Beyond* . . . , the postal code. The center of that code, the "postal principle," communicates with what is perhaps the essence of philosophy, the gesture of *setting up*, of *Setzen, thesein, ponere*, while at the same time suggesting that this act, far from being originary and constitutive, is an "effect" of a network of relays, of a circulation that never succeeds in coming full circle. This would be the "athesis" demonstrated by Freud's speculations. But the formulation of this "athesis" seems still inextricably bound up with the deconstructive demasking of a determining intention:

Perhaps he who bears the name of Freud can neither appropriate the speculative (moment) of this singular speculation, nor identify himself with the speculator of this speculation, without precedent or precursor, nor yet exclude it, detach himself from it, deny (disown: *renier*) the one or the other. (*La Carte postale*, 297)

If Freud, then, perhaps never entirely succeeds in sending himself that fateful letter, in prepaying the charges of that return-to-sender, he also, it would seem, can never stop trying, either. And the point of departure of that impossible, if ineluctable, attempt, is "the promissory note (*lettre d'engagement*) that [Freud] *believes* he can send himself circularly, round-robin, specularly" (*La Carte postale*, 303; emphasis added).

But does Freud begin his speculations with such a *belief*? Does he begin by writing—by writing off his debt to philosophy, in order to gain the means with which to speculate? If his "speculations" entailed, "within the 'same' word—speculation—. . . a translation . . . from the philosophical concept of speculation in its dominant determination . . . to something else [which], in allowing itself to be excluded [from the philosophical concept] has never ceased to belabor it in the most domestic fashion" (*La Carte postale*, 296)—if Freud's speculations ential such an *intraverbal* translation, we may assume that the mechanism of such a translation will, perhaps, also be situated within what appears to be a single word, thereby opening and dividing that word, as well as the code to which it seems to belong.

If the master-word of the postal code that imposes itself in and on "*Spéculer—sur 'Freud'* " is that of *position*, the philosophical act par excellence, it is not surprising that the beginning of Freud's speculations, in *Beyond the Pleasure Principle*, should be described in such terms. Freud introduces that text, you may remember, with a brief survey of the current state of psychoanalytical theory, in particular concerning the pleasure principle: "In the theory of psycho-analysis we have no hesitation in assuming that the course taken by mental events is automatically regulated by the pleasure principle" (*S.E.* 18.7). Derrida remarks that Freud thus begins on a note of uncertainty that will pervade his entire speculations, imparting to them a character of undecidability that will place them beyond the pale of traditional theory and theorems; what we have, right here at the outset, he writes,

is neither a confirmation nor a questioning of the well-foundedness [of the pleasure principle]. But that will never become—this is my hypothesis here—either a confirmation or a refutation. Nonetheless, for the moment let us take note (*prendre acte*) of the following: Freud presents this state of theory as the possibility of an assumption which can be imprudent: "we assume *unbedenklich*," without wincing, as if it were self-evident, the authority of the pleasure principle. (*La Carte postale*, 294)

And, Derrida continues, Freud's manner in thus describing the imprudence, the *Unbedenklichkeit*, of this *assumption* serves to suspend its validity, and with it, that of the "law of avoidance" (*loi d'évitement*)—whether the avoidance of tension, *Unlust*, or Freud's own avoidance of his philosophical antecedents—or rather, the manner in which that law functions and its significance.

It is precisely such a suspension—of the governing assumptions of psychoanalytical theory—that distinguishes the speculations of psychoanalysis from their philosophical counterparts (or homonyms). Having begun by describing the nature of the pleasure principle within analytical theory, Freud goes on to assert, as Derrida puts it, that such " 'speculative hypotheses' " are radically distinct from those of philosophy because they claim no a priori status or validity.

But if their status is determined neither by the dominant, philosophical notions of speculation nor by any other deductive or inductive scheme, by what is it determined? It is here that the intervention, or imposition, of the "postal code" demands our attention. For what is at work in Freud's "speculative hypotheses" is not simply an imposition, but a *superimposition*, and one that leaves the most suggestive—most *bedenklichen*—traces. The phrase by which Derrida translates Freud here, thereby drawing him back toward the "philosophy" he ostensibly seeks to "avoid," as well as into the postal code—marks a slight but significant shift from the German text. Freud describes the pleasure principle not as a "spekulative Hypothese," as the French translation might lead us to believe, but rather as a "spekulative *Annahme*," a word that repeats and continues the verb, *anzunehmen*, with which Freud began his considerations on the state of analytical theory.

Why all this fuss about the translation of *Annahme* by *hypothesis*? Not merely because Freud, in *Beyond the Pleasure Principle*, repeatedly resorts to this word, rather than to *Hypothese*, perfectly available in German, to designate the *assumptions* with which psychoanalysis is destined to operate, but also because the root of the word sets it apart from that which characterizes "hypothesis," from the "setting up" or "posing" of a *thesis*.[9] At the core of "assumption," *Annahme*, is not *Setzung*, but *Nehmen*, and the difference is *bedenklich* indeed. For "to take," or "take on," denotes an "activity" that is by no means the same as "setting: up, out, upon. . . ." Indeed, it is hardly even certain that this *Nehmen* should be called an "activity" at all, for it also entails receptivity, a certain passivity or readiness, as much as any spontaneous and clearly delimited "act."

Thus, if Freud begins *Beyond the Pleasure Principle* by both describing and at the same time in a certain sense "suspending" the guiding principles of psychoanalytical theory, by underscoring their character as "assumptions"—and assumptions as such are always to some extent assumed *unbedenklich*, unreflectively—it is not indifferent if he retains the word to designate, in their entirety, the tenuous character of metapsychological concepts. Such *Annahmen*, Freud remarks, apparently to reassure his readers, unlike those of philosophy, have been arrived at "in an attempt to describe and to account for the facts of daily observation in our field of study" (*S.E.* 19.17). However, one need only recall that such "daily observation" in the "field" of psychoanalysis is, like perception itself, a function of borrowed languages, *Bildersprachen*, to realize how tentative the "descriptive" or "observational" status of psychoanalytical assumptions must necessarily be.

It is this precarious, tentative aspect of psychoanalytical thinking that leads Freud, at the conclusion of his brief, introductory résumé, to declare that in such matters, "the least rigid [loosest, most flexible] assumption (*die lockerste Annahme*) will, I believe, be the best one" (my translation; Strachey uses "hypothesis").

If, then, the story of Freud's speculations is not so much one of "hypotheses," or even of "theses," but of *Annahmen*, this modifies the very "postal code" that seeks to impose itself upon it. And it modifies it by revealing a certain process of *imposition* at work. This process installs a peculiar indebtedness at the very core of psychoanalytical thinking. For *to assume assumptions* is not merely to open oneself and one's thought to an exteriority that comes from without: it is to accommodate something that remains, in a certain sense, alien, strange— *fremdartig*, as Nietzsche would say. It is to install a debt at the core of cognition, *owing* at the heart of *knowing*. Such accommodation can only be ambivalent, however, since it inevitably entails a resistance to that which imposes itself, but which can never be simply assimilated or appropriated.

This is why an *Annahme* can never be simply "loose" or *locker*, however desirable that might be. For the force with which it *takes hold* is irresistible: this at least is what emerges at decisive points in the speculations of *Beyond the Pleasure Principle*. This is already explicit in the opening pages of the text, where it becomes clear that, if the pleasure principle has succeeded in installing itself as an *unbedenkliche Annahme*, it is because of its ability to overwhelm any and all resistance: the assumption, Freud writes, has been "forced upon us by psychoanalytic work" (*S.E.* 18.8).

This is also why, when an *Annahme* is suspended, it is generally only through the force of another, more powerful "assumption." This is the case with the move "beyond the pleasure principle": what replaces the pleasure principle is not, as Derrida has emphasized, another principle or thesis, or even a hypothesis, but rather the very process of *imposition*, of *assumption* itself. To assume, *unbedenklich*, in order to "account" for the "facts" of an impossible observation—an "observation" which in fact is nothing but the *reading* of a borrowed, figural language—is to engage in the very process that Freud "thematizes" under the ostensibly descriptive term "repetition-compulsion." The latter does not merely *designate* the irresistible, repetitive movement of the *drives*: it *imposes* itself upon Freud with and as the very same movement it describes:

"Here the idea cannot but force itself upon us, that . . ." (my translation; in *S.E.* 18.36, it appears as "At this point we cannot escape a suspicion . . .").

If the gesture that marks Freud's speculations is that of an irresistible imposition of *Annahmen*, then this may explain why and how Freud can at the same time deny, acknowledge, and dispatch his indebtedness with that matter-of-factness that so fascinates Derrida. To record the movement of such *assumptions* is to retrace one's dislocation by forces that one can neither determine nor identify; to "assume," in this sense, is both to admit an irreducible dependency, and also to refuse that dependency as a mere "assumption": to recognize the "other" at the very moment one tries to take hold of it.

It is this ambivalent character of the process of assumption, by which its "taking on" is also and inevitably a "taking off," that may account for the curious place *Annahme* occupies within the postal code. For, in German at least, when a letter is returned to its sender, it is often with a stamp affixed to the envelope, which reads: *Annahme verweigert*. In this case, however, the question: "Who, in short, pays? The addressee or the sender?" is a lure, for neither pays. Or both. For it is the postal system itself that is left holding the bill, which is probably why such systems can never make ends meet.

VI

This almost brings us back full circle to our point of departure, the collect call from Martin(e) or martini Heidegger. The call, you remember, was refused, after the "chemistry" of a calculation impossible to summarize, but for reasons we have in the meanwhile *perhaps* begun to envisage.

And yet, what results when a collect call made in the name of Martin, Martine, or martine Heidegger is refused? "This morning, I thought that I ought not to pay. . . ." But in refusing to accept the charges — *Annahme verweigert* — was the debt reduced?

In the chain of readings in which "Speculer — sur 'Freud' " is situated, Heidegger is doubtless the most important of the missing links. The divisibility of place and the reversibility of time, the superimposition of "fort" upon "da," the destination of the postal network, its "exappropriative" structure — all can be retraced to Heideggerian notions of *Geschick* and "*Da*," of *Enteignung* and *Ent-fernung*, and of a space in which backward and forward, front and back, near and far, are no longer defined by opposition to each other. The debt to Heidegger is clear, and, in a certain sense, assumed. Why, then, is the collect call, made in his name, refused?

A hint of where the elements of a response might be sought is inscribed in, and around, the same long footnote in which Heidegger and Nietzsche are mentioned in regard to the notion of an unrequitable debt — the note that ends with the promise, or threat, to "refer *Sein und Zeit* to *The Genealogy of Morals*, insofar as *Schuldigsein* (being guilty) is concerned"—but to do it "elsewhere (*ailleurs*)" (*La Carte postale*, 282). The phrase that occasions this long note reads as follows: "One can be guilty of that of which one considers oneself essentially innocent; indebted to that of which one always feels oneself redeemed in advance" (ibid.). And the ensuing footnote refers the reader to "the existential analytics of Dasein," which "situate the structure of originary *Schuldigsein* (being responsible, being forewarned, or the capacity-of-being responsible, the possibility of having to answer-for before every debt, every fault, and even every determinable law) this side of all subjectivity, of every relation to an object, [prior to] all cognition and above all, prior to all consciousness" (ibid.; compare Heidegger, *Being and Time*, sec. 58, pp. 325-35).[10]

One can be *schuldig*—guilty, responsible, indebted—independently of any act or feeling, intention or awareness, that one may have or do—for instance, the act of refusing to accept a collect call. But when the call is made in the name of a certain Heidegger—however dubious its authenticity may be—that *name* obliges its addressee at least to take note of the discussion of debt, or rather, of being-*Schuldig*, in *Being and Time*.

If, therefore, we follow the hint, promise, or threat, and go to the section of *Being and Time* indicated (sec. 58), what we find is not merely a discussion of debt, or being guilty, but also—and perhaps above all—a scene that is almost the uncanny double of that said to have taken place the morning of August 22, 1979.

For the discussion of *Schuld* in *Being and Time* is also the analysis of a "call" (*Ruf*), or rather, of an "appeal" (*Anruf*). Or perhaps of a telephone call. Indeed, coming to section 58 with that other call in mind, it becomes impossible *not* to read the *Anruf* of conscience (*Gewissen*) as just such a telephone call. In the first place, the call is very definitely long distance: "The call is from afar unto afar" (*Gerufen wird aus der Ferne in die Ferne*) (*La Carte postale*, 316). Second, the call is in a certain sense uncalled for, it comes as a surprise, interrupting and deranging. Third, if the call deranges, it is because, ultimately, nothing is said: "The call asserts nothing, gives no information about world events, has nothing to tell" (*La Carte postale*, 318). It announces nothing, except perhaps a certain nothingness of the called, of the addressee. That is, it recalls the latter to or before its irrevocable *Schuldigsein*—a term whose translation I shall defer, for a moment, but only in order first to proceed to another untranslatable word, which bears even more immediately on our problem. This word concentrates, as it were, the duplicit, uncanny but also witty, perhaps even *farcical* relation of the two calls, long distance and collect. For the essence of the call of conscience, in *Being and Time*, is that caller and called are, ultimately, the *same*—although by no means simply identical. The call comes from *Dasein* to *Dasein*. In short, "Es (Dasein) hat sich selbst gewählt" (which the English translation presents as, "It has chosen itself" [*Being and Time*, 334]. The untranslatability of this phrase is like that of a good joke. For *wählen* does not simply mean "to choose, elect"; it also, and particularly in combination with "call," means: "to dial." In the long-distance call that says nothing, but calls up a certain debt, *Dasein* therefore *dials* itself. And it is above all the nature of this dialing that suggests why, and in what way, that other collect call had to be refused, by one whose "private relation to Martin does not go by the same line" (*La Carte postale*, 26).

For it is precisely a question of *standards*: of equivalents, as with Nietzsche, but also of telephone lines, exchanges, and operators (*standardistes*). *Dasein*, we recall, does not simply *dial itself* in *Being and Time*. It dials itself *directly*, without intermediary. Indeed, it is this ability of direct dialing that determines the possibility of the call, as that which interrupts *Dasein*, recalling it to its *Schuldigsein*: "The possibility of its thus getting broken off lies in its being appealed to without mediation (*unvermittelten*: unaided)" (*Being and Time*, 316). The ineluctability of a certain *Vermittlung*, however—and the word also designates the *telephone exchange*—is what *La Carte postale* is all about. There is no call, no dispatch, no missive, letter, or communication, without a *Vermittlung*; indeed, the former is an effect, and defect, of the latter. This, too, is recorded and recounted in the annotated story of the collect call that was refused.

> All this should not create the impression that there is no telephonic communication which ties me to the ghost of Heidegger, as well as to more than one other. On the contrary, the network of my connections . . . is rather cluttered and more than one exchange is required to absorb in the overload. Simply, my correspondents of this morning should know that . . . my private relation to Martin does not go by the same line. (*La Carte postale*, 26)

That "private relation" does not go by the "même standard" for the simple reason that it does not go by *le standard du même*, not at least as that *standard* operates in the direct dialing of *Dasein*. For what enables Dasein to call itself directly, without the intermediary of any exchange or any operator, is a certain *sameness*, which notwithstanding the remoteness that separates *Dasein* from itself, nevertheless substantiates the assertion that caller and called are ultimately the *same*.

> Indeed, the call is precisely something which *we ourselves* have neither planned nor prepared for nor voluntarily performed, nor have we ever done so. "It" calls, against our expectations and even against our will. On the other hand, the call undoubtedly does not come from someone else who is with me in the world. The call comes *from* me and yet *from beyond me*. (*Being and Time*, 320)

To be sure, *Dasein* as the "called" (*als angerufenes*) is differently *da*, there, from the *Dasein* that calls. And indeed, the entire effect of the call operates within the space of this difference. However, what is essential in remarking the distinction between the call of *Dasein*, recalling its *Schuldigsein*, and the collect call refused in *La Carte postale*, is that the call of *Dasein* takes place, takes its place, *without the intervention of an operator*. This means that there can never be any doubt as to the nature of the call, of the caller, and what the call recalls: namely, a *Schuldigsein* whose "owner," as it were, is unequivocally determined, as "Dasein itself" (*Dasein Selbst*).

Of course, such clarity is not characteristic of the actual call itself: the Self of *Dasein* that receives the call "remains indefinite and empty in its 'what'. . . . And yet the Self has been reached, unequivocally and unmistakably," even though "That which calls the call, simply holds itself aloof from any way of becoming well-known" (*Being and Time*, 319). But if the Called and the Caller are both indeterminate, the certitude with which the call attains its addressee indicates a level of determination that exceeds that of the call as experienced, that of its "*existentielles Hören*." For the "*existenziale Analyse*," by contrast, both Caller and Called can be unequivocally determined, and indeed, such absence or elimination of equi-vocation is the condition of the Call itself.

To understand this unequivocal quality of the Call, we must recall the manner in which it operates, without the mediation of operators or exchanges. *Dasein* dials itself, but the Self that it dials is not that which dials. The Self that is called is one that is *lost*—lost in the "one" (*das Man*) of itself, lost in, and as, *one*-self. It is this Self, lost in its *Oneness*, that is interrupted and disrupted by the unexpected, unerring call. The Self is thereby called back and forth, not alternatively, in an oscillating or rocking motion, but at the same time. It is this back-and-forth, back-*as*-forth, that comprises the silent, unuttered message of the call: what Heidegger designates as *Schuldigsein*. Let us, finally, take a closer look at just what this word denotes in *Being and Time*.

The *Schuldigsein* that is called up in the call of conscience addresses *Dasein* in its ability-to-be (*Seinkönnen*); that ability-to-be, however, is characterized by a certain *Nichtigkeit* (nullity, notness). What marks the being of *Dasein* as *schuldig* is that it is inseparable from being-*not*. Not only is *Dasein* "thrown, *not* brought by itself into its There" (as "geworfenes, *nicht* von ihm selbst in sein Da gebracht"), but its very ability-to-be confounds it in a choice (*Wahl*) of possibilities that is ineluctably marked by those it necessarily must reject, the possibilities *not*-chosen:

> In having a potentiality-for-Being, it always stands in one possibility or another: it constantly is *not* other possibilities, and it has waived these in its existentiell projection. Not only is the projection, as one that has been thrown, determined by the nullity of Being-a-basis; *as projection* it is itself essentially *null* [not]. . . . The nullity we have in mind belongs to Dasein's Being-free for its existentiell possibilities. Freedom, however, *is* only in the choice of one possibility—*that is, in tolerating*

one's not having chosen the others and one's not being able to choose them.
(*Being and Time*, 331; emphasis added in final sentence)

Dasein is thus "as such *schuldig*" because its mode of being is determined by the possibilities it rejects, does *not* choose, as much as by those it does.

The call of conscience, then, recalls *Dasein* to its most basic being, which is to be the basis of a notness or nullity. It is only on this basis, as *Grundsein einer Nichtigkeit*, that *Dasein* can truly care, and take care of its Self. By being thus recalled to this basic "notness," *Dasein* calls upon itself *to accept* the not-possible, that is, "even that thrown entity which it is (*selbst das geworfene Seiende, das es ist, existierend zu übernehmen*)" (*Being and Time*, 333). However "uncanny" this call may be, however indeterminate the caller, however strange and unexpected, there can never be any doubt, for the discourse that articulates the existential analysis – that is, at the level of the "existenzial" – that the call is a house call that *Dasein* pays upon itself. Indeed, within the economy of *Being and Time* this is precisely the *interest* of the call. For it is this call that enables the argument to proceed from the analysis of being-to-death, which establishes the *general possibility* of an authentic existence, to the demonstration that such a possibility is also a *specific demand* that *Dasein* makes of itself. From the standpoint of the existential analysis, the call *bears witness (bezeugt), attests* to this demand (*Being and Time*, 311). The significance and value of this testimony can thus be presented as unequivocal insofar as the transaction takes place within *Dasein* itself, between *Dasein* and its Self. Through this call, *Dasein* bears witness to its proper calling, to the propriety and the property of its notness. If the call thus testifies to the indebtedness and responsibility of a being that only can *be* in accepting (i.e., excluding) and supporting what it is not, there is never any doubt that the debts thus incurred are *Dasein's own*.

It is this *claim* that provides the background – or is it the foreground? – of the decidedly inauthentic refusal to accept the collect call from one Martin, Martine, or martini Heidegger. Instead of assuming a debt that would ultimately prove to be his own, the narrator calculates, maneuvers, seeks to negotiate – and decides, "very quickly to refuse." The call, he tells the operator, is only "a joke." What he might have added, was that it probably was not for him in the first place. For if the caller gave his, her, or its name, that of the called is not mentioned, not at least in the story we are told. The call, in short, seems not to have been: *person-to-person.*

Which is why, *perhaps*, the call of *La Carte postale*, in contrast to that of *Being and Time*, was not to be accepted, but only *assumed* anonymously in and as a *story*. For what was lacking was the name, the proper name. And yet, that name was also *there*, all the time. Where? *Da*:

Naturellement je ne l'ai jamais accepté, ni toi, ce n'etait pas possible, mais je le veux encore. . . . J'accepte, ce sera désormais ma signa-

ture, mais que cela ne t'inquiète pas, ne t'inquiète de rien. Je ne te voudrai jamais aucun mal, entends bien ce mot en toutes lettres, c'est mon nom, que j'accepte, *et tu pourras compter, y compter comme sur les clartés capitales, de toi j'accepte tout. (La Carte postale,* 31)

Naturally I never accepted it, nor you, it wasn't possible, but I still want it. . . . I *accept*, henceforth this will be my signature, but don't let that worry you, don't worry about anything. I will never wish you any harm, take this word literally, it's my name, that *I accept*, and you can count . . . on it. . . . from you I accept everything.[11]

Chapter 9
Ambivalence: The Humanities and the Study of Literature

Allow me to begin with an anecdote. Shortly before I sat down to complete this paper, I found myself writing a letter to the organizers of a conference to be held in Vienna in which I had been asked to participate. The meeting was sponsored by an institution that seeks to bring together scholars from different cultural, linguistic, and political areas – above all, although not exclusively, from Eastern and Western Europe – in order to facilitate communication between groups that do not often have the opportunity for discussions with one another. The name of this institution is the *Institut für die Wissenschaften vom Menschen*; in English: the Institute for the Sciences of Man. This title caught my attention for a number of reasons. First of all, it sounds quite unusual in German, almost like a neologism. In this respect, it reminds me of a similar designation that came into vogue briefly in the early seventies in West Germany, but which has since vanished from the academic scene: the phrase, *Humanwissenschaften* ("human sciences"), which in turn was an attempt to find a German equivalent for the French notion of *les sciences humaines*. Paradoxically enough, it was French structuralism that did much to popularize the term *sciences humaines* – paradoxically, because of course it was also French structuralist writers, such as Foucault and Lacan, who mounted a powerful and probing challenge to the normative value of the notion of Man, of the Human.

This first line of thought – but perhaps "association" would be the better word – provoked by the rather bizarre resonance of the Viennese *Institut für die Wissenschaften vom Menschen*, led me on to a second series of considerations, which involved the question of the Human: the question, that is, of its scope or rather of the *universality* generally attributed to it. In *Les Mots et les choses* (*Words and Things*), Foucault argues that the Human is a peculiarly modern notion, one that could be historically situated and delimited, and which hence cannot simply be accorded the kind of universal validity long regarded as self-evident. In this perspective, the idea of the *sciences humaines* can be understood only in terms of an effort to discern and establish the limits of the human and thereby render it a suitable object of scientific investigation. In the French "human sciences," therefore, the epistemological accent had to be placed on the *sciences*, not on the *human*. And although the situation was somewhat less clear-cut in Germany, inasmuch as the "Humanwissenschaften" never succeeded in articulating themselves as extensively as in France, the tendency there was no doubt similar. The prestige enjoyed by the term *Wissenschaftlichkeit*—"scientificity"—in academic discourse is indicative of a cognitive ideal that equates "scientific"—*wissenschaftlich*—with rigorous, coherent inquiry and knowledge, no matter what the domain.

To be sure, *Wissenschaft* and, in French, *science*, have very different connotations from our English word *science*. How, otherwise, could the entire discipline of literary studies be designated as *Literaturwissenschaft*, as "the science of literature"? And yet, what is instructive for our purposes, as we gather here to discuss "The Ends of the Humanities," is that one if not *the* decisive reference traditionally used to define, or at least to situate the "Humanities" in the English-speaking world—that which opposes it to the "Sciences"—is inoperative in the French and German universes of discourse. And this, in turn, may explain what it is that has led me down this rather curious, semi-anecdotal detour in approaching the question of the Humanities: the fact that there is nothing, in French or German academic discourse, that really corresponds to the English notion of the Humanities; nothing in their discourse, and also nothing in their institutions. What takes the place of the Humanities in Germany are, of course, the *Geisteswissenschaften*; however, it is not the opposition to science that is at work here, but rather that of Spirit (or Mind), on the one hand, and Nature on the other. Although this is not entirely foreign to our tradition of the humanities, which also has defined itself in opposition to nature and to natural science, it by no means is identical to it either. The English idea of the humanities is not centered on the Spirit, not at least in the sense of Hegel or of Dilthey, nor is it focused primarily on "the life of the mind." Rather, it is closer to the ideal of Renaissance humanism, which in turn is related to the Roman origins of the word in the emphasis it places on the more practical, social, and civic virtues felt to derive from the cultivation and mastery of certain "arts."

And this brings me to the third and last train of thought set in motion by my letter to the *Institut für die Wissenschaften vom Menschen*. It is surely symptomatic of the difference separating these "sciences of man" from our "humanities" that the topic of the conference to be held in Vienna should be entitled "The

Question of the Subject—Between Neo-Structuralism and Hermeneutics." The "Question of the Subject," as you will have noticed, is a question that can be comfortably situated within the epistemological sphere of the *Geisteswissenschaften*, the sciences of the mind. "The Ends of the Humanities," for better or for worse, can not.[1]

But where then *are* those Ends located? What space do they imply? What place do they occupy? Where do the questions we have been asked to address come from? And where are they going? Let us look for a moment at some of those questions. They begin, to be sure, with what is a familiar scenario: "What values and functions are accorded to the humanities in contemporary society?" More often than not, in the past fifty years at least, discussions of the humanities have started—and usually ended—with the question of "values and functions." The second question, however, although appearing, at least initially, to continue this scenario, in fact begins to diverge from it. It asks about "the institutional role of the humanities today." The traditional manner in which this role has been discussed may be gleaned from the following passage drawn from the beginning of R. S. Crane's very readable lectures, *The Idea of the Humanities*. Crane is speaking of the difficulty in defining just what it is that the humanities really are: another leitmotiv of this topic. Their elusive essence, he suggests, is masked rather than revealed by the received idea that the humanities must be defined in opposition to the sciences. As an example of such an "external" way of construing the humanities, Crane recounts "the jibe current in the University of Chicago several years ago to the effect that the humanities were merely what was left over after all the departments which wished to be thought scientific had organized themselves in the three other divisions." But, Crane concludes, "the matter isn't as simple as that."[2] And yet, when, some ten lectures and 150 pages later, after surveying the history of Western humanism from Cicero and Quintillian to Irving Babbitt, it comes time to arrive at a conclusion about just what the humanities are or should be, the institutional "setting" has long since disappeared from the stage, as behooves something whose ultimate function is construed as that of an external framework within which something far more essential, far more valuable takes place. The University of Chicago, and universities in general, are worth a good jibe, but not too much more. For Crane, in short, the "idea" of the humanities resides elsewhere.

And yet, once the term "institutional role" is more precisely described, it becomes clear that this role cannot be construed in the traditional terms of humanistic discourse, as the external if indispensable frame or framework of an *idea* or of an *ethos*. Indeed, to pose the question of the institutional role of the humanities in the terms of "power" and "desire" is to move our attention in a direction very different from that which has hitherto determined discussions of this kind. It is this direction that I want to explore with you today, in however halting and tentative a fashion.

And I would like to begin this exploration by reformulating what I take to be implied in the series of questions that articulate our topic. These I shall reduce to the following: First, how is the problem of the humanities an institutional problem? And second, in what way do its institutional implications entail power and desire? To this reformulation I would then wish to make one addition and one emendation. To describe the "institutional role" of the humanities in terms of power and desire is necessary, but not sufficient. Insofar as the institutional role of the humanities is inseparable from the university, it must also be considered in relation to an element it has often tended, deliberately or not, to exclude from its discourse: that of *cognition*. The question I would add, then, is: What is the place of cognition, alongside desire and power, in the institutional role of the humanities today? The emendation I have in mind is less substantive and more syntactic in character. It concerns the use of the disjunctive conjunction "or," which occurs twice in the questions we are to discuss. First, in the formulation: "what forces of power and desire are questioned *or* affirmed by this role?" Might it not be conceivable, however, that certain forces of power, desire, and cognition are *both* questioned *and* affirmed by the institutional role of the humanities? Similarly, when the final two questions are cast in the mode of an alternative—"Is there a crisis in the humanities . . . or are (they) engaged in constructing other truths . . . mapping new spaces for activity?"—I would like to suggest and even argue that *both* parts of the alternative may obtain. And that in fact, the one may be intimately related to the other, the "new spaces" a product of the "crisis," even of the "dead ends." Indeed, perhaps it is the very way in which the humanities have begun to question the deeply ingrained logic of binary opposition, of mutual exclusion, that can account for the possible emergence of such "new spaces"? Perhaps.[3]—Perhaps the humanities, which have traditionally been concerned with values, have become the arena in which the logic of opposition that has determined the value of values is being replaced—that is, relocated, not merely eliminated—by something else.

But before I attempt to describe just what that other, nonoppositional movement might look like, let me try to situate it with respect to the "crisis of the humanities." It is surely significant to recall that wherever the humanities have imposed themselves as an issue of academic discussion, at least in the United States, it has been in a context of crisis. From Irving Babbitt's and Paul Elmer More's defense of the "new humanism" in the twenties and thirties, to the more recent Report of the Rockefeller Commission, the humanities have been regarded as in jeopardy. The very first words of *The Humanities in America*, the report of the Rockefeller Commission, reflect this concern: "A profound disquiet about the state of the humanities in our culture moved the Rockefeller Foundation in April 1978 to sponsor a commission to assess the humanities' place and prospects."[4] This sense of crisis has generally been interpreted along two distinct, but interrelated lines. On the one hand, it has been situated in the context of the opposition to the sciences: the latter are generally regarded as the model of cognitive rigor whereas the humanities, preoccupied with values and standards, make their own evaluation difficult if not impossible. If man is the measure of all things, what is the measure of man? The challenge of the sophists to philosophy is replayed here, although with important alterations. For the scientific method is respected not so much for the manner in which it attains objective truths, but rather for its capacity to produce the tools of social, and above all, technological power. On the other hand—but it is, perhaps, merely the other side of the same hand—the crisis of the humanities has long been seen not merely as what might be called an "external" problem caused by its relation to the sciences, but also as an internal one. "The most serious threats to the humanities," Crane stated in his 1953 lectures, "come from within rather than from without" (*Idea of the Humanities*, 13). These "internal enemies" he described as "dogmatism" and "the spirit of reduction," which, he asserted, tend to betray what he took to be the essence, the "idea" of the humanities: the concern with "the multiplicity and diversity of human achievements" (*Idea of the Humanities*, 14). Since this conception of the humanities is by no means limited to Crane, but has, in one form or another, pervaded most attempts to approach this question, let me pursue some of its ramifications.

What is striking in Crane's lectures is the manner in which they seem compelled to recur to the opposition of the sciences and the humanities in order to delimit the latter:

> There is a very real sense . . . in which the direction of the humanistic arts, when they are properly cultivated, is the opposite of the direction properly taken by the sciences of nature and society. The sciences are most successful when they seek to move from the diversity and particularity of their observations toward as high a degree of unity, uniformity, simplicity, and necessity as their materials permit. The humanities, on the other hand, are most alive when they reverse this process, and look for devices of explanation and appreciation that will enable them to preserve as much as possible of the variety, the uniqueness, the unexpectedness, the complexity, the originality, that distinguish what men are capable of doing at their best from what they must do, or tend generally to do, as biological organisms or members of a community. (*Idea of the Humanities*, 12)

The sciences, in short, generalize, universalize, they seek the invariant and attain it by reduction. The humanities, on the other hand, seek "to preserve *as much as possible* of the variety, the uniqueness, the unexpectedness" that Crane identifies with the productions of a humanity free from biological or social constraints.

The question, of course, is: just how much is possible? And it is here that the question of knowledge, of the cognitive function of the humanities, must be confronted. In the course of his lectures, Crane makes it clear that he would like to have it both ways: he wants to assign the humanities a normative, value-setting function and this leads him back beyond the etymological origins of the humanities in the Roman orators, to Greek philosophy, to Plato, and above all to Aristotle.[5] On the other hand, such normative performance is hardly conceivable without cognitive capability, as one of Crane's concluding statements makes quite clear: the task of the humanities, he declares, is

> to study . . . poems as poems, histories as histories, philosophical works as philosophical works—and each kind in terms, not of its lowest common denominator in language, thought, or experience, but of the principles by which it is constructed and achieves its distinctive excellence. (*Idea of the Humanities*, 169)

The normative power of the humanities to preserve "distinction" as much as possible from the leveling of scientific generalization still requires the recognition of what things are: of what makes a poem a poem, of what distinguishes "histories as histories, philosophical works as philosophical works." Such awareness, in turn, is difficult to conceive without recourse to the very generalizing procedures that the humanities, according to Crane, should seek to avoid.

We find a very similar argument in the Rockefeller report:

> The humanist often proceeds by progressively inclusionary acts that make the precise field of inquiry hard to fix. The scientist and technician normally proceed through a series of systematic exclusions toward precise proofs and laws. (*The Humanities in America*, 15)

Here, the opposition between generalization and specification becomes that of exclusion and inclusion. The scientist excludes: the humanist includes. And yet, the very same questions arise here as in the case of Crane: can there be any sort of "inclusions," however "progressive," comprehensive, or totalizing they may be, that would not necessarily proceed by selection, and hence by exclusion? And is any sort of specification or particularization conceivable that would not necessarily entail recourse to conceptualization, and thus to generalization?

The ambiguous and indeed ambivalent attitude of humanistic discourse toward its great rival, the experimental sciences, provides us with an exemplary response to these questions. As we have seen, Crane attempts to characterize the opposition to the sciences, together with the institutional context in which that opposition is situated, as a superficial and "external" factor incapable of disclosing the true "idea of the humanities." And yet, he is forced constantly to return to that opposition in order to describe this idea; that is, in order to *demarcate* it, to set it off and apart from what it is not.

What I want to suggest is that this procedure, which I take to be highly characteristic of the organization of knowledge in modern society, has developed with problematic intensity in what we call the humanities, in particular within that portion of it dedicated to literary studies; and further, that what we call the crisis of the humanities is inextricably related to what I will term *the ambivalence of demarcation.*

The passages we have already cited from Crane and the Rockefeller report indicate the character of this ambivalence. To defend the humanities, the Rockefeller report attempts to describe them as a method of "progressive inclusion," one that is indispensable to society precisely because of its capacity to surmount difference, conflict, and competition by "including" and "integrating" *(The Humanities in America,* 22) while at the same time "transcend(ing) divisive ideological terms" *(The Humanities in America,* 24). Yet both explicitly and implicitly, such a description of the inclusive nature of the humanities necessarily proceeds by distinguishing and demarcating them from what they are *not,* from the "exclusionary" activity of science. In short, the inclusive description of the humanities is articulated as the *exclusion of exclusion.* A similar process is at work in Crane's assertion that the distinctive merit of the humanities is or should relate to their capacity to avoid the dogmatic, sectarian reductionism of the sciences and yet still to "treat poems as poems."

What results is a strategy of demarcation that cannot but be highly ambivalent. For in the process of distinguishing the humanities, the marks of distinction imperceptibly but inexorably *demark* themselves. The particular concern with the particular, the unpredictable, the unexpected, defines itself through a heterogeneity from which it can never entirely extricate itself. Such marks thus remain determined by what they are not even when they seek to conceal this unrequitable indebtedness. It is in the highly conflictual force field of this demarcation that the crisis, but also the *chance* of the humanities, have their respective places.

In order better to delineate the conflictual tendencies to which I have alluded, I want to return to a text that deals with the very problems that have emerged in the course of the previous discussion: above all, with that of understanding how knowledge of the "unexpected," of the particular, comes about. I am referring to Kant's *Critique of Judgment,* a text that offers considerable insight both into the situation of the humanities today, and also into the peculiar position of literary studies among the humanistic disciplines.[6]

The general problem addressed by Kant in his Third Critique is precisely that which Crane and others have placed at the center of their consideration of the humanities: How is knowledge of the particular possible? Or, to transpose the question into terms closer to Kant's text: Is there an a priori rule that presides over our acts of judgment, acts, that is, by which we subsume the particular under a general rule? If there is, Kant argues, this rule cannot itself be constituted by any objective concept, since it would then be unable to account for the process of subsumption as such. Every substantive concept would only defer consideration of just how concepts in general are applied to particulars.

For this reason, Kant introduces a distinction between two sorts of judgment, which he calls "determinant" and "reflective":

> Judgment in general is the faculty of thinking the particular as contained under the universal. If the universal (the rule, the principle, the law) be given, the judgment which subsumes the particular under it . . . is *determinant*. But if only the particular be given for which the universal law has to be found, the judgment is merely *reflective*.[7]

That is, if we are confronted by the unknown, the unusual or the unexpected, or in fact by anything that the concepts we have at our disposal are incapable of subsuming, the principle that guides our judgment is not substantive, it does not serve to determine an object but rather to allow the judging subject to pursue its investigation, its search for the missing general rule. These judgments are "reflective" inasmuch as the "law" they follow in moving from the particular to the general is based not on the object as such—for, in the absence of a given concept, this is precisely what must be determined—but rather on a relation of the subject to itself. If there is any sort of regularity to reflective judgments, and Kant argues that there is, it can be based only on a law that this judgment takes "from and (gives) to itself." (*Critique*, 16). This kind of law can be neither objective, since it precedes all determination of the object, nor purely subjective, in which case it would never lead to any valid judgment whatsoever. It would be merely solipsistic, a product of subjective fantasy, leading not to knowledge but to wish fulfillment and presumably to self-deception.

If there is any doubt that the Kantian notion of reflective judgment, with all the problems it entails, is related to the dilemma of the humanities, we need only recall the very striking literary citation with which the Rockefeller Commission begins the first chapter of its report:

> Nailed to the ship's mast in *Moby-Dick* is a gold doubloon stamped with signs and symbols "in luxuriant profusion." The coin is Captain Ahab's promised reward to the crewman who sights the white whale, but in its emblems each man reads his own meaning. As Ahab says, "This round gold is but the image of the rounder globe, which, like a magician's glass, to each and every man in turn but mirrors back his own mysterious self."

And the report comments:

> Like the bright doubloon, the humanities mirror our own image and our image of the world. Through the humanities we reflect on the fundamental question: what does it mean to be human? The humanities offer clues but never a complete answer.

However, the passage from *Moby Dick* goes much further, and is far more disquieting than this commentary would suggest: for what is in question is not merely the "completeness" of the answer to the "fundamental question," but the question itself. If the humanities are like the gold doubloon, what they provide is a reflection, a mirror image of the viewer. Yet, to see one's mirror image and to arrive at self-knowledge are, needless to say, not necessarily identical.

In another context this has been put very well recently by Jacques Derrida:

> What happens when acts or performances (discourse or writing, analysis or description, etc.) form part of the objects they designate? When they can give themselves as examples of that of which they speak or write? There is certainly no gain in self-reflexive transparency, on the contrary. An accounting is no longer possible, an account can no longer be rendered, nor a simple report or compte rendu given. And the borders of the whole are neither closed nor open. Their trait is divided.[8]

It is precisely this division that is at work in what I have called the process of ambivalent demarcation, to which I shall return in a moment.

But before I do, I want to recall two further aspects of Kant's discussion of reflective judgment. They concern the peculiar relation of such judgment to cognition. First of all, those not familiar with this text may be surprised to learn that what Kant has in mind in introducing the notion of reflective judgment is above all the situation of the experimental sciences, where the goal precisely is to move from an investigation of particulars to the establishment of general laws. This is of great interest in our context since up to now we have stressed the similarity of reflective judgment to the approach traditionally associated with the humanities: the confrontation of the particular, the unexpected, or the heterogeneous, of everything not yet subsumed by "given" concepts. And yet, precisely this situation Kant attributes to the sciences. What this suggests, therefore, is that the opposition of the humanities and the sciences may in fact be less pertinent than their underlying common effort to apprehend the particular and to make it the substance or object of a judgment, which, if it is not itself a cognition, nevertheless always entails a relationship to cognition.

It is the necessity of this relationship that explains why—and this brings me to the second aspect of the discussion of reflective judgment—Kant should find the most exemplary, most significant instance of such judgment not in the realm of scientific practice but in that of aesthetic evaluation:

> This perplexity about a principle [that is, a principle of reflective judgments, where no objective cognition is produced or presupposed—S. W.] presents itself mainly in those judgments that we call aesthetical, which concern the beautiful and the sublime of nature or of art. (Preface, 5)

Kant's entire philosophical interest in aesthetic judgments, therefore, derives from the peculiar "perplexity"—or, more properly, the peculiar *embarrassment* (*Verlegenheit*)—that characterizes judgments of beauty or of the sublime, where concepts precisely are not "given" and where cognition therefore is not a constitutive factor.

In thus characterizing aesthetic judgments as those in which the particular imposes itself at the expense of preexisting universals, Kant's critical philosophy bequeaths to the modern discipline of literary studies, and in particular to literary criticism and theory, a fateful and ambiguous legacy. Literary and aesthetic judgments are assigned a decisive position within all the cognitive activities, inasmuch as such evaluations appear to be exemplary instances of the judgmental process as such. In this sense, Kant can describe the Third Critique, centered on the critique of the judging subject, as nothing less than "the propaedeutic of all philosophy" (*Critique of Judgment*, 31). And yet at the same time aesthetic judgments provide no "knowledge of its objects" (ibid.), and hence they cannot themselves be made the content of any substantive theory or discipline. In the light of critical philosophy, then, 'critical theory' in the contemporary American sense is a contradiction in terms. There can be no theory of criticism, any more than there can be a theory of taste. There can be an empirical history of taste, but its theoretical value would be nil. And what is worse, such a history would have to miss the distinctive singularity that makes an aesthetic judgment aesthetic, or—as Crane would have put it—what makes a poem a poem.

In short, the very dignity and significance of the aesthetic judgment as one in which the singularity of the object resists all attempts to subsume it under general concepts also precludes the establishment of a discipline of literary studies or of literary criticism. It is precisely this conclusion that Crane refused (understandably) to draw, although his insistence on the nongeneralizable aspects of the humanities, and of literature in particular, tends precisely in this direction. The question can be formulated more emphatically if we refer to a remark made by Wayne Booth in his introduction to Crane's lectures:

> Surely one of the tasks of the humanities is to come to terms with
> such wondrously uncommon creations as escape the generalizing mind
> because they are not, as the scientists say of *their* experiments, replica-
> ble. But if this is so, a method committed to proper differentiations is
> needed if we are to avoid reductions to a common ground.[9]

If we hope to be able to articulate what Booth refers to as "proper differentiations" in regard to the humanities, however, we will have to confront the paradox that, although the findings of humanists may not be "replicable" in the sense of the experimental sciences, they are nevertheless and necessarily *repeatable*, or, to use a term that Derrida has elaborated in his debate with John Searle, they are *iterable*.[10] The notion of iterability allows us to resituate one of the decisive distinctions between the humanities and the experimental sciences: whereas the latter inscribe their operations in a continuum of repetition through the establishment of control instances, such controls are in principle excluded from the sphere of the humanities. The iterability of a literary—or a psychoanalytic—interpretation, for instance, entails alteration as much as it does recurrence. If it produces insight, it is of the kind hinted at by that philosophic heretic, Charles Sanders Peirce, when he declared that "cognition arises by a process of beginning, as any other change comes to pass."[11]

Cognition as a process of "change" is, to be sure, very different from what the classical notion of truth as *adequatio intellectus et rei* was designed to survey. And yet the dynamic conception of knowledge as change is not without its own precursors. Indeed, although it hardly was intended in that way, Kant's notion of reflective judgment must ultimately be understood along such lines. To take the opposition of determining and reflective judgment as though it implied two mutually exclusive operations; to imagine that concepts could be "given" in a way that would make their application to a particular case unproblematic; or conversely, that we could even so much as apprehend a "particular case" without some reference to general terms, is to ignore the irreducible divergence of identity and difference without which any judgment whatsoever would be simply superfluous. What Kant's notion of reflective judgment suggests, without stating it as such, is a situation in which "given" concepts do not suffice to identify or "subsume" the particular case, and hence in which the latter requires a reorganization and reworking of those concepts. If such a reworking is what constitutes the a priori principle of judgment, then its product, whether it is cognitive or aesthetic, will always entail an element of *change*, of *transformation*.

This notion of *transformation*, never mentioned by Kant, is nonetheless what might be called the *deregulative idea* of the *Third Critique*. Here I want to elaborate one aspect of that idea, which seems of particular relevance to the questions we are discussing: the ends of the humanities and the place of literary studies in regard to them.

Kant refers to the humanities only once in *The Critique of the Power of Judgment*, at the very end of his discussion of aesthetic judgment. The context is that of an *Anhang*, an appendix entitled "On the Methodical Doctrine (*Methoden-lehre*) of Taste." Kant begins by reiterating that a "science of the beautiful" is impossible, that "judgments of taste are not determined by principles," and hence that there can be no methodical doctrine in such matters. Taste, in short, cannot be taught or transmitted methodically, but only through what today would be called exemplary learning. The problem, however, which Kant, here as elsewhere in this text, recognizes and struggles to resolve, concerns the status of such models. Inasmuch as they inevitably entail objectification, they necessarily tend to obscure what they are designed to preserve: the irreducible singularity of the "beautiful." In short, the very need that produces such exemplifications of the beautiful tends to immobilize them in objectifications that remain alien to the essence of the aesthetic judgment of taste. And yet, if that essence is first and foremost *subjective*, it is also understood by Kant as being *universal*. The fact that Kant feels himself constrained to return to this question again and again is indicative of its unresolved state in this text. It is the articulation of this irresolution that deserves our attention.

The situation described by Kant is one in which taste is transmitted by exemplification, but in which care must be taken to prevent the example from becoming a rule. This would stifle the imagination and ultimately make both the production of new works of beauty and judgments of taste themselves impossible. The indispensable condition of both resides in the imaginative apprehension of the difference that separates the "aesthetic idea" from all possible conceptualization. And yet, the problem here as elsewhere in the Third Critique is to find a way of accounting for the universality of those "ideas," particularly as it finds expression in the relative constancy of aesthetic taste over the years, without abandoning the notion of conceptual and cognitive heterogeneity that an a priori principle of judgment requires.

It is in this context that Kant invokes the humanities:

> The propaedeutic to all beautiful art, in respect to the highest degree of its perfection, seems to lie not in precepts, but in the cultivation of those spiritual powers (*in der Kultur der Gemütskräfte*) by means of the pre-cognitions (*Vorkenntnisse*) called the humanities (*Humaniora*): presumably because *humanity* signifies on the one hand the universal *feeling of taking-part* (*Teilnehmungsgefühl*), and on the other, the power of being able to *impart oneself* (*mitteilen*) in the most inward and universal manner; which properties in combination comprise the *sociability* of human beings, by which they distinguish themselves from the limited character of animality. (*Critique*, Section 60, p. 201. Translation modified)

The humanities, for Kant in this context, entail not so much the cultivation of particular arts, nor even the aims and preconditions of such arts, which Bernard in his translation renders as "sympathy" and "communication." Rather, if I have rendered *Teilnehmungsgefühl* and *mitteilen* more literally, as "taking-part" and "imparting," it is in order to render legible what the two German words used by Kant have in common and what I take to be the distinctive feature or "property" of the humanities as he invokes them here: *partiality*. What distinguishes the sphere of the human from the more restrictive one of mere animality is not simply that the former is less limited than the latter, but rather the nature of that limitation: that of a taking-part and of an imparting that never entirely overcomes its particularity.

An example of such partial imparting is afforded precisely at this point by Kant's text itself. In the first edition of the *Critique*, we find the word that I have retained in my translation, *Geselligkeit*, used to describe the peculiarly human trait produced by the combination of the two "properties," taking-part and imparting, as "sociability." In subsequent editions, however, the word is replaced by *Glückseligkeit*, "happiness" or "bliss." The "secondary revision" that supplants "sociability" by "bliss" calls attention to the conflictuality of a sociality in which the particular can never be entirely transcended, and yet in which it can also never simply persist in its isolated partiality.

The *Third Critique* can thus be read as inscribing the cultivation or culture of the humanities in precisely the place where the partiality of man partakes and imparts itself by a process of self-effacement that is never entirely successful and that—like Freudian repression, to which it is related in more than one way—always leaves traces.

In the light of Kant's text, then, the crisis of the humanities could be understood as an inevitable outgrowth of their aporetic ends: the participation in and imparting of the particular, the partisan, and the partial. At the same time, however, it is precisely this aporetic operation—"the reciprocal imparting of ideas" in Kant's words—that spans a society, from its "most cultivated part" to its "crudest," and holds it together.

Thus, Kant's invocation of the "humaniora" here serves not so much to reaffirm the traditional notion of the humanities as a socializing force, as to bring to the fore the ambivalent character of such socialization. This can help explain why in recent years the humanistic disciplines have manifested an increasing interest in questions relating to their own institutional status and in institutional issues more generally. Such an interest would not simply be an empirically contingent response to "external" factors. Rather, it would be inscribed in the aporetic project of the humanities as described by Kant: that of *imparting the particular*. Questions involving "the institutionalization of knowledge" reflect the desire to come to terms with the partiality of the project, but they have generally tended to avoid rather than to address the difficulties discussed.

An illuminating instance of this is provided by one of the leading contemporary historians of knowledge, the Berlin sociologist Wolf Lepenies. Writing of the methodology of the burgeoning discipline of the history of disciplines, Lepenies observes that the historian's point of departure must be "the cognitive, historical and institutional environment" in which the discipline first sought "to formulate, systematize and institutionalize a set of ideas and of practices," thereby enabling it to "distinguish itself from other disciplines."[12] The difficulty with such a self-evident statement is that the determination of the "environment" to which Lepenies refers must remain problematic and open-ended; or rather, it must remain problematic and *ambivalent*. For the environment cannot simply be left open, it must also be determined, borders must be fixed and maintained, whether by the discipline as such or by the individual historian who seeks to re-trace its history. But such a retracing will itself take part in what it is seeking to retrace, by virtue of the fact not only that any selection or delimitation made will necessarily be partial and not the whole, but also because that partiality, which founds the possibility of cognition and insight, does so only insofar as it ignores—or *represses*—its own particularity. And yet the process does not end, or start, there: as with the repression described by Freud, such cognitive repres-sion does not entail the pure and simple effacement of what is thereby excluded from one's field of vision or of consciousness: rather, *the exclusions persist qua exclusions*, and they must be so maintained if they are to delimit what falls within the scope of our determinations.

The result, then, is what I have called ambivalent demarcation. The demarca-tion is ambivalent because it does not merely demarcate one thing by setting it off from another; it also de-marks, that is, defaces the mark it simultaneously inscribes, by placing it in relation to an indeterminable series of other marks, of which we can never be fully conscious or cognizant.

Let me illustrate this with two examples, both of which, significantly enough, involve language. The first relates to the process of learning a foreign language. Initially, we use dictionaries that translate unknown foreign words back into our mother tongue. As we develop a certain proficiency, we begin to use dictionaries that remain within the foreign language (German-German or English-English lexica, for instance). When we first begin using these foreign dictionaries, we are liable to be confronted with an experience that can be either disconcerting or exhilarating, depending upon one's situation or mood. We look up the mean-ing of a word only to find that the defining word is equally obscure; or we dis-cover that certain aspects of the word are unclear and that we are constrained to choose between meanings without being certain of which criteria we should use.

What I want to suggest through this very banal example is that such uncer-tainty may well be symptomatic of something very essential in the way language works: words are determined only by their being referred to other words, which in turn must be referred to yet other marks, usages, contexts, and the like. This process is intrinsically endless, and yet in order for it to function at all we must *arrest* it. The fact that we do this (most of the time without a second thought) and that our lives are generally organized precisely in order to defend against such arresting second thoughts does not change the basic operation: namely, that even in the most prosaic use of language, we must in a certain sense *split our minds* in order to *think* at all, in order to articulate. We must both refer the defin-ing terms to other marks that can never be fully defined for us and at the same time—but this precisely fractures the Sameness of that Time—we must "forget" this irreducibly undefinable vestige, this set of exclusions that is neither entirely indeterminate nor fully determinable.

This problem of demarcation—and I come to my second example—is articulated in a most instructive manner in Saussure's *Course in General Linguistics*. The example is of particular interest in our context inasmuch as it brings together the problem of language with that of the institution of a discipline, linguistics. Saussure's entire enterprise is one of demarcation, and moreover, one dictated by the desire to establish the foundation of linguistics as an autonomous discipline. In its previous historical, comparatist, and philological form, Saussure argued, linguistics could never achieve this aim since its object was far too "heteroclite," that is, not sufficiently homogeneous and self-contained. This is his reason for constructing—i.e., for differentiating—language as a semiotic system, *la langue*, from language as an empirically observable phenomenon, from *le langage*. But what is curious and remarkable in Saussure's work is that the effort to demarcate *la langue* from *le langage* as well as from speech, *la parole*, produces an object so self-contained that it threatens to implode entirely, or rather, to dissolve.[13]

The process, again one of ambivalent demarcation, turns on the notion of linguistic difference. As a system of signs, Saussure asserts, language is entirely self-contained and constitutes an adequate foundation of and object for an autonomous discipline. Thus, the value of a linguistic sign, signifier or signified, is determined not by the extralinguistic entity, material or conceptual, that it designates, but rather by the ensemble of differences that distinguishes the signifier from its milieu, its environment. The value of a linguistic entity for Saussure is determined by that which "*surrounds*" it—an argument we rediscover in the passage cited from Lepenies. The only problem, however—but it is crucial—is how that environment in turn is to be determined. If language consists of "pure difference," as Saussure begins by asserting, where is the principle that will delimit the play of pure difference and impose upon it the rules of the game, the borders of a system?

The question, as Derrida remarks in *Of Grammatology*, is not resolved by Saussure; it is simply avoided, but the form in which it is avoided is paradigmatic both for Western thought in general and for the establishment of autonomous disciplines in particular. What Saussure does is simply to replace the notion of "pure difference" with that of "opposition" in order then to derive the structure of what he calls the "totality of the sign." And this "totality," in turn, is the product of what in a strange and revealing equivocation he calls "linguistic institution," whose task it is "to maintain the parallelism between these two orders of difference," that is, between signifier and signified. The equivocation of the term "linguistic," which can refer here to either language or to linguistics, is revealing inasmuch as it suggests that the establishment and maintenance of the *object* of a discipline—language as a system—is a task that only the discipline itself, *qua institution*—that is, linguistics—can perform. And yet this only displaces the problem. For a discipline legitimates itself through the operations it performs upon objects held to be *different* from it; otherwise, cognition is threatened by redundance, truth converges with tautology, and we find ourselves once again confronted by Ahab's uncanny gold doubloon.

Once again, the issue is one of demarcation. It is a problem that imposes itself all the more imperatively, the less securely established a discipline is, the less clearly it is situated with regard to the prevailing academic division of labor. An instance of some of the problems this may entail is furnished by the American historian and political theorist Louis Hartz, in the preface to his remarkable study, *The Liberal Tradition in America*. Hartz reflects on

> the curious failure of American historians, after repeating endlessly that America was grounded in escape from the European past, to interpret our history in the light of that fact. There are a number of reasons for this . . . but one is obvious at the outset: the separation of the study of American from European history and politics. Any attempt to uncover the nature of an American society without feudalism can only be accomplished by studying it in conjunction with a European society where the feudal structure and the feudal ethos did in fact survive. This is not to deny our national uniqueness, one of the reasons curiously given for studying America alone, but actually to affirm it. How can we know the uniqueness of anything except by contrasting it with what is not unique? The rationale for a separate American study, once you begin to think about it, explodes the study itself.[14]

But Hartz's own argument also answers itself: if the comparative aspects of American Studies—or of anything else, for that matter—"explodes the study itself" as an independent discipline, it is hardly curious that American historians would be reluctant to take this route. For to do so would be to put into question their own authority and competence, based on what I have elsewhere[15] sought to analyze as the *professionalist paradigm of knowledge*. The regulative idea of this paradigm is that of the *absolute autonomy of the individual discipline*, construed as a self-contained body of investigative procedures and of knowledge held to be universally valid within the confines of an unproblematized field.

Without a theory capable of problematizing the demarcation of such fields and at the same time of calculating the ambivalent effects and potentialities of their maintenance, it is difficult to envisage any transformation of the professionalist paradigm or any intervention that would not reinforce the already dominant technological tendency that is rapidly replacing the traditional humanist notion of disinterested "scholarship" with a productivist model of "research and development."

It is in this respect that it may prove useful to reconsider the Freudian notion of ambivalence. In order to be productive, however, such reconsideration must begin by bracketing the very familiarity of the term, which serves to conceal rather than reveal its implications. Ambivalence, for Freud, entails not merely the static opposition of conflicting emotions, but rather a constantly shifting dynamic of drive and prohibition:

> The drive is constantly shifting in order to escape from the impasse and endeavors to find substitutes—substitute objects and substitute acts—in place of the prohibited ones. In consequence, the prohibition itself shifts about as well, and extends to any new aims which the forbidden impulse may adopt. Any fresh advance made by the repressed libido is answered by a fresh sharpening of the prohibition. The mutual inhibition of the two conflicting forces produces a need for discharge, for reducing the prevailing tension, and to this may be attributed the reason for the performance of obsessive acts. In the case of a neurosis these are clearly compromise actions. . . . It is a law of neurotic illness [literally, of neurotic falling-ill, *neurotischer Erkrankung*—S. W.] that these obsessive acts fall more and more under the sway of the drive and draw even closer to the originally prohibited action.[16]

Although Freud is here discussing what is generally called individual psychology, the processes he describes are anchored in the relation of human beings to language, and more specifically, in the relation of *cognition to articulation*. The affinities Freud observed between social taboo and obsessional neurosis, between ritual acts and compulsive recurrence, are grounded not in the peculiarities of the individual psyche but in the structural dynamics of identification, understood in the broadest sense of the word, and of its relation to institutionalization.

The term I have tried to elaborate to indicate what is at stake in that relation, *ambivalent demarcation*, allows me, in lieu of a conclusion, to pose a question: Is it possible to envisage institutions, academic or otherwise, that would *assume*—in all the sense of this loaded and equivocal term[17]—the effects of the ambivalence described here without thereby resorting to the kind of archaeo-teleological self-determination that Freud suggests is a factor in provoking neurotic illness? Are institutions of inquiry conceivable in which the relation to the exclusions that enable all inquiry to pose its questions and pursue its problems—in which this process of enabling exclusion is assumed as a structuring factor and as a "regulative idea"? In which the relation to those limits is experienced in a manner other than that attributed by Marx to capitalist accumulation and appropriation, for which "the conquest of each new country signifies a new frontier";[18] and hence, for which, conversely, each new frontier signifies only a new country to be conquered?

We may find the hint of a response in Freud's discussion of ambivalence in *Totem and Taboo*. At the end of the chapter devoted to this subject, Freud returns to the similarity of ambivalence in taboo and in neurosis—this time, however, in order to distinguish the two: that is, to distinguish an ambivalence that performs a socializing function from one that tends to isolate individuals. Freud's point of departure is an apparent paradox: the violation of the taboo-prohibition entails the expectation that the violator will be punished, either spontaneously (by illness, fate, etc.), or by the acts of the community. The other is thereby held responsible for the transgressive acts performed. In the case of obsessional neurosis the situation is different: whereas the taboo produces a mode of behavior that appears to be "egoistic," the neurotic seems to behave "altruistically": he worries that his transgression may bring harm to some other, innocent person. Behind this apparent altruism, however, Freud discerns the aggressive desire to destroy the other; the altruistic fear is in reality "brutally egoistic" in that it has *already* performed phantasmatically the very aggressive act against which it defends, precisely by projecting it upon the other and thereby *identifying* him as a possible object of aggression.

Whereas the neurotic's concern for the other conceals an incapacity to accept the other's alterity (and to assume one's own aggressive desires), the "egoistic" attitude provoked by the violation of the taboo, Freud asserts, is in fact far more social in its assumption of the otherness of the other. The other is identified not primarily as *another ego*, as someone to be eliminated in order that his place be taken and his property be appropriated—but rather as an *agent*, acting in the name of a transgressive desire acknowledged to be as dangerous as it is seductive: seductive because it is shared by all members of the community, and dangerous, because if indulged it would threaten the very bounds that structure that community.

The other, in this narrative, is punished only when and because he attempts to become the same: only when transgression seeks to become appropriation. In this case, "the envied transgressor must be deprived of the fruit of his enterprise," while those who carry out the punishment "will not infrequently" share in "committing the same outrage under the cover of an act of expiation" (*Totem and Taboo*, 72). The ambivalence associated with the taboo, then, is distinguished from that of the obsessional neurotic by the manner in which the other, or rather, the *transgression of the other*, is *assumed*: behind the drive to punish (and thus, to participate in) the other's transgression, lies the acknowledgment of the transgressive other as model of the self. Paradoxically, the punishment administers the law of the other even while violating it, and herein resides the socializing force of the taboo. This force arises from a desire whose object is not just another subject, but *a movement of transgression on the verge of effacing itself* and thus *of giving rise to a subject*. Perhaps it is not overly excessive to read this *arrested effacement* as the trace of *another* kind of institution.

What would that kind of institution be like? And, as a related question: Can we conceive institutionalized practices of a "discipline" that would assume the ambivalent demarcations that make it, and them, possible?

I shall, in conclusion and as briefly as possible, risk a partial response to these questions. Starting with the second question first, let us return one last time to Kant's *Critique of the Power of Judgment*. In his discussion of the principle of reflective judgment, Kant arrives at the following conclusion: faced with the extreme complexity and indomitable heterogeneity of "nature," the reflecting subject gives itself a law that is neither objective, nor purely subjective. This law is what Kant calls "the principle of formal purposiveness" and it consists, quite simply, in treating the particularities that we seek to judge but do not yet comprehend, "in accordance with such a unity as they would have if an understanding (although not our understanding) had furnished them to our cognitive faculties, so as to make possible a system of experience according to particular laws of nature" (*Critique of Judgment*, 16). In short, we treat the singularities *we* do not understand as though they were the products of *another* understanding, like our own and yet unlike it (for it has produced precisely what we do not understand).

What Kant is here describing is surely an experience we have all had at one time or another: faced with an enigma, be it a hermetic piece of poetry, a contemporary painting, a puzzling coincidence, we almost instinctively tend to interpret the question, "What does it mean?" as: What did its author mean, or, what's "behind" it? As a reaction to our own bewilderment, we suppose a consciousness that is like our own, only less bewildered. Yet it is also here that the difference between what we do more or less spontaneously and what Kant is describing emerges. For, immediately after he has described this supposition, Kant goes on to qualify it:

> Not as though, in this way, such an understanding should really be assumed, (*Nicht als wenn auf diese Art wirklich ein solcher Verstand angenommen werden müsste . . .*) (for it is only our reflective judgment to which this idea serves as a principle — for reflecting, not determining); but this faculty thus gives a law only to itself and not to nature. (16–17)

The fictionality of the Kantian *als-ob*, the "as-if," thus becomes the condition of all knowledge of the particular. But it is a singular condition, one we "assume" without "really" assuming it, since it is "only" what we might call a "heuristic device." And yet, can we be sure that the discoveries made possible by such a device are themselves any more reliable or any less fictional than the "assumption" from which they proceed? What assurances can we have that such discoveries will be anything other than the image reflected in Ahab's gold doubloon? It is significant that today, almost a half-century after Wimsatt and Beardsley mounted their attack on the "intentional fallacy," the belief in the extraterritorial authority of the Author is still alive and well in literary studies on both sides of the Atlantic. And yet at the same time we have also seen readings of literary and critical texts in which the assumption of authorial authority is itself explored or even staged as a problem of reading itself. Not the least interesting aspect of such readings is that they are difficult to classify in terms of the received oppositions of fiction and nonfiction. Nor can they easily be claimed for the domain of literary criticism. Rather, they tend to suggest notions of *theatricality* that are not necessarily at home within the space of the university, especially insofar as this space is defined in terms of teaching and scholarship. I am thinking here of a text such as the "Envois" from Derrida's book, *La Carte postale*, as well as of much of the work of Paul de Man.

That literary studies should find themselves in the middle of such questions is a development anticipated by Kant in his Third Critique. Although that Critique begins using examples drawn primarily from the domain of visual perception, it is increasingly drawn or impelled toward what it calls *Dichten—* poeticizing—as Kant seeks to account for the irreducible singularity involved in the aesthetic judgment of taste. The most striking example of this tendency occurs when Kant explains the power of "genius" to create beautiful art in terms of its capacity to produce "aesthetical ideas"; these he describes

> as a representation of the imagination associated with a given concept (and) bound up with such a multiplicity of partial representations in its free employment that for it no expression marking a definite concept can be found.[19]

Such ideas, Kant observes, are therefore "unnameable" (*unnennbar*), but they are precisely *not* "ineffable," as Bernard translates. For they can only be conceived as a function of language, although language in this case does not function as an instrument of denomination. Rather, it is poetic language, *Dichtung*, that Kant describes as the privileged medium of aesthetic ideas, even though he has previously associated poetry with an imaginative activity whose freedom is scarcely compatible with the universality required of all judgments, including aesthetic judgments of taste.

If, however, the study of literature has in fact been influenced by the "unnameable" operation of such "aesthetic ideas," it is not entirely surprising that it has also become an area in which the question of institutionalization is increasingly discussed. For that question is, as I have already suggested, another way of exploring the processes and mechanisms by which a certain degree of unity— of names or terms—is imparted to that "multiplicity of partial representations" which Kant described as characteristic of the aesthetic idea.

As to the first question, concerning alternative forms of institutionalization, a possible example is the recently founded Collège International de Philosophie, which embodies the attempt to institutionalize research that might be described as transgressive inasmuch as it questions the defining limits of the established disciplines. Indicative of the Collège's relation to its own institutionality is the fact that membership in it is to be limited to no more than four years. Its first years of existence have been marked by an intense and apparently quite productive activity.

To be sure, no one institution, here or elsewhere, can be cited as anything other than an incitation to further reflection. Ultimately, the general question that emerges from the previous discussion can be formulated thus: Is a redefinition of "interdisciplinarity" conceivable and practicable that would allow for the assumption of a certain transgressivity—if not of transgression itself—mindful of the fact that such an assumption, at least in a cognitive-pedagogical space, could never be quite *real*?

The future of the humanities may well depend on the capacity of American society, within and without the Academy, to admit and accept the fictionality of what it assumes to be real, as well as the reality of its fictions.

Afterword
Religion, the State, and Post(al) Modernism
Wlad Godzich

For some time now, increasingly frequent, and strident, predictions of the end of theory have been made and greeted, predictably, with glee among those who saw the theoretical onslaught of recent years as one more plague that a merciless god was visiting upon them. They drew solace from what may well be the manifesto of this tendency, Walter Benn Michaels and Steven Knapp's tract, "Against Theory" (*Critical Inquiry* 8, 4 [summer 1982]: 723–42), in which a call for "an end to theory" was issued and theoreticians were lambasted for being at best no more than apologists for their own practices and at worst power-hungry academics posing as adjudicators of the claims made by others while studiously avoiding the production of any work that could be used to indict their own views. The antitheorists, as they have become known, are particularly virulent against what they view as the social and political disengagement of much recent theory, by which, it generally turns out, they mean deconstruction. They are not alone in this denunciation: even defenders of the theoretical enterprise, indeed of the very necessity of theory, such as Frank Lentricchia, view this as the gravest shortcoming of deconstruction, and one that, by implication, has given all theory the bad name it now bears:

> In what goes by the name of deconstruction, he [William E. Cain, author of "English in America Reconsidered: Theory, Criticism, Marxism, and Social Change," published in the same volume as Lentricchia's response to it] sees a political cop-out—an elaborate theory

which tries to undercut any and all justification of political choice, including the choice to work against "cruelty, suffering, and exploitation." As a theory, deconstruction (in effect, if not in explicit intention) works on behalf of quietism and political enervation. . . . These are points that I would not quarrel with, since in *Criticism and Social Change* I make them myself. ("On Behalf of Theory," in *Criticism in the University*, edited by Gerald Graff and Reginald Gibbons [Evanston, Ill.: Northwestern University Press, 1985, pp. 105–6])

These charges are not new, nor do they appear subject to modification even in the face of such empirical evidence as the remarkable consistency of Derrida's political position during France's rightward swing or his personal and intellectual involvement in the antiapartheid movement where he has been joined by precious few of those who thunder against deconstruction's apoliticism. One may well wonder at the reasons behind this attitude, especially since it does not seem to be the preserve of the foes of deconstruction. Even well-disposed students of deconstruction, such as Jonathan Culler, while acknowledging the political potential of its stances, pay scant attention to the work in which this potential is being realized.

A case in point is Samuel Weber's earlier work, in particular his first English-language book, *Unwrapping Balzac* (Toronto: University of Toronto Press, 1980). To be sure, Weber would be more aptly described as a theoretician of deconstructionist bent than a strict, undo-or-die, deconstructionist—if there are any such outside the imagination of deconstruction's enemies. He trained with Paul de Man, became sufficiently well acquainted with Adorno to be entrusted with the task of co-translating, with Shierry Weber, the essays in the collection *Prisms*; held the position of Assistant at the University of Berlin under the philologist and hermeneuticist Peter Szondi; translated, and introduced to readers of German, the work of Jacques Lacan; took part in the Western discovery of the Bakhtin Circle, before turning his attention to the theoretical and critical scene in the United States. The Balzac book, derived from his Cornell University dissertation, is remarkable in several respects. To begin with, it is one of the earliest instances of the poststructuralist study of literature. Weber challenges Roland Barthes's famous opposition between Balzac and Flaubert—the opposition upon which Barthes was attempting to construct his periodizing concept of the modern by distinguishing between readerly and writerly practices of literature. Using a mode of reading in text segments, which Barthes was to adopt and make famous some time later when he revised his earlier view of Balzac in *S/Z*, Weber brings out the complex interplay of elements that constitutes not only the economy of Balzac's *La Peau de chagrin* but a broader semiotic, social, and literary economy as well. Nor does Weber's work give any comfort to those antitheorists who assert that all theory is but the disguise of a will to power. In his work on Freud, originally in German and then in his own revision of the text into English, Weber examines this particular conception of theory and shows that the notion of theory as mastery, over the world or over texts, is untenable; it is rather a reading practice that relies on the polemical for the articulation of its stances, thus putting forward what are, in the language of this book, ultimately assumptions. To read Weber, then, is a challenge, one that would not permit some of the facile generalizations about either deconstruction or the end of theory currently being broadcast. It is also, inevitably, to enter in a polemic with him.

Paul de Man, reflecting upon the critical practice of a number of eminent thinkers, from literary critics like Georges Poulet to philosophers like Martin Heidegger, saw a curious interplay of blindness and insight in the production of these thinkers' most important critical ideas: the blindness, far from being disabling, was constitutive of the insight yet nonetheless remained a blindness to the person affected with it. It was this predicament of critical activity that led de Man to formulate a more properly theoretical stance in which the mechanism of blindness and insight would be understood without being disabled, or at least not in such a way as to render further insights impossible. De Man's solicitude in the preservation of the mechanism had something profoundly disquieting, if not downright scandalous, about it. Our impulse, bred in the bone by several centuries of education, is to correct error when we come across it. De Man's willingness to let it be marked a profound break with a major component of the Western cognitive tradition, one that is the motor of the disciplines, especially the scientific ones. And it was the more puzzling as de Man did not shy away from polemics in which he did reprove others for making mistakes, of reasoning, of reading, or even of fact. Yet in spite of the apparent arbitrariness in the willingness to countenance a blindness while correcting a mistake, de Man was highly consistent, if not clear to impatient readers. A blindness constitutive of an insight was far more interesting than the result of its correction would be: at best, the latter would smooth out the argumentative path through which the insight was obtained; at worst, it would erase the traces of the functioning of a cognitive mechanism that forced anyone examining it into wondering about the provenance of insight, and thus of the workings of cognition in general. Correcting errors sets the record straight, eliminates impediments to thought; reflecting upon blindness, on the other hand, forces thought into a reflective judgment about its own tortuous and discontinuous path, the very blindness of which consists in the fact that it has no guide to warn against its vagaries.

Sam Weber distinguishes between these two modes by means of the category of institution, within which he differentiates between institutional functioning on the one hand, which corresponds to error-correction in de Man's formulation, and instituting on the other, which is precisely what thought is engaged in when it proceeds blindly, in de Man's sense, to cut a path where none had been traced before. Weber then properly links this problematic to the organization of knowledge and the constitution of the disciplines that are its building blocks. Since, as he had already shown in his *Unwrapping Balzac*, the organization of knowledge is far from indifferent to the organization of society, this concern with the instituting function of institutions is a gateway to the rich field of social and political reflection, the absence of which in deconstruction we saw being deplored, if not vilified, earlier. Yet even here one ought to be wary and continue using the distinction between institutionalized functioning and instituting acts that Weber has drawn. Far too often, what is meant by the political, and even the social, among literary critics and theorists falls under the former—not that that there is no value to this sort of politics or social thought, but its localization within the demarcation of the institution should make clear that its political program can only consist in a change of personnel in dominant positions, and its social program can only have a reformist outcome if it is ever implemented once the political project is carried out.

We tend to think of institutions as apparatuses, that is, as constituted bodies with their internal procedures and delimited field of intervention. But an institution is first and foremost a guiding idea, the idea of some determined goal to be reached for the common weal; it is this goal that is sought according to prescribed behavior and by the application of set procedures. The idea itself is adopted by a group of individuals who become its public possessors and implementers. This group then becomes the institution as a result of the combining of the guiding idea with the set procedures. The members of the group are shaped by the guiding idea they seek to implement and the procedures they apply; they adopt common behavior, develop similar attitudes, all of which tend to unify them into a determinate and identifiable group and give the institution its distinct unity. An institution, then, is a social crucible, and it may be something as traditional as a church or as contemporary as a mode of watching television. The role of the guiding idea is all important, however, for without it we have forms of social behavior like all others rather than an institution. The guiding idea is precisely what seeks to avoid the blind path taking that so interested de Man in the arrival at insight. In short, the insightful path is turned into a beaten one, with the subsequent development of procedures within and by the institution being akin to road improvement. The trailblazing, or, in Sam Weber's terminology, the instituting, becomes a moment of odd standing in the now constituted institution. Its necessity is acknowledged, for without it the institution would not exist, but it no longer really matters except insofar as the marking out of the line that brought point of departure and point of arrival together is concerned. In other words, the instituting moment, which endows the entire institution with signification and meaning, is held within the institution as both proper to it and yet alien: it is its other, valued to be sure yet curiously irrelevant to immediate concerns.

In its day-to-day functioning, the institution manages to ignore this constitutive otherness within itself, and yet it cannot forget it since it stands as its foundational moment. Instituting and institution are not, then, two facets of the same entity, as some structurally minded sociologists would maintain. A particular relationship conjoins them, one that defines not only the institution as a social phenomenon but the social itself. Institutions are fundamentally instruments of reproduction, not in the simple mechanical sense, but rather in that they ensure that regulative processes take place so as to contain what otherwise could threaten to turn into anarchic proliferation. The accomplishment of this task is far from mechanical; it requires a specific form of intellectual activity which consists in the reconduction of what appears particular through the paths of the general, or, more precisely, through that instituting insightful path which is no longer treated as particular but as general now that it has been widened, had culverts laid in, bridges thrown, and generally been turned more and more into a reliable and safe all-weather thoroughfare. To this specific form of intellectual activity, we have long given the name interpretation, and Weber is particularly keen on showing the role that it plays in institutions. He also shows that this role is not confined to reproduction in the sense that I have been using, however.

Interpretation, when it is carried out with the rigor that it demands, inevitably goes beyond the procedural ground of the institution to encounter that of its instituting. Inasmuch as interpretation is itself a process of "meaning-discovery," it has to venture onto the ground where such meaning as is available within the institution that regulates it has been constituted. This is the second relationship of institution to instituting that Weber explores, striking out himself on territory that has hardly been explored. Interpretation, beholden as it is to the institutional framework that both authorizes and empowers it, finds itself indebted to the instituting act that enables it. It is this recurrent theme of debt that I find most interesting in the essays that make up this book.

Paul de Man's complex of blindness and insight, developed in relation to the critical propositions of individuals, has now been reworked in the context of the delimitation of disciplines as institutions, into another complex whereby meaning is located outside the institution, or discipline in the academic context, that manages it on behalf of the society. Whereas de Man noted that there was a gap between the blindness and the insight and that, furthermore, there was little prospect of their overcoming it on their own since it was constitutive not only of their respective positions but of their cognitive efficacy and, as a result, sought to delimit a theoretical space within which the mutual relations of the blindness to the insight could be described, Weber, already functioning in that theoretical space, takes the relationship to be not one of mutual ignorance but of active denial, generating guilt and indebtedness. At this stage of the reflection, we find not only that, in the institutional framework, meaning is sufficiently remote to warrant the elaboration of specific discovery procedures but that it is other, and an other to which we are indebted.

In the chapter entitled "The Debts of Deconstruction," which provides the most elaborated exposition of this problematic, Weber makes explicit the link between what may at first appear to be an obscure point in epistemology and the socio-political concerns that were our point of departure. He does so by means of Nietzsche's own heuristic myth on the origins of the gods. It will be recalled that Nietzsche views this as a socio-psychological process whereby all that we have today is attributed to the inventiveness of ancestors, who, as they recede into the past must grow in stature so that they may indeed be viewed as the originators of all that has been developed since. Although Nietzsche himself makes no claim of veracity of behalf of this myth, it contains features that have found independent support in ethnographic material. For example, one of the most vexing questions in the study of the relationship between thought and material conditions has been the lack of any traces left by the invention of agriculture, surely a major conceptual and material accomplishment with considerable consequences for the very survival of the species and its mode of acculturation. Yet all ethnographic inquiries come up short: agriculture goes back to time immemorial, just as the rest of the culture's materials do, and its invention is attributed either to the founding ancestors or to a gift from the gods. We do seem to have here the sort of denial and indebtedness that Weber theorizes on the basis of Nietzsche's indications.

What is perhaps even more important about Nietzsche's myth is its methodological rigor: if the gods are truly human creations, as he believes, then one should not appeal to some other transcendental category, such as "natural" necessity, to account for their constitution. And since it is precisely the status of the transcendental that is at issue in this invention, one can hardly proceed in an ontological way either, even if one were so inclined, which Nietzsche definitely was not. Thus the only recourse left is the socio-psychological realm. This methodological rigor is important for it locates the realm of the constitution of the gods as the social—thereby rejoining Durkheim's own conclusions in the matter before *his* lack of rigor pushed him to transcendentalize necessity—in such a way as to raise the question that Weber is implicitly seeking to answer in the essays of this book: what is the social stake of constituting meaning as other and as external to the society? The last part of the question does not represent an unwarranted extension of the earlier discussion on the externality of meaning to institutions: modern society has long been defined as a society of institutions; the externality of the meaning to them must then be seen as constitutive of this society itself.

What indeed is the stake? This is the question that haunts anyone who begins to reflect upon the social function of religion and wishes to go beyond the purely psychological reasons for the maintenance of religion as an institution to inquire

into its instituting. We must begin by observing that if there is a social decision—whatever the actual nature of that decision-making mechanism is, I have
no competence to determine—to attribute the origin, the mode of organization,
the self-understanding, and the cultural accomplishments of a society of whatever magnitude, be it a small tribe or a large state, to gods conceived of as inhabiting a distinct ontological realm, then this decision represents a desire and
a determination to split the society from its first causes in such a way as to make
the latter inaccessible to human intervention or tampering, as the many tales of
woe befallen to those humans who have tried attest. As a result, the principles
that preside over the organization of society and animate its rules are beyond its
ken. They may be precious and are indeed highly valued, but they are inaccessible in precisely the same way that meaning is inaccessible to institutions in Weber's description, the scope of which is becoming apparent. What this means is
that no one within the society—the status of strangers is much more problematic
as the reception of Cortéz has shown—may claim the legitimacy of these principles as his or her own, and even less so to speak from the society's foundational
locus since the latter is beyond the reach of any human member of that society.
This means that no one can occupy the seat of meaning, and therefore that of
power since, as we saw earlier, meaning is empowering. Again, anthropologists
have long remarked on the ambiguous status of the traditional tribal chief who
claims no authority for himself and generally is hardly better off than his com-
patriots (see Pierre Clastres, *Societies against the State* [New York: Urizen
Books, 1980]). Both Nietzsche's myth and the reflection on religion point to the
fact that society is constituted through the operation of exclusion whereby the
foundational principles are set in a realm that transcends the society. A number
of consequences derive from this: Since this realm is beyond the society, it is
impossible for the society as a whole, or for anyone within it, to be in a position
to reflect upon the society and its organization, hence the sense that the existing
order is the only possible one and should be left alone. Furthermore, the organization of the society is meaningless to human cognitive powers: since meaning
resides outside the society, it is not at all surprising that any effort to uncover
it within should end with the conviction that arbitrariness or senselessness prevail, although a more appropriate and self-reflective conclusion would admit instead to the inadequacy of human powers for such a task. The third consequence
is implicit in the earlier two: a society has no capacity to act upon itself; it cannot
change itself, and least of all by acts of institutional or collective will. If change
is to come, either it must have been programmed in the foundational principles,
or it is the result of an intervention from this other realm.

The mechanism at work in these three consequences is twofold: first the acknowledgment of a separation, and then the attribution of value to that which
is now cut off from society. The thread common to all three is power (to know,
to endow with meaning, to alter). It is easy to see that what is involved here is

the separation of power from the rest of human society and then the proclamation of its inaccessibility to the society. It would be even easier to be cynical about this and remark upon who profits from a conception in which power is not denied but access to it is. Such cynicism is very much exterior to a society ruled by this conception, however, and would beg the question by virtue of its location. Rather we need to observe that from within the society an important result obtains: if power resides eminently outside the society, there is no power for anyone inside the society to hold, and thus no one can hold power; all are equally powerless—as far as these three social facets of power are concerned. Indeed the sharing of this powerlessness is what constitutes the people's commonality and establishes them as the members of that society. This has always been the strongest point of religious thought, one that is necessarily lost in the institutional forms through which we know religion: all humans are equal with respect to the true powers of the universe because they are barred from power.

But it is also a very fragile one since it acknowledges the reality, and the experience, of power, and therefore its immediacy, only to proclaim its unattainable remoteness. The precarious balancing act between the two propositions calls for a safety net, that provided by a mediating instance. The individual, or group of individuals, who occupy this new position will represent themselves as the bridge between the powerless and the realm of power. As mediators, they are *of* the powerless but partake in the power whose effects they propose to channel. Perhaps even more important, they now span the gap between the two realms: they have made themselves, at least partially, other in order to ensure continued communication with the realm of the other. Mythological thought is well acquainted with these demi-gods who empower humans, are hated by the gods in whose realm they trespass and from whom they steal such things as fire or the secret of knowledge, and are both admired and dreaded by the humans. The separation between same and other has grown more complex, and since it is the mediators that one deals with in everyday experience, it is their otherness that comes more and more into view. The rulers, or more simply the state since this is the mediating instance I am speaking about, are no longer on the side of the powerless: they have access to knowledge, to meaning, and the power to change the society, and they have the authority of their mediating status to do so. The constitutive split whereby society came into being as the collection of all those who lived by certain principles forever beyond them is appropriated by the state, which represents itself as, literally, the interpreter of these principles. The instituting of society (by the split from its foundational principles) is now institutionalized and becomes highly irrelevant as all sorts of new questions emerge: who is fit to be a mediator-ruler? how is continuity in this position to be ensured? are there taboo domains or is all of the social realm open to state intervention? and so on. If religious thought is, in relation to power, an acknowledgment of its existence and then its neutralization by its expulsion from the realm of human attributes, the state is its complementary acknowledgment and appropriation by some humans. It both reverses religion and upholds it. Power continues to be felt immediately though it is mediated, but it is no longer remote. Mediation has made it more pervasive, and with this pervasiveness has come the breakdown of equality: there are now those who know, mean, and alter, and those who can only submit. Social division and the inequality that results from it find their justification here.

The principal difference between a society that submits to what I will call, for lack of a better term, a religious order and one that submits to a state-organized one lies in their attitude to otherness. It is immediately apparent that the first type makes the other an absolute other, whereas the second turns into an inner component of the same. Yet it is not enough to remark upon the position of the other in both systems; we must also note that they differ in the way in which they believe that the other came to be. Nietzsche's account makes clear that the gods are the products of the society, and one can therefore speak of the social production of this otherness even though the form it takes is not a pro- but an ex-duction. And since this act of production of the other is at the same time the production of the society, we have a collective determination of the boundaries of the social and of the other. By contrast, in a state-organized society, the determination of otherness no longer directly affects the constitution of the social since those who hold state power first co-opt individuals, thereby making them other with respect to the rest of the society, and then let the state as an apparatus of power determine the configuration of the social. Thus neither the production of the other nor that of the social is collective; indeed in such an order there will be strong prohibitions on this type of production, as we shall shortly see, since it is the prerogative of the state. We are then in the following situation: for a society to constitute itself it must know where its legitimacy lies; furthermore it must have a sense that its order is neither anarchic nor nonsensical but must be, in some ways that may well be beyond our ken, the realization of a true order; although its intelligibility is a challenge to our limited cognitive means, it must possess it in principle. If all these conditions obtain, order and change are both possible and the society is assured of continuity. But for that to occur, the foundational principles cannot be found in the society at large but must be located in a space of otherness that ensures that they remain beyond the reach of human desire and temptation. This space of otherness is either absolute or mediated through the institutions of the state. In other words, as Nietzsche had already seen and Weber reminds us, the society carries a heavy burden of debt to this space of otherness: it owes its meaning, its organization, its capacity to act upon itself, and thus its ability to manage order and change. This is the foundational debt of meaning that pervades all institutions, including the academic disciplines that Sam Weber is concerned with.

It is in relation to this state of affairs that the social dimension of deconstruction becomes more apparent. Institutions behave as if they did not carry this debt, as if the meaning they dispense was the result of their own activity or that of recognized meaning producers such as authors and critics as far as the institution of literary studies is concerned. When antitheorists claim that individual preferences or orientations determine the critical bent of literary judgments, they reaffirm this institutional conception with which they identify unbeknownst to themselves. To pursue the financial metaphor, institutions do not acknowledge the debt as their own but collect the interest on it, thereby fostering the formation and the maintenance in dominant position of a privileged class. This is the target of deconstructive practice, which aims at nothing less than, in a first stage, the restoration of a universal indebtedness since this appears to be the only ground on which equality, as a social fact, can be thought of. In this connection, it is worth observing that the privileging of the epistemological model in recent theory derives from the fact that the ethical model no longer had the capacity to produce equality and, again, those who are presently advocating a return to the ethical, and who frequently justify this return by their distaste for theory, are choosing a ground that cannot but result in inequality since it is always located in a postinstituting moment. The epistemological ground favored by deconstruction permits the assertion of an equality between all human beings by virtue of their dispossession from the domain of meaning. The insistence on aporia, undecidability, the fact of the dependence of our thought processes upon language and its tropological games, all convey the same sort of human powerlessness that obtained within religious thought, without any of the latter's transcendental dimension. Sam Weber gives the best exposition of this conception when he describes the exemplary constitution of psychoanalysis as both an acknowledgment and a repudiation of debt. The model of assumption that he then disengages is precisely the one by which all disciplinary and institutional thought authorizes itself in such a way that is appears to be legitimate and yet beholden to no one for this legitimacy.

As a deconstructionist, Weber then has to describe that which constitutes the equality we all have and which institutions destroy. He does so by means of Derrida's reliance upon a communicational model that is autonomous from those who are its "users" in *La Carte Postale*. It is a giant Postal Service that uses us as the relays for the impulses it sends along its circuits, impulses that we insist on taking for messages from the relay that immediately precedes us. What matters here is not so much the accuracy of this description—something we do not have any standards for in any case—but rather its originating impulse: against the inequality fostered by the state we have the assertion of a fundamental equality; against the inequality-producing and distorting claims of empowerment of modernity, the dispossessing equality of postmodernity—or perhaps more accurately since it is clearly directed against the state and its institutions and therefore still functions within the parameters of modernity—a postal modernity, which, as everyone knows, is characterized by the nonaccessibility of sender and receiver. The failure of the Postal Service deconstructs far more than any other enterprise the claims of legitimacy of the state since it shows that it cannot play the role of mediator which is its ground. If it cannot ensure the transmission of messages from same to same, what is the likelihood that it can do so with those that have to travel from other to same?

Yet in order to challenge the state in this way, deconstruction must hypostasize a postal system that is autonomous and beyond the ken of human powers. One may well wonder whether this is the best way of challenging the state and whether it is not more vulnerable elsewhere. The state itself has always shown an inordinate fear of the literary. One need only recall Plato's expulsion of the poets from his ideal state, the reluctance of Puritans on this score and the difficulty that Philip Sidney found in mounting a defense of them. Plato's reasons are the most telling. Prior to the *Republic* his concerns are epistemological: we learn and we know that we do not know. In the *Republic* this cognitive concern moves to the issue of knowing that which is, that which truly is, a question that forces him to consider how we know that we know and brings him to the Form or Idea. What is to be known, then, is being as determined by the Idea and as Idea. Knowing is essentially theoretical. It is in this context that Plato turns to a consideration of mimesis. Mimesis will be considered in the relation of theater to truth, and this relation is taken to be a theoretical one. Plato will indeed treat it at the theoretical level but on a political ground, somewhat in the fashion that the arguments in this essay have unraveled.

Plato begins to inquire into art and theater from a political perspective, that is, he evaluates art in relation to its position in the state, according to the essence of the state and the latter's foundation in relation to truth. Plato knows that poetry has the capacity to alter, to transform, and it must therefore be kept under surveillance. When he turns to the theater he is already suspicious, and this suspicion colors his reflection. What is the poet up to in drama? The poet provides the diegesis of events that may be past, present, or future and thus plays the role of witness. But the poet also engages in mimesis, that is, he or she utters speeches under the name of someone else, of another, speeches to which one then conforms. This other is created by the poet; mimesis creates otherness.

Mimesis does not take place, then, against a backdrop of some reality that one copies. It is neither the imitation nor the representation of a reality. To consider it in such terms is to take Plato in terms of the *adequatio* that Weber identifies as an obstacle to modern scientific thought in his introduction. For Plato, mimesis is far more worrisome than is generally suspected: through mimesis one can create otherness, and through it the distinction between real and apparent melts into air. Mimesis gives being to that which does not have it; it is a labor of presentation such that something other comes into being, which would not have existed without this labor. We experience mimesis as a mode of rendering, one in which the distinction between real and unreal is undecidable. Poets are dangerous, then, because they give being to that which does not have it; they produce otherness instead of placing themselves, and therefore all of us, in its debt. They serve as constant reminders of the fact that otherness, constitutive or otherwise, is a human production, and thus they empower us to think, to know, to give meaning, and to act upon our society. It is for this reason that poets must themselves be expelled into otherness and that their "messages" must be processed, like certain cheeses, through institutions. The persistent concern with epistemology and the literary in deconstruction derives from a social concern rather than represents a turning away from it as the accusers pretend.

Notes

Notes

Introduction

1. Gaston Bachelard, *Le Nouvel Esprit scientifique* (Paris: Presses Universitaires de France, 1934). Hereafter cited as *NES*. My translation.

2. Far from being contradicted by the rhetoric of "interdisciplinarity," such autonomy is almost always presupposed by it.

3. *NES*, 41.

4. Ibid., 116.

5. Although this term itself is not to be found in Bachelard's text, it formulates in condensed form an essential parameter of his argument. The relation between the notion of enabling limits and foundational thinking is discussed in "The Limits of Professionalism," printed in this volume.

6. *NES*, 80. Pauli's "exclusion principle" has been described in nontechnical terms as stating that "no two electrons could share identical quantum numbers or . . . share the same quantum state" (Daniel J. Kevles, *The Physicists, The History of a Scientific Community in America* [New York: Vintage, 1979], 161).

7. *NES*, 24.

8. Ibid., 28. Deformation (*Entstellung*) is also a salient feature of unconscious articulations and hence a distinctive trait of psychoanalytic hermeneutics. See "The Blindness of the Seeing Eye," chapter 6 of this volume.

9. *NES*, 126.

10. Ibid., 59.

11. Ibid., 75.

12. "une pensée se faisant un appui de son mouvement" (ibid., 133).

13. Ibid., 126. A related and only apparently trivial instance of this tendency can be seen in the widespread use of the exclamation, "Really?!" in English. Often employed as a kind of "filler,"

"Really?!" can be understood as an attempt to fill the very void in "reality" that its equivocal grammatical status—half affirmative, half interrogative—and its defensive indifference toward the particular situation ostensibly being addressed confirm.

14. "Le trouble de la désignation objective," *NES*, 126.

15. Ibid., 142.

16. Ibid., 76.

17. Commenting on the way in which the traditional manner of conceiving the reflection of light—rays "rebounding" on contact with a solid, opaque body—changes with "the quantic interpretation of the phenomenon," Bachelard observes: "The vibration that touches the molecule does not rebound like an inert object, any more than like a more or less stifled echo: its timbre will be different by virtue of the multiple vibrations that will have joined in" [including those of the "body" itself, whose molecules are also "vibrating"—S. W.]. But even this image is too materialistic to account for the quantic interpretation of the phenomenon. Is it truly a spectrum of light that emerges from the molecule that has been touched by a ray? Or is it not rather a *spectrum of numbers* that the new mathematics transmit to us from a new world? In any case, when one gets to the bottom of quantic methods, one discovers that what they involve is not shock, rebounding, or reflection, any more than a simple energetic quid pro quo, but rather exchanges of energy and of light established according to a double play of writing (*un double jeu d'écriture*) that in turn is regulated by complicated numerical arrangements (*convenances*) (*NES*, 74).

18. Ibid., 51.

19. Ibid., 177-78.

20. Ibid., 128.

21. See "Capitalizing History," infra.

22. *NES*, 12.

23. To which one would have to add the struggle to outstrip competitors, the "synchronic" aspect of the agonistics of science, which Bachelard considers only in its "diachronic" dimension. A spectacular instance of such competition has recently been provided by the controversy that has arisen around the naming of the AIDS virus, in which the respective claims to (chronological, and thus: juridical) priority in its identification, and hence to the enormous property rights at stake, made by the two research teams involved: that of the Institut Pasteur in Paris, led by Luc Montagnier, and that of the National Cancer Institute directed by Robert Gallo, turn on the recognition accorded the respective names given the virus by each group (LAV by the French, HTLV 3 by the Americans). For details, see: "How Gallo Got Credit for AIDS Discovery," *The New Scientist*, February 7, 1985.

24. See Bruno Latour and Steve Woolgar's study of the Salk Institute, *Laboratory Life* (Beverly Hills, London: Sage Publications, 1979), and B. Latour, *Les Microbes, guerre et paix, suivi par Irréductions* (Paris: Editions A. M. Métailié, 1984). Latour's analyses can be read as pursuing Bachelard's polemical, antirealist approach, while attempting to rid it of its idealist vestiges. Contemporary science thereby emerges as a function of "relations of forces" whose conflictual, partial, and partisan character science does its best to conceal. In this latter respect Latour's position converges with certain arguments developed in "The Limits of Professionalism," chapter 2 of this volume.

25. See Latour and Woolgar, *Laboratory Life*, passim.

26. *NES*, 109-10. Bachelard's description of the *exclusionary* basis of the traditional scientific community converges not only with the account of Freud—for whom the "sociality" of the Joke depends on shared "inhibitions" (or repressions): i.e., on what is *proscribed* rather than *prescribed* (see "The Blindness of the Seeing Eye," chapter 6 of this volume)—but also with the implications of the text in which "the community of interpretation"—a notion that has enjoyed a certain popularity in recent years—was first elaborated in English: Josiah Royce's *The Problem of Christianity* (1913). As opposed to recent advocates of "the community of interpretation," Royce leaves no doubt that the unifying and constitutive principle of this "community" must be *external* to it, and hence that

its origin can be conceived only as the result of "some miracle of grace." The concept of community — whether of interpretation or of anything else — can describe the stage on which divergences play themselves out, but never the principle of their adjudication, much less that of their resolution. (Cf. Josiah Royce, *The Problem of Christianity* [Chicago and London: Univ. of Chicago Press, 1968], 130.)

27. *NES*, 17.

28. René Lourau, *L'Analyse institutionnelle* (Paris: Editions de Minuit, 1970), 137. This functionalist conception of the institution also marks the theoretical writings of Michel Foucault, despite the emphasis placed on the exclusionary procedures by which "discursive practices" establish themselves. The opening scene of Foucault's inaugural lecture at the Collège de France is in this respect unmistakably clear. It is the voice of "the institution" — as such and in general — that seeks to assuage the "uneasiness" provoked by "discourse in its material reality": "But you need have no fear of beginning; we are all here to show you that discourse is in the order of laws; that its appearance has been long awaited; that a place has been reserved for it which honors it but also disarms it; and that if it should happen to have any power, this comes from us and from us alone" (Michel Foucault, *L'Ordre du discours* [Paris: Gallimard, 1971], 9–10; "The Discourse on Language," in: Michel Foucault, *The Archaeology of Knowledge* [New York: Harper Torchbooks, 1980], 215–37). (Translation modified.)

29. For a discussion of "setting-apart," a process that entails not just exclusion, but also attempted integration and assimilation through hierarchical subordination, see: Samuel Weber, *The Legend of Freud* (Minneapolis: Univ. of Minnesota Press), 1982, 32–60.

30. Roland Barthes, *Image, Music, Text*, translated by Stephen Heath (New York: Hill & Wang, 1971), 147.

31. Ibid., 148.

32. See my essay on W. Iser, "Caught in the Act of Reading," *Glyph* 9 (Minneapolis: Univ. of Minnesota Press, 1986).

33. "The author . . . constitutes a principle of unity in writing . . . a point where contradictions are resolved" ("What Is an Author?" in Michel Foucault, *Language, Counter-Memory, Practice*, edited by Donald Bouchard [Ithaca N.Y.: Cornell Univ. Press, 1977], 128).

34. The specificity of reading is thereby neutralized and its operation assimilated to that of an unproblematized notion of direct perception — bulwark of that 'intuitive thinking' which Bachelard's 'new scientific spirit' challenges, but only within the relatively limited area of its own practice. A recent instance of such neutralization, which also reveals some of its political and ideological implications, is offered by William J. Bennett's Report on the State of the Humanities in American Higher Education: "To Reclaim a Legacy." The return to the Great Books advocated by Bennett is presented in terms of intuitive perception: "Teachers who can make the humanities live" are described as those "who can guide students through the landscape of human thought," so that they may "not wander aimlessly over the terrain," but instead find their way quickly and efficiently to "the landmarks of human achievement," and of "civilization's lasting vision" (*The Chronicle of Higher Education* [28 November 1984]: 17.) The model that ultimately informs this secularized conception of reading as direct perception is, of course, a theological one: that of divine revelation.

35. L. Wittgenstein, *Philosophische Untersuchungen* Par. 156–71 (Frankfurt am Main: Suhrkamp, 1967), 82ff.

36. Foucault, "Author?", 116.

37. I. Kant, *Critique of Judgment*, translated with an introduction by J. H. Bernard (New York: Hafner Press, 1951), 15.

38. "Judgment in general is the faculty of thinking the particular as contained under the universal" (ibid., 15).

39. Preface (ibid., 5).

40. Ibid., 16. Emphasis added; translation altered.

41. Ibid., 20.

42. Ibid.

43. On the problematic necessity of such self-effacement and some of its contemporary consequences, see "Ambivalence: The Humanities and the Study of Literature," chapter 9 of this volume.

44. W. K. Wimsatt, Jr. and Monroe Beardsley, "The Intentional Fallacy," in *The Verbal Icon* (New York: Noonday, 1954), 18.

45. Read in this perspective, Kant's "repulsive style" and "wearisome" repetitions, as his translator, Bernard, puts it (Kant, *Critique*, xiv), prove to be a more effective medium for the conflictual scenario that plays itself out in *The Critique of Judgment* than any direct expression could ever provide.

1. Texts/Contents: Closure and Exclusion

1. The Marxian critique of capitalism, for which Nietzsche of course had little sympathy, describes a similar process: the competitive aspect of capitalist economy is increasingly reduced by the latter's inherent tendency toward concentration and oligopoly.

2. The remarks leading up to this conclusion deserve to be cited in their entirety. "Three observations are worth making on the subject of language games. The first is that their rules do not have their legitimation in themselves, but that they are the object of a contract, whether or not it is explicit, between the players (which is not to say that the players invent the rules). The second is that in the absence of rules there is no game, that even a minimal modification of a rule modifies the nature of the game and that a move (coup) or an utterance that fails to comply with the rules does not belong to the game defined by those rules. The third remark has just been suggested: every utterance must be considered as a "move" in a game." (J.-F. Lyotard, *La Condition postmoderne* [Paris: Minuit, 1979], 22–23).

3. C. S. Peirce, *Collected Papers* 5 ed. Charles Hartshorne and Paul Weiss (Cambridge, Mass.: Harvard Univ. Press, 1931–35) Par. 213. References to this work will henceforth be provided in the text, with the volume number followed by the paragraph number.

4. In a letter to Christine Ladd-Franklin, Peirce wrote that "pragmatism is one of the results of my study of the formal laws of signs." (Cited in: John J. Fitzgerald, *Peirce's Theory of Signs as Foundation for Pragmatism* [The Hague: Mouton, 1966], 10)

5. See Jacques Derrida, "Signature, Event, Context" in *Glyph* 1 (Baltimore: Johns Hopkins Univ. Press, 1977), 172–97; and "Limited Inc," *Glyph* 2 (Baltimore: Johns Hopkins Univ. Press, 1977), 190 and *passim*.

6. "A court may issue *injunctions* and *judgments* against me and I not care a snap of my finger for them. I may think them idle vapor. But when I feel the sheriff's hand on my shoulder, I shall begin to have a sense of actuality. Actuality is something *brute*. There is no reason in it. I instance putting your shoulder against a door and trying to force it open against an unseen, silent, and unknown resistance. We have a two-sided consciousness of effort and resistance. . . . I call that Secondness" (1.24).

2. The Limits of Professionalism

1. Jacques Derrida, *"Le Parergon,"* in *La Vérité en peinture* (Paris: Flammarion, 1978), 23–24: my translation.

2. "Texts/Contents: Closure and Exclusion," chapter 1 in this volume.

3. C. S. Peirce, *Collected Papers* 5 (Cambridge, Mass.: Harvard Univ. Press, 1934), 416. Unless otherwise indicated, references are to this edition, with volume and page numbers given in parentheses.

4. C. S. Peirce, *Collected Writings*, edited by Philip P. Wiener (New York: Dover Publications, 1958), 332. References to this edition will be given in the text as "Wiener," with page number.

5. *Philosophical Writings of Peirce*, edited by Justus Buchler (New York: Dover Publications, 1955), 79. References to this edition will be given in the text as "Buchler," with page number.

6. Robert Wiebe, *The Search for Order* (New York: Hill & Wang, 1967).

7. Quoted by Burton Bledstein, *The Culture of Professionalism* (New York: Norton, 1976), 29. Further references to Bledstein's book will be given in the text.

8. John Higham, "The Matrix of Specialisation," in *The Organization of Knowledge in Modern America, 1860–1920*, ed. Alexander Oleson and John Voss (Baltimore: Johns Hopkins Univ. Press, 1979), 3–4.

9. Within philosophy, for instance, such a progression can be traced from the later Wittgenstein, through Austin, to John Searle, for whom the conception of language as "rule-governed" behavior is a founding premise, itself never subjected to critical reflection.

10. Samuel Weber, *The Legend of Freud* (Minneapolis: Univ. of Minnesota Press, 1982).

11. Sigmund Freud, *Inhibitions, Symptoms and Anxiety*, Collected Works 20 (London: The Hogarth Press, 1959):120. Hereafter cited as "Freud," with page number.

12. Alfred North Whitehead, *Science and the Modern World* (New York: Mentor Books, 1959), 179.

3. The Debt of Criticism: Notes on Stanley Fish's *Is There a Text in This Class?*

1. Stanley Fish, *Is There a Text in This Class?* (Cambridge, Mass.: Harvard Univ. Press, 1980), 1. Hereafter cited in the text with page number.

4. Capitalizing History: *The Political Unconscious*

1. For reasons clearly foreseen by Hartz himself, and that liken the position of his work to that of Freud, whom he obviously knew well (although he seldom refers to him). Concerning the reception of his theories, Hartz predicted that "the liberal society [= Hartzian] analyst is destined in two ways to be a less pleasing scholar than the Progressive: he finds national weaknesses and he can offer no absolute assurance on the basis of the past that they will be remedied. He tends to criticize and then shrug his shoulders, which is no way to become popular, especially in an age like our own" (Louis Hartz, *The Liberal Tradition in America* [New York: Harcourt, Brace, 1955], 32. For a latterday confirmation of Hartz's prediction, see: Dorothy Ross, "The Liberal Tradition Revisited and the Republican Tradition Addressed," in John Higham and Paul J. Conklin, editors, *New Directions in American Intellectual History* (Baltimore and London: Johns Hopkins Univ. Press, 1979), 116–30. Ross, who seeks to demonstrate the superiority of Pocock's vision of American history, in which "the central issue" is "the survival of the virtuous republic," over that of Hartz, whose arguments she simplifies to the point of caricature, arrives, at the end of her article, at a "paradox" that precisely the work of Hartz could do much to explain: "The real paradox of Progressive thought is that historicism, with its desire to secure values within history, ended in an ahistorical social science that had adopted the objective voice and strove to be value-free" (Ross, "Liberal Tradition," 128). The reading of Jameson in this article may, in this light, be considered as a Hartzian attempt to explain such a "real paradox of Progressive thought."

I would like to express my gratitude to James Siegel for calling the work of Hartz to my attention.

2. This term was introduced in a second book, *The Founding of New Societies* (New York:

Harcourt, Brace, 1964), which Hartz published together with a number of collaborators and in which he undertook to generalize, by the comparative study of a number of emigrant societies (the United States, Latin America, South Africa, Canada, and Australia), the process of fragmentation.

3. Hartz, *Liberal Tradition*, 14.

4. Stanley Fish, *Is There a Text in This Class?* (Cambridge and London: Harvard Univ. Press, 1980), p. vii. For further discussion, see chapter 3 of the present volume, and also S. Weber, "How Not to Stop Worrying," in *Critical Exchange*, No. 15 (Winter 1984):17–25.

5. When Fish, at the conclusion of his book, claims that he has provided "a principled account of change," (*Text*, 367) he states, by antiphrasis, the problem. For his theory of institutional determination is just as unable to account for change as the theories of the autonomy of literature it sets out to criticize, but whose basic category—that of monadic (individualist) self-identity—Fish preserves, displacing it simply from the "work" to the "institution." From the perspective of the insider, change is never entirely explicable (which does not imply that the outsider is any better off).

6. Hartz, *Liberal Tradition*, 14 (my italics).

7. In those areas of intellectual activity where social power is directly determined by the production of knowledge, the understanding of the latter is far less "constative" and far more "performative," both playful and agonistic; in the humanities and social sciences, by contrast, where the pressures of social justification cannot be answered by direct reference to the economic and technological power that results from research (and that determines it as well), a constative notion of "truth" and associated ethical "values" play a far more conspicuous role.

8. See Samuel Weber, "It," *Glyph* 4 (Baltimore, 1978), 9ff.

9. "Socialism is largely an ideological phenomenon, arising out of the principles of class and the revolutionary liberal revolt against them which the old European order inspired. It is not accidental that America which has uniquely lacked a feudal tradition has uniquely lacked also a socialist tradition. The hidden origin of socialist thought everywhere in the West is to be found in the feudal ethos. The *ancien régime* inspires Rousseau; both inspire Marx" (Hartz, *Liberal Tradition*, 6).

10. Fredric Jameson, *The Political Unconscious* (Ithaca, N.Y.: Cornell Univ. Press, 1980), 13. Hereafter cited in the body of the text.

11. In *Inhibition, Symptom and Anxiety*, Freud describes "isolating" as one of the "techniques" that the ego can substitute for repression to attain similar results. Instead of the objectionable idea being simply excluded from consciousness, "its associative connections are suppressed or interrupted." Freud emphasizes that such a tendency is to be found in normal thought as well, where "concentration provides a pretext"—or an occasion—"to keep away not only what is irrelevant or unimportant, but, above all, what is unsuitable because it is contradictory." Contradiction, here, excludes dialectical synthesis (Sigmund Freud, *Inhibition, Symptom and Anxiety* [New York: Norton Library, 1959], 46–47). I have discussed the more general implications of "isolating" in my *Legend of Freud* (Minneapolis: Univ. of Minnesota Press, 1982), part 1.

12. Karl Marx, *Grundrisse* (Berlin: Dietz Verlag, 1953), 377.

13. Sigmund Freud, *The Ego and the Id* (New York: Norton Library, 1960), 16. Translated by James Strachey.

14. Ibid., 15.

15. Sigmund Freud, *The Interpretation of Dreams* (New York: Avon Books, 1965), 563. Translated by James Strachey.

5. The Critics' Choice

1. Richard A. Lanham, *Tristram Shandy. The Games of Pleasure* (Berkeley and Los Angeles: Univ. of California Press, 1973), 13.

2. In *The Great Tradition*, cited by Ian Watt in his introduction to *Tristram Shandy* (Boston: Riverside Press, 1965), xxxi.

3. V. Sklovskij. "The Parodistic Novel: Sterne's *Tristram Shandy*," in *Texte der russischen Formalisten* 1, ed. Jurij Striedter (Munich: Fink Verlag, 1969), 299.

4. From *Boswell's Life of Johnson*, cited in *The Norton Critical Edition of Tristram Shandy*, edited by Howard Anderson (New York and London: Norton, 1980), 484.

5. Watt, xxxii.

6. From Nietzsche, *Werke in drei Bänden* 1, ed. Karl Schlechta (Munich: 1962), 780–81.

7. Cited in Lanham, 9.

8. Ibid.

9. Ibid, 98.

10. For an incisive discussion of this matter, see Irving Wohlfarth, "Krise der Erzählform, Krise der Erzähltheorie—Überlegungen zu Lukács, Benjamin and Jauss," in *Erzählung und Erzählforschung im 20. Jahrhundert*, ed. Rolf Kloepfer and Gisela Janetzke-Dillner (Stuttgart/Berlin/Cologne/Mainz: Kohlhammer Verlag, 1981), 269–86.

11. Cited in Lanham, 15.

12. Ibid.

13. References to *Tristram Shandy* give first the book, then the chapter numbers.

14. Lanham, 113.

15. Ibid., 49.

16. Samuel Weber, *The Legend of Freud*.

17. Emile Benveniste, "La Nature des pronoms," in *Problèmes de linguistique générale* (Paris: Editions de Minuit, 1966), 256.

18. Sigmund Freud, *The Joke and Its Relation to the Unconscious* (New York: Norton Paperback, 1963), 60.

19. Ibid.

20. Watt, xxxiv.

21. Ibid.

22. This will be a major concern of a projected study of *Tristram Shandy*, to which this text is an introduction.

23. Lanham, 128.

24. Ibid.

25. Ibid., 166.

6. The Blindness of the Seeing Eye: Psychoanalysis, Hermeneutics, *Entstellung*

1. Sigmund Freud, *Standard Edition* 23 (London: The Hogarth Press, 1978), 275. Hereafter cited as *S.E.*

2. Sigmund Freud, *Studies on Hysteria* (New York: Basic Books), 117n.

3. Cf. *S.E.* 19.142–43 and my discussion in *The Legend of Freud* (Minneapolis: Univ. of Minnesota Press, 1982), 22ff. The present chapter brings together a number of considerations developed in that book, as well as in the essay *"tertium datur"* (published in Friedrich Kittler, editor, *Die Austreibung des Geistes aus den Geisteswissenschaften* [Paderborn: Schöningh, 1980], 204–21), in order to explore their hermeneutical ramifications.

4. "We might well lend the word 'Entstellung' (distortion) the double meaning to which it has a claim but of which today it makes no use. It should mean not only 'to change the appearance of something' but also 'to put something in another place, to displace'." *SE* 23.43.

5. Sigmund Freud, *The Origins of Psychoanalysis* (New York: Basic Books, 1977), 421ff.

6. Cf. Weber, *Legend of Freud*, 44ff.

7. See ibid., 84–117, for a more extended discussion.

8. Sigmund Freud, *The Joke and Its Relation to the Unconscious* (New York: Norton Paperback, 1963), 139.

9. Sigmund Freud, *Inhibition, Symptom and Anxiety* (New York: Norton Library, 1966), 47.

7. Reading and Writing—*chez* Derrida

1. Martin Heidegger, *Erläuterungen zu Hölderlins Dichtung* (Frankfurt am Main: Vittorio Klostermann, 1951) 50.

2. Ibid.

3. Jacques Derrida, *La Carte postale* (Paris: Flammarion, 1980), 37–38.

4. Ibid., 385.

5. Ibid., 10.

6. Maurice Grevisse, *Le Bon Usage* (Paris: Gembloux, 1949), 748.

7. Jacques Derrida, *Speech and Phenomena* (Evanston: Northwestern Univ. Press, 1973), 104; *La voix et le phénomène* (Paris: 1967), 117. Translated with an introduction by David P. Allison.

8. Emile Benveniste, *Le Vocabulaire des institutions indo-européennes* (Paris: Editions de Minuit, 1969) 1.295.

9. Derrida, *Speech*, 16; *La Voix*, 16.

10. Ibid., 57/51.

11. Derrida, *La Carte postale*, 417.

12. Derrida, *Speech*, 55; *La Voix*, 50.

13. Ibid., 97/109.

14. Ibid., 52/57.

15. Ibid., 96–97/106–8.

16. Derrida, *La Carte postale*, 305.

17. Ibid., 302.

18. Ibid. 373–74.

19. Ibid., 425.

20. Ibid., 382.

21. Ibid., 366.

22. Ibid., 410.

8. The Debts of Deconstruction and Other, Related Assumptions

1. J. Derrida, "My Chances/Mes Chances: A Rendezvous with Some Epicurean Stereophonies," in *Taking Chances: Derrida, Psychoanalysis and Literature*, edited by Joseph H. Smith and William Kerrigan, translated by Irene Harvey and Avital Ronell (Baltimore and London: Johns Hopkins Univ. Press, 1984), 31; translation modified.

2. L. Sterne, *Tristram Shandy* (Boston: Houghton Mifflin, 1965).

3. F. Nietzsche, *Ecce Homo* (New York: Random House, 1967).

4. In the original French: "Freud en prend tellement à son aise dans une situation aussi embarrassante, il décline la dette avec une assurance si empressée, une légèreté si imperturbable qu'on se demande: s'agit-il de sa propre dette? Ou de la dette d'un autre? Et si la dette était toujours d'un autre? Comment se sentir et ne pas se sentir à la fois, d'avance, acquitté et coupable de la dette d'un autre quand celui-ci, en soi logé par l'effet d'une singulière topique, revient à soi selon une filiation dont tout reste à penser? Comment spéculer sur la dette d'un autre à soi revenant?"

5. In the original French: "Si l'on tient à surnommer Oedipe la figure du *fort: da*, telle que nous

l'avons vue fonctionner l'autre fois, c'est en y *remarquant* une matrice nébuleuse et plus qu'abyssale de l'un seulement de ses effets ou si vous préférez de ses rejetons. C'est comme si on la tirait, cette matrice nébuleuse à fusions ou fissions en chaine, à permutations et commutations sans fond, à disséminations sans retour, par un seul de ses fils. *Il est vrai que cette tentation (un seul de ses fils pour former le trait) n'est pas une limitation contingente dont on puisse se dispenser de rendre compte*. Car c'est comme si l'on voulait faire revenir à l'un de ses fils, autrement dit à la mère matricielle, à une mère qui ne serait que ce qu'elle est."

6. *Protokolle der Wiener Psychoanalytischen Vereinigung* 1 (Frankfurt: S. Fischer, 1976), 338. In regard to Freud's relation to philosophy and philosophers, one can consult with great profit the studies of Paul-Laurent Assoun, including: *Freud, la philosophie et les philosophes* (Paris: P.U.F., 1976), *Freud et Nietzsche* (Paris: P.U.F., 1980), *Introduction à l'épistémologie freudienne* (Paris: Payot, 1981).

7. Concerning the minimal "exteriority" and distance required by the strategy of deconstruction, see *Of Grammatology*: "I wished to reach the point of a certain exteriority in relation to the totality of the age of logocentrism. Starting from this point of exteriority, a certain deconstruction of that totality which is also a traced path, of that orb which is also orbitary, might be broached" (161–62).

8. F. Nietzsche, *On the Genealogy of Morals*. Translated by W. Kaufmann and R. J. Hollingdale (New York: Random House, 1967). Translation occasionally modified. Page references are to this edition.

9. The distinction between hypothesis and assumption—*Annahme*—is by no means new to the history of philosophy. It is, for instance, at the core of Hans Vaihinger's *Philosophy of the As-If*, first published in 1911. Vaihinger, who discusses *Annahmen* within the framework of a general theory of *fictions*, himself refers to Alexis von Meinong and Heinrich Maier as convergent theorists of *Annahmen*. This aspect of Freud's theoretical practice thereby discloses its affinities with certain contemporary philosophical versions of neo-Kantianism, a point that has been explored by Paul-Laurent Assoun.

10. M. Heidegger, *Being and Time*, translated by J. Macquarrie and E. Robinson (New York: Harper and Row, 1962). Page references are to this edition; translation modified.

11. But the circle would not be complete were I not to point out, here at the end and in passing, that not only is the proper name of the "sender" inscribed there, in the *Envois*, but also the very term I have suggested was missing, and which seems to denote the exact opposite of that "name": *Annahme verweigert*! (acceptance [or assumption] refused). For indeed, this term was *there*, all the time. Where? On the very first page of the very first envoi, which begins as follows: "Yes, you were right, henceforth, today, now, at every instant, at this very point on the card, we are only a minuscule remnant 'left unclaimed, rejected, disclaimed, refused' (*laissé-pour-compte*): of what we said to each other, of what—don't forget—we made of each other, did to each other, wrote to each other. . . . 'Left unclaimed'—I would have preferred to say of what we *destined*, solely, for each other" (11–12).

The phrase *laissé-pour-compte* is thus the first explicit citation or quotation of the book. It designates the "we" of the *Envois*—from the perspective of the "I"—as unclaimed vestige, remnant of what "we" "said," "did," "wrote," but above all, *sent to, destined* for each other. And yet, we will not be entirely surprised any longer to discover that it is in another place—another text—that this destiny plays itself out, a play in which the "left-over" is both assumed and refused, assumed-as-refused.

This, then, is the beginning (itself a repetition and reproduction) of: Hans-Joachim Metzger's German translation of: Derrida, *Die Postkarte, Von Sokrates bis an Freud und jenseits* (Berlin: Brinkmann and Bose, 1982): "Ja, Du hattest recht, wir sind künftig, heute, jetzt, in jedem Augenblick, an diesem Punkt hier auf der Karte nichts als ein winziges Überbleibsel, dessen 'Annahme verweigert' wurde: . . . 'Annahme verweigert' würde ich lieber von dem sagen, was wir uns einer dem anderen, einzig, geschickt haben" (13).

9. Ambivalence: The Humanities and the Study of Literature

1. "The Ends of the Humanities" was the title of a conference held in the fall of 1984 at the University of Miami (Oxford, Ohio) for which this text was initially written. The following three paragraphs refer to a "position paper" outlining the issues the conference proposed to discuss.

2. R. S. Crane, *The Idea of the Humanities* (Chicago and London: Univ. of Chicago Press, 1967), 17.

3. "The fundamental belief of metaphysicians is *the belief* in the opposition of values. It may be questioned whether there are indeed any oppositions at all . . . rather than simply foreground estimations, preliminary perspectives. . . . Indeed, it might even be possible that *what* comprises the value of those good and respected things is precisely that they are insidiously related, tied to, interlaced with those wicked, seemingly opposed things, and perhaps even of the same essence. Perhaps! But who is willing to worry about such dangerous perhapses." F. Nietzsche, *Beyond Good and Evil*, translated by W. Kaufmann and R. J. Hollingdale (New York: Random House, 1967), 10; translation modified.

4. William J. Bennett et al., *The Humanities in America*, (Berkeley, Los Angeles, London: Univ. of California Press, 1980).

5. Plato and Aristotle are said to have been "at once humanistic in their concern with criteria of excellence, and philosophical in the manner of their statement and derivation" (*The Idea of the Humanities*, 157).

6. It is not indifferent for our context that the habitual translation of the *Kritik der Urteilskraft* sacrifices the work's decisive problem for convenience and for readability; what is in question is not *judgment*, in the sense of an accomplished *act*, but rather the *power*—the "Kraft"—to judge.

7. Immanuel Kant, *Critique of Judgment*, translated by J. H. Bernard (New York: Hafner Press; 1951), Introduction, section iv, 15.

8. Jacques Derrida, *La Carte postale* (Paris: Flammarion, 1980), 417.

9. Crane, *Idea of Humanities*, p. xvi.

10. Jacques Derrida, "Limited inc. abc . . . ", *Glyph* 2 (Baltimore: Johns Hopkins Press, 1978), passim.

11. Charles Sanders Peirce, *Collected Papers* 5, edited by Charles Hartshorne and Paul Weiss (Cambridge Mass.: Harvard Univ. Press, 1931–35), Par. 263. See also chapters 1 and 2.

12. W. Lepenies, *Actes de la recherche en science sociale* 47/48 (Paris: Maison de Sciences de l'homme, 1983), 39.

13. For a more detailed account of this process, see my article "Saussure and the Apparition of Language," *MLN* 91 (1976): 913–38.

14. Louis Hartz, *The Liberal Tradition in America* (New York: Harcourt, Brace, 1955), 4.

15. Samuel Weber, "The Limits of Professionalism," chapter 2 in this volume.

16. Sigmund Freud, *Totem and Taboo* (New York: Norton, 1950), 30. Translated by James Strachey.

17. Some of these senses I have sought to work out in "The Debts of Deconstruction and Other, Related Assumptions," chapter 8 in this volume.

18. Karl Marx, *Das Kapital*, vol. 1, ch. 3 (Berlin: Dietz Verlag, 1961), 139 (my translation).

19. Kant, *Critique*, section 49, p. 160.

Index

Index

Samuel Weber is professor of comparative literature at the Universities of Minnesota and Massachusetts (Amherst). He has taught in the Humanities Center at Johns Hopkins University and at the Free University of Berlin, and has also served as visiting professor at the University of Strasbourg. Weber is the author of *The Legend of Freud* (Minnesota, 1982), *Unwrapping Balzac: A Study of "La Peau de Chagrin,"* and *Rückkehr zu Freud: Jacques Lacans Ent-Stellung der Psychoanalyse*. A founding editor of *Glyph: Textual Studies*, he also edits its German counterpart, the yearbook *Fugen*.

Wlad Godzich teaches comparative literature at the Université de Montréal and at the University of Minnesota, where he is director of the Center for Humanistic Studies. He is co-editor, with Jochen Schulte-Sasse, of the series Theory and History of Literature.